The Making of Arthur Wellesley

The Making of Arthur Wellesley

ANTHONY S BENNELL

Sangam Books

SANGAM BOOKS LIMITED
57 London Fruit Exchange
Brushfield Street
London E1 6EP, U.K.

By arrangement with
Orient Longman Limited
3-6-272 Himayatnagar, Hyderabad 500 029

© Anthony S Bennell, 1997

Published by
Sangam Books Limited 1997

ISBN 0 86311 601 9

Typeset by
OSDATA, Hyderabad 500 029

Printed in India at
Bindu Art, Mumbai 400 011

Contents

Acknowledgement

This short study has been long in gestation. My first steps in Indian history were taken under the guidance of C.C. Davies and Sir Cyril Philips.

Over a prolonged period I have received assistance from two Librarians to the Dukes of Wellington, the Librarians and staff of the Institute for Historical Research, the Universities of Southampton and Nottingham, the British Library (both the Manuscript and the Oriental and India Office Record Departments), the National Army Museum, the London Library, the Ministry of Defence, the National Libraries of Scotland and Wales, and the Record Offices of Kent, Devon, and Somerset.

The final manuscript was read, to its very considerable advantage, by Malcolm Yapp and Gordon Johnson. Since I elected not to take some of the excellent advice I received, the normal disclaimer is very much in order: the responsibility for the text is solely mine.

As matters proceeded, my friend and former colleague Brian Robson believed in the book and urged its author onwards; I valued his support. I have also benefitted greatly from the sympathy of my wife in this venture, who has understood that her partner has to live in 1803 as well as in 1996.

March Square   Anthony S Bennell
Chichester

December 1995

1

The Man and the Setting

In the eighteenth century, when extended travel was a rarity, it took many months to travel from Europe to India. Broken only by a stay at the Cape of Good Hope, or at St Helena, the traveller endured many weeks on a heaving East Indiaman, until at last he was either carried ashore at Madras, or his vessel came to anchor in the Hoogly in steamy heat, alongside Fort William, Calcutta and a small city of Palladian villas.

The foundation of the Indian career of Arthur Wellesley, later Duke of Wellington, lay in the Governor-Generalship of India of his elder brother Richard Wellesley, who as the second Earl of Mornington was appointed to the position in mid-1797, and arrived in India in April 1798. Arthur Wellesley, to use the spelling of his surname he adopted that year, had arrived in the East with his regiment in 1797. He commanded the 33rd at the age of twenty-eight with the rank of Colonel, following a series of purchases of military appointments made possible by financial provision by his elder brother and by aristocratic connection.

Richard Wellesley was the third Governor-General to serve in India under the political structure created by the India Act of 1784, introduced by William Pitt after the Whig attempt to reform the administration of India—the India Bill introduced by Fox and Burke,—had failed in 1783. It was a position, if its holder elected so to treat it, of very wide power. This followed in part from the distance; instructions took many months to travel between London and Fort William, Calcutta. While answering in form to the Court of Directors of the East India Company in Leadenhall Street, a

Governor-General could exercise wide authority, especially if he was confident of the support of Ministers of the Crown. For the period 1784 to 1801 this meant that of Henry Dundas, who headed the Board of Control and treated Indian matters as his exclusive preserve.

Of the three British Presidencies in India, Calcutta, Madras and Bombay, it was Calcutta alone that controlled a substantial hinterland, acquired earlier in the century. This gave to the Company land revenue income which supported its armies, not only in the Bengal Presidency but also in other parts of India. The East India Company needed a policy towards the 'country powers', the independent Indian states. Of these in 1798, as Richard Wellesley arrived in India, the dominant was the Maratha Confederacy, a loosely grouped system of rulers, owing the most nominal allegiance to Peshwa Baji Rao in Pune. The whole of western India, the northern Deccan and the lands between the Godavari river and the Jumna, was controlled by the various Maratha rulers of whom Daulat Rao Sindia, Raghuji Bhonsle, and Jaswant Rao Holkar were effectively independent. The Nizam of Hyderabad, who had been defeated in a contest with the Marathas in 1795, was a far weaker power, with the ruler of Oudh the survivor of the subordinate authorities of the Mughal Empire. Mysore was ruled by Tipu Sultan, unreconciled to his defeat by the Company under Cornwallis in 1792, when he had lost territory and been forced to pay a substantial indemnity. In both Oudh, the modern Uttar Pradesh, and in the Carnatic, the modern Tamilnadu, surviving Indian rulers, previously subordinate to the Mughal Emperor in Delhi, had become dependent on Company support and were close to a condition of clientage to the Company.

Richard Wellesley set himself at once, in the short timespan of a single Governor-Generalship, to alter drastically this political structure. His objective was to create a scheme of alliances, known as the subsidiary alliance system, which would place the British Company in a dominant position in India, and would make possible the exercise of controlling power. By this, in return for a defensive guarantee, the East India Company stationed troops within the territory of the country power, paid for by that state, but available for general political purposes, as defined by the Company. Since the protected state had lost the right to an independent foreign policy—if it followed the requirements of the alliance—the advance of this system led to British paramountcy.

On the strength of his achievements during his Governor-Generalship, Richard Wellesley looked to establish for himself a political career in London, which would take him towards the highest offices. Of this intention he made no secret, and wrote freely to members of the Government in London. There was nothing modest about the initiation of the venture and, furthermore, the style of the Governor-Generalship was autocratic. The dominance was that of character and temperament, in an age when aristocratic title was highly regarded. There was also a heavy measure of intellectual conceit.

The instruments in the hand of Richard Wellesley were the administration of the Company, and its armies. Young men with connection in London were appointed writers to the three Presidencies, made or failed to make themselves masters of the commercial or revenue matters to be handled, and served for a life career which, if their health stood up to the climate and the intemperate habits of the age, brought them to a medium level of financial security at a relatively early age. The armies of the Company, predominantly sepoy but including an element of European infantry, were officered by a long service cadre, appointed similarly, who served for many years before attaining senior rank, and who suffered from the superior authority of 'Kings Officers' appointed by the Horse Guards. There were a limited number of Kings units, infantry and cavalry, serving in India; they had been reinforced in 1798, at the point at which Henry Dundas believed that the objective of the French invasion of Egypt could be an attack on India. Almost all Europeans within the boundaries of Company territory were its employees, military or civil.

Beyond, in the world of the country powers, some Europeans and those of mixed race, served in the armies of the Indian states; these were the European adventurers who were to give a measure of justification to the contention of Richard Wellesley that they constituted a threat to the British control, and were the potential supporters of a French attempt to regain predominance in India. On his arrival, Richard Wellesley saw the position of the East India Company in India in 1798 as one of crisis, even before he knew of the French invasion of Egypt. In a series of bold measures in the years 1798 to 1802, in which he showed scant patience with those who did not share his quickly formed analysis of situations, he disbanded a French officered force at Hyderabad and replaced it by a Company force, prepared an attack on Mysore, and after a most nominal attempt at negotiation, invaded the lands of Tipu Sultan and secured his defeat and death in the capital fortress of Seringapatam in May 1799.

Richard Wellesley followed these achievements by tightening the bonds of alliance with the Company of the Nizam of Hyderabad, seizing a substantial part of the territory of the Nawab of Oudh, and displacing the Nawab of the Carnatic, subsequently taking almost all his lands into direct Company rule. He also attempted to secure the acceptance by the Peshwa, the nominal head of the Maratha confederacy, of a defensive alliance, but this objective eluded him at first. All this represented a formidable attempt to impose on the country the political structure which Richard Wellesley believed that the British position required, and which he had probably devised, during a period of observation and lack of opportunity to act, when he served in London as a junior member of the Board of Control.

In 1797 Arthur Wellesley was virtually without military experience. He had served in garrison duty in Ireland, and in 1794 had been briefly involved in a campaign in the Netherlands. He had come to India because he had purchased the colonelcy of the 33rd. He had written to his elder brother before he knew of the appointment to the Governor-Generalship, suggesting that if the opportunity of nomination presented itself it should be seized. Arthur Wellesley would have hoped that his own relationship to the prospective Governor-General would strengthen his career prospects in India.

Following the opening of the Governor-Generalship, Arthur Wellesley was moved with his regiment to Madras, and busied himself as an interested observer in the preparation of a threat to Mysore created in the autumn of 1798 which led on to its invasion in February 1799. He was placed in command of a brigade which included forces of the Nizam of Hyderabad, allied with the Company in their attack on Tipu Sultan. Although not a participant in the assault on Seringapatam, he was appointed both to the Commission on the affairs of Mysore—the instrument created by Richard Wellesley to determine the settlement of the defeated territory—and subsequently to the command of British forces in

Mysore. In the task of settlement and pacification he worked with Barry Close, the first Company Resident. In the autumn of 1800 Arthur Wellesley led the movement of Company and British forces which culminated in the defeat of a guerilla leader of some importance, Dhondiah Vagh, in the lands north of Mysore. He was involved in the initial preparation although not the ultimate command of a body of troops in Ceylon intended at first for an attack on Mauritius, but subsequently sent under another commander to the Red Sea. By the autumn of 1802 Arthur Wellesley had served in India for five years, and had recently been gazetted a Major General. He was thirty-three years of age.

In 1802 the turbulent affairs of the Maratha Confederacy led to the opening for British intervention which Richard Wellesley had sought. Jaswant Rao Holkar, a guerilla leader of genius, avenging the murder of his brother by the Peshwa, threatened the territory Baji Rao directly ruled, and was victorious in a battle before Pune on 25 October. Peshwa Baji Rao fled to the coast near Bombay, while remaining in his own territories. On the morning of the battle, Baji Rao had accepted in outline the terms of a subsidiary alliance treaty which, as Resident, Barry Close had been seeking to secure for some months.

This is the setting for the most critical period of the Indian career of Arthur Wellesley, which is here surveyed.

2

The Creation of the Treaty of Bassein (October-December 1802)

"European government were, until very recently, guided by certain rules and systems of policy, so accurately defined and generally known, that it was scarcely possible to suppose a political event, in which the interest and conduct of each state would not be as well known to the *corps diplomatique* in general, as to the statesmen of each particular state. Asiatic governments do not acknowledge and hardly know of such rules and systems."

Arthur Wellesley, October 1804

The formidable achievements of the earlier years of the Governor-Generalship of Richard Wellesley had, by October 1802, brought the East India Company to the point of a major challenge—a political and military confrontation with the Maratha Confederacy. Given his presuppositions, this had been pre-destined since the outset of the Governor-Generalship of Richard Wellesley; it was certainly projected in the letters which he wrote to Henry Dundas from the Cape of Good Hope in February 1798.

Northern and central India existed under various degrees of feudal overlordship of the Marathas, which had been evolving for more than a century. The surviving pageant rule of the Mughals was intertwined with Maratha overlordship. The powerless Mughal Emperor in Delhi, whose rule was almost literally confined to a fortress, was at Maratha discretion, and his position acknowledged by the holding by their chiefs of Mughal titles. But the Marathas themselves practised pageant rulership: the position of the Peshwa, himself a hereditary first minister to the Raja of Satara, was both absolute and uncertain, and had been weakened by the prolonged period of direct domination of Pune by the Sindias. Standing against the Sindias were other Maratha chiefs, the Raja of Berar, whose capital was at Nagpur, and the Holkars of Indore, whose position was complicated by a disputed succession, with the Peshwa and Daulat Rao Sindia supporting a rival. Throughout the Confederacy there were feudal chiefs at different levels, their positions both precarious and secure, precarious in that 'even the king is served of the field' and the harvest and, therefore, land-revenue income was uncertain; secure in that marauding armies could be created and were the means of securing this income by the most direct of means, military action which shaded into brigandage.

The outcome of a battle outside Pune on 25 October 1802 gave Richard Wellesley the opportunity, which he was quick to seize, to intervene actively in the Maratha polity. He was shortly to receive from Addington as Prime Minister and Castlereagh as President of the Board of Control, a somewhat hesitant offer of continued support in his post. This support from London, which was in response to a resignation sent by Richard Wellesley in February 1802, was qualified, markedly cool, and accompanied by a reminder of the importance of economy in the administration of the affairs of the British Company in India. The support was endorsed by the Chairman and Deputy Chairman of the Company. This was important because senior members of the ruling Court of Directors had been alienated from Richard Wellesley by his action in attempting to introduce a measure of 'private trade' in place of the monopoly of the Company. But the promise from Addington was not genuine in the sense that he could not deliver support; his position in the House of Commons required the backing of the 'India interest' in the House of Commons. The moment of decision for Richard Wellesley in his Maratha venture came in mid-November 1802. It was not until three months later, in February 1803, that he received the message from Downing Street. Taken together with private correspondence, he could read the uncertainty within it. His mandate from London was uncertain, and the creation of a revised political structure within India would need to be secured speedily.[1]

What Richard Wellesley wished to achieve was a pacified Maratha Confederacy that recognised British overlordship. This was to be the climax of his Governor-Generalship, the ultimate restructuring of the political system of the country powers in India, and the basis of his claim to high political office when he returned to England. His agents in the venture were to be the politicals on whom he had relied before, including Edmonstone, Barry Close and John Malcolm. But central to the evolution of the policy was to be his relationship with Arthur Wellesley.

The prospect of intervention in the Maratha Confederacy arose from the conflict between the Sindias and the Holkars, the central fault line of the polity of the Maratha people. Late in October 1802, in the battle of Hadapshar outside Pune, Jaswant Rao Holkar defeated the army of Peshwa Baji Rao, and some troops provided by Daulat Rao Sindia. Baji Rao fled from Pune and after a period of hesitation accepted the personal security of a small force of troops provided by the East India Company at Bassein, in Maratha territory but close to Bombay. Shortly before the battle of Hadapshar, Peshwa Baji Rao had sent to Barry Close, the British Resident at his court, an agreement or *sanad* accepting military support in return for the cession of territory. It was this agreement, once he had heard about the outcome of the battle and the events immediately following it, that Richard Wellesley at once wished to convert into a full subsidiary alliance. This was achieved by Barry Close in the Treaty of Bassein concluded on the last day of 1802.

Richard Wellesley was in no doubt as to his objective in his Maratha policy: it had been implicit in his dealings with the Confederacy from the outset of his period in India. He believed that the Marathas would accept the overlordship of the Company and the loss of their freedom of action. In return they would receive the advantages of a cessation of the perennial feuding and warfare between members of the Confederacy. But acceptance of these advantages, evident to Richard Wellesley, would be contrary to Maratha nature. Further, this change would move far forward the political and military frontier of the Company, and involve it in the disputes and contests of vast areas of which the British knew very little. Scepticism of the whole project was entirely in order, and this Arthur Wellesley was not alone in expressing. At the outset this perhaps mattered little, but later when the younger brother was to be drawn centrally into the execution of policy, these differences became of note.

Much depended on the presuppositions of British policy. It was questionable whether it was realistic to see an alliance with the Peshwa, when achieved, as an alliance with the whole Confederacy. Alternatively, it might be possible to hope that the individual members of the Confederacy would accept the relationship of subsidiary alliance with the Company. Arthur Wellesley certainly saw the alliance with Baji Rao as of limited value. His own experience beyond the Maratha frontier, in the context of the campaign against Dhondiah Vagh in late 1800, had given him adequate insight into the limited degree to which the Peshwa could be said to be the ruler of southern Maharashtra.

The outcome of the battle of Hadapshar outside Pune on 25 October 1802 marked the point at which the British East India Company ceased to be observers of the conflicts of the Maratha rulers and became principals. On the morning of the battle, as Barry Close the British Resident pointed out, 'to be prepared for every event' Peshwa Baji Rao sent him a statement of cession of territory of the annual value of Rs. 25 lakhs. In return Peshwa Baji Rao sought 'a corps of British troops consisting of six native battalions, with their proportion of artillery.'

That evening, Close wrote from Pune to the Governors of Madras and Bombay, and also to the British Resident at Hyderabad, the court of the Nizam. These letters initiated contingent military preparation. From their form it is possible to deduce the response which Close expected Richard Wellesley to make following the opening into Maratha politics which Peshwa Baji Rao had now given him. In writing to the second Lord Clive, Governor of Fort St. George, Madras, Close pointed out that he expected the Governor-General to direct that a considerable force be put in readiness against the need to support the government of Baji Rao. He was sending this forewarning in secret, because he thought it likely that Clive would wish to take possible measures in advance of orders from the Fort William Secretariat. 'If the troops be called for, it is probable that they will be ordered to move in this direction from the Toombuddra' (Tungabhadra). The Governor of Bombay, Jonathan Duncan, was advised that the state of the negotiations with the Peshwa had reached a point where he should 'hold in readiness to be employed in the Konkan, when called for, as large a body of British troops as you can with convenience collect.'[2]

The Resident at Hyderabad, James Kirkpatrick, was recommended to make discreet preparation for the movement of the Company
subsidiary force, stationed at Hyderabad at the cost of the Nizam,
but available for purposes of British policy. Baji Rao may have
hoped that his essentially casual request for military assistance
would not give an opening for the construction of a British position
within the Maratha Confederacy, and that this danger could later
be averted by negotiation. The prompt response to the recommendations in these letters of Barry Close for discreet preparation for
military movement made it the more certain that the political
benefits would be secured that could accrue to the Company.[3]

As soon as the outcome of the battle was at all predictable, Baji
Rao fled, retreating southeastwards away from Pune to Singhar. He
still had with him the principal persons in his court, about 7000
cavalry, a small force of infantry and five guns. Close advised Peshwa
Baji Rao that evening to seize the pass through the western Ghats
above Mahad (Mhar) and so 'secure his communication with the
sea.' He reported that Baji Rao seemed anxious that the Resident
should move to Bombay, but that he had given only the most
generalised reassurance of continued contact. Close still thought
it possible that Jaswant Rao Holkar would be able to capture Baji
Rao, as he was sending out cavalry parties from Pune to intercept
him. While Close hoped to leave for Bombay, he felt it appropriate
to ask for permission from Jaswant Rao Holkar, a significant action
in itself, and when he sought this permission it was refused.

Although Close probably thought it likely that Richard Wellesley
would accept the agreement for the cession of territory as the
opening move in the negotiation of a treaty of subsidiary alliance
which he had been seeking for so long, it was possible that an
entirely new policy towards the Marathas might be appropriate.
Close noted that Baji Rao retained some freedom of action, since
his move to Mahad had placed him beyond 'the grasp of Jaswant
Rao Holkar.' Few of those with Baji Rao knew of his attempted
negotiation with the Company, much less of the agreement that
had been reached. His entourage were urging upon Baji Rao
reliance on the continued support of Daulat Rao Sindia. Close at
this stage believed that 'Holkar will fail in his view to effect a
revolution at Pune, if he ever really entertained such a view, and
ere very long he may be removed from this neighbourhood, either

by the actions of Sindia or by effecting an accommodation with the Peshwa.'

Close took it that the immediate objective of Holkar had been to secure the person of the Peshwa and this attempt having failed, Holkar might still seek a negotiation with Baji Rao. He noted also that 'if Sindia from any cause be unable to collect a force sufficient to defeat or match Holkar, and the Berar government remain passive, the Peshwa's hopes of being restored to his government must rest solely on the aid he may derive from the Company's government.'[4]

Two agents of Baji Rao arrived in Bombay in the first days of November 1802, and sought asylum there for their master. Duncan, Governor of Bombay, hesitated, but after consulting John Malcolm, then in Bombay, placed a vessel of the Company at the disposal of the Peshwa. Its captain was to provide security for the Peshwa if it was sought, but not to press it upon him. This decision was countermanded almost at once after further advice reached Duncan from Barry Close at Pune. The advice given by John Malcolm gives an analysis of recent events as seen by one of the politicals who had been working closely with Richard Wellesley on relations with the country powers. It is probable that John Malcolm had been involved in the drafting of the detailed instructions of June 1802 which were the last considered statement of British policy towards the Marathas available to Barry Close at the time of the battle of Hadapshar.

Malcolm saw the conduct of Baji Rao since 1798 as 'more that of an enemy than a friend.' The Peshwa had kept the negotiations with the Company alive 'with a view to alarming the other Maratha states' but had deliberately avoided bringing them to a conclusion. He would 'never enter into subsidiary engagements with the English until reduced to a state in which he dreads the loss of his life or liberty and cannot indulge a hope of being extricated by any other power.' The conclusion of an alliance with Baji Rao was significantly in the interests of the Company. Peace in Europe, news of which had recently arrived, opened 'a scene for intrigues in India.' Sindia would be led by the current Maratha crisis to move his force south of the Narbada, 'covering the Maratha provinces in the Deccan with hordes of banditti, which must soon exhaust that already desolate country.' These horsemen would soon be 'forced by necessity if not invited by policy to invade either the territory of the English government or that of its allies.' It was therefore worth a considerable risk to secure an alliance. But Malcolm considered that the Peshwa was seeking asylum and an association with the Company in part to strengthen his political position in relation to the other leading members of the Maratha Confederacy, and only a last resort as a means of securing his personal safety. It was important not to safeguard his position, because he was likely to conclude an agreement only under the stimulus of fear for his safety. It was therefore important so to act as not to 'extricate the Peshwa from his difficulties.'

Malcolm sent a copy of his memorandum to Calcutta, adding that he expected that Richard Wellesley would elect to take a decided part.[5]

From Pune, Close advised Duncan that the Peshwa should be recommended to stay in his own territories. The Governor of Bombay should 'discourage him from seeking an asylum in the territory of the Company until you shall hear from the Governor-General.' If Baji Rao felt insecure, he should be advised to travel by sea to Bassein, still in his own territory, but protected by nearness to Bombay. This would leave ambiguous the extent to which the Company proposed to support him. Agreeing with Malcolm, Close added

'the desire I repeatedly expressed that the Peshwa should continue as long as possible in his own territory refers to the following consideration.... It is desirable that we should have a plea, or rather a right, to interfere in the Maratha dominions in the Deccan; such right we now possess by virtue of the agreement lately delivered to me by the Peshwa. Our object therefore is to preserve this right and the means of acting upon it ... our right of interference must be extinguished or rendered nugatory should His Highness fall into the hands of his adversaries ... the circumstance of my having accepted his paper of agreement ... and having recommended him to secure himself at a spot communicating with the sea, must inspire him with a hope of protection from the British government.'

Duncan had this advice before him as he and John Malcolm interviewed the two agents of Baji Rao on 9 November 1802. In this discussion, the two envoys were assured that the Company vessel which was intended either to convey Baji Rao northwards along the coast, or to give him security, was about to sail, and with it a boat intended to carry him to Bancoote. It was pointed out that it was in Baji Rao's own interest 'to maintain his position where he was, or in any other safe and eligible position in his own territories, rather than abandon them for an asylum in another country.' This advice appeared to be acceptable to the *vakils*; they believed that only extreme necessity would bring Baji Rao to Bombay.[6]

Detained in Pune by the unwillingness of Jaswant Rao Holkar to allow him to leave, Close reported on the attempt being made to create a new Maratha polity. The half-brother of Baji Rao, Amrit Rao, had been brought reluctantly to Pune, and been joined by former officials who had been associated with Nana Phadnavis, a former Chief Minister to the Peshwas, who had died in 1800. Close believed that Jaswant Rao Holkar and Amrit Rao intended to persuade the widow of Mahdu Rao, the Peshwa who had died in mysterious circumstances in 1795, to adopt Amrit Rao's son as her heir and then place him on the Peshwa's throne. Holkar meantime was 'subject to severe pressure at present from want of cash.' Close believed that Holkar would by now have realised that Daulat Rao Sindia would 'soon make an effort to assist the Peshwa and retrieve the reputation of his arms.' In Pune it was believed that Baji Rao was 'wholly guided by the vakils of Sindia, who continue to give him promises of support, and that should he be induced to embark, it will be with the intention of proceeding to Surat from whence to join Sindia.' Close added that he saw some support for this view in that a recent letter from Baji Rao to Duncan made no mention of the agreement that had been sent to Close on the day of the battle outside Pune.[7]

The letters which Close had written to Hyderabad and Madras now began to generate formidable military support for what was still an assumed British intention to intervene in Maratha politics. In Hyderabad, the Resident warned its commander that he should 'hold in readiness ... as large a proportion of the subsidiary force as can with any convenience be prepared.' He would himself seek from the court of the Nizam agreement to the contingent move westwards of at least two-thirds of the force stationed there. Kirkpatrick later indicated to John Malcolm scepticism of the whole venture; 'if we espouse the cause of the Peshwa, what assurance or security have we either for his steadiness and adherence, or of his not being deserted in such event by the very chieftains who at present side with him?' He reported to Calcutta that when he received the letters from Close he had given secret mobilisation instructions to the commander of the subsidiary force; he assumed that the Governor-General would wish to deploy 'as large a proportion of the subsidiary force as can with convenience be spared,' without direct violation of the rights of the Nizam or the taking of actions directly contrary to his wishes. At the same time he reported that the chief minister of the Nizam had asked for, and not been given, details of the negotiations with Peshwa Baji Rao.[8]

From Madras, Clive reported to the Governor-General that immediate steps were being taken to assemble a field force on the Mysore frontier of the Company territory adjoining the southern Maratha lands. It would comprise about 1800 European infantry, 6000 Indian infantry, five companies of artillery and seven regiments of cavalry. This was the force that was to be commanded by Arthur Wellesley when it moved into Maratha territory in March, 1803.[9]

Close continued to be puzzled by the situation at Pune. On 10 November 1802 he gained the agreement of Jaswant Rao Holkar that he should leave for Bombay, but he was not confident that this undertaking would be honoured. Close reported that he believed that Holkar despaired of securing the return of the Peshwa to Pune, and was therefore anxious to proceed with the placing of the son of Amrit Rao on the throne of the Peshwa.

> This extreme mode of proceeding however is opposed by that chieftain (Amrit Rao) who shows himself hopeful that the Peshwa may be conciliated and yet be induced to come back to his capital. The persons of most consideration here ... discourage for the present all attempts to effect a revolution and the Berar *vakils*, though sparing of their sentiments, incline to the same part.[10]

On 16 November Close visited Jaswant Rao Holkar and Amrit Rao. Amrit Rao urged on Close the reasonable contention that Baji Rao had failed the Maratha statehood by failing to adjust the claims of Jaswant Rao Holkar against Daulat Rao Sindia. He had also refused to return to Pune when pressed to do so. Amrit Rao asked Close for advice. Close responded that he was under orders to retire to Bombay, which he almost certainly was not, although he was correctly anticipating the orders he was soon to receive from Calcutta. Ready acceptance of his departure by Amrit Rao, he somewhat disingenuously argued, would lead Richard Wellesley to 'be satisfied of his amicable intuitions.' Amrit Rao repeated the request for Close to remain at Pune, and further asked him to use his influence with Baji Rao to induce him to return there.

To these points Close did not respond. He finally secured the permission that he had sought—to leave Pune. He explained to the Governor-General the factors that had weighed with him in planning to retire to Bombay.

'Under the present uncertainty relative to the real inclinations and designs of leading individuals, the amount of force Sindia may be able to exert for recovering his credit and influence, the time that may elapse before he be enabled to act, and the course that Holkar's numerous and increasing army may be obliged to take to procure subsistence, it shall be my aim to keep the field of adjustment or accommodation as open as possible, in order that on giving your attention to the existing state of Maratha affairs, your Lordship be enabled to avail yourself of as many combinations as possible, towards effecting your views ... giving order and permanency to the Pune state, and thus laying the foundations of general tranquillity in India.'

Close warned Duncan that he believed that Baji Rao was 're-solved to avoid a connection with the English and to adhere to Sindia for support.' If there was to be any question of Baji Rao being granted an escort of a British vessel to proceed to a port in his own territories, as distinct from seeking asylum in Bombay itself, he should be 'interrogated' on the intention of the transmission of the agreement of 25 October, 1802. Only if this were done, would the Governor-General gain sufficient information on the intentions of the Peshwa. Close reminded Duncan of the main elements of the subsidiary alliance with Baji Rao that had been sought.[11]

These events had been closely watched by the Fort William Secretariat in Calcutta, dependent on dispatches taking about three weeks to reach them from Pune and Bombay, carried via Hyderabad. By mid-November 1802, both the outcome of the battle before Pune, and the contents of the agreement given to Close by Baji Rao were known. Barry Close was informed immediately that Richard Wellesley approved of his conduct 'during the late negotiation' and considered that the Peshwa had 'in fact concluded a defensive alliance with the British government.' The Governor-General intended to effect 'that part of the engagement to which the British government is pledged.' It would be important to supplement the provisional agreement with an engagement in the form of preliminary articles and subsequently by a definitive treaty. Orders which would initiate military movement, of the type of which Close had already given forewarning, would be issued.[12]

Fresh instructions were also sent to the former Resident with Sindia who had been withdrawn following an ineffectual attempt at negotiations in early 1802. He was to return to the court of Sindia. The Governor of Bombay was instructed to follow the directions of Close on military movement relating to the support of Baji Rao; it was assumed that he had already taken steps to protect the Peshwa. From these instructions it was at once clear that Richard Wellesley was not considering the variant policy options that Close had been concerned to keep it open for him. He was determined to proceed to a treaty relationship with Baji Rao.[13]

These despatches were elaborated a few days later. The Governor-General was anxious to avoid 'all contest with either Holkar or Sindia' and wished British action 'to refrain from checking the progress of the present warfare between those chieftains'. If Company forces were moved at once to protect the Peshwa, it could result in hostilities with Jaswant Rao Holkar, or suppression of the conflict between Sindia and Holkar by depriving them both 'of the object for which they contend.' While there was no doubt as to the outcome of such a contest, it would be 'inconsistent with the pacific views which have uniformly regulated ... conduct in seeking to combine the principal powers of Hindustan in a general system of defensive alliance and guarantee.' Some delay in protection of the Peshwa would not hazard the gains to the Company following from the engagement into which he had already entered. Clearly these instructions were based on the premise, reasonable in the light of events of the previous two years, that the contest between Sindia and Holkar would not be resolved readily. Delayed intervention would give an opportunity to improve the alliance with the Peshwa, and to offer a defensive alliance to Sindia. Troops would meanwhile be assembling, and the decision to call them forward was delegated to Close. The Peshwa should be required to enter into a formal treaty before the British troops moved into the Maratha territory.[14]

After reports from Close—of as late a date as 9 November, 1802—had reached Calcutta, guidance was further revised. It was correctly assumed that Close had discouraged the Peshwa from retiring to Bombay because of uncertainty as to the extent to which the Governor-General wished to support him. Given the decision that had been taken to reestablish the authority of the Peshwa, withdrawal to Bombay should be sought rather than avoided. If the Maratha rulers themselves seemed likely to combine to restore Baji Rao—without British assistance—this would have to be accepted, even though it would involve the abandonment of 'all prospect of concluding with any of the Maratha states those defensive engagements which are essential to the complete consolidation of the British power in India and to the future tranquillity of Hindustan.' This danger could be forestalled by the rapid conclusion of an alliance with the Peshwa. Once concluded, the nature of this alliance was to be made known to both Sindia and Holkar, and an attempt made to concert with them regarding the restoration of the Peshwa 'to the due exercise of his authority under the stipulations of the defensive alliance.' Provided that the Peshwa relied on the aid and influence of the British Company 'every practicable exertion' was to be employed to reestablish his authority. The instructions concluded with an expression of confidence in the judgement of Close in their interpretation.[15]

The Resident with Sindia, whose journey from Fatehghar on the Jumna to resume his position at that court would take at least a month, was ordered to keep his negotiations in step with those undertaken by the Resident with the Peshwa. He was to rebut any attempt on the part of Sindia to argue that he had a right to be consulted by the Peshwa in the conclusion of a new relationship with the British because of his position as heir to the mediator of the Treaty of Salbai which had ended the Anglo-Maratha war in 1782. 'His interest and his station, as a member of the Maratha state, are sufficiently considered by the offer of admitting him to be a party to the defensive treaty with the Peshwa, or of concluding separate engagements between him and the British government.'

Although the Resident with Sindia had discretion to vary the elements in the defensive alliance that was to be offered to him, he was to stress the security which Daulat Rao Sindia would derive from it, whether independently or in association with the Peshwa.[16]

These successive instructions from Calcutta, received by Close in December, form the basis of the policy towards the Marathas prior to the Treaty of Bassein. But they also gave guidance on the policy after the conclusion of the treaty. It was to the Resident with the Peshwa that authority had been delegated, and it was he who planned the steps leading to the restoration of Peshwa Baji Rao to his capital in May 1803.

Close reported his last four days in Pune from the 24 to 28 November in detail, if only because it was important to record the anxiety of Jaswant Rao Holkar to retain him there as Resident. Close believed that he was delayed in Pune pending the outcome of an attempt made by Mir Khan, one of Jaswant Rao Holkar's commanders, to seize Peshwa Baji Rao by force, and that authority to leave was given only when this venture was known to have failed. In what was to be the final interview of Jaswant Rao Holkar with one of the 'politicals' of the Company until John Malcolm met him in December 1805, Close declined an invitation to mediate between Holkar and the Peshwa without the prior agreement of Baji Rao. Holkar, in allowing Close to leave, 'spoke of his wish to accommodate the Peshwa, who he said obstinately slighted him and countenanced Sindia, although his house was as old as Sindia's and at least of equal rank.' Close finally left Pune on 28 November, 1802 and arrived in Bombay on 3 December, 1802.[17]

While Close travelled from Pune to Bombay, Baji Rao, under continued threat of attack, moved north along the coast from Mhar to Bancoote and later to Suvarnadurg. The progress was a leisurely one, since religious scruples prevented Baji Rao from taking food on board ship. He was in his own vessel, but escorted by two British ships. A minister, Raghunath Rao, privy to his engagement with the Company, travelled separately to Bombay.

It was at this point that Close received the critical first set of instructions, those of 16 November, 1802, from the Fort William Secretariat. It was now clear that he was authorised to develop from the agreement sent to him on 25 October the subsidiary alliance that Richard Wellesley had always wished to secure. Close considered that the statements made by Baji Rao to the captain of the

British vessel escorting him showed that he was 'sincerely disposed to conclude the proposed general defensive alliance, according to the assurances which I received on his part from Raghunath Rao at Pune.' But given the prolonged uncertainty which Close had faced at Pune in negotiation before the battle, he had concluded that it would be possible to 'adjust a treaty or conduct business with him with any degree of certainty' only when Baji Rao was 'under the immediate protection of a British corps.' Close knew that most of the surviving members of the entourage of the Peshwa were unaware of the agreement into which Baji Rao had entered, and probably favoured an alliance with Sindia. He feared that this group would 'continue to influence his conduct until he be rendered wholly independent of them.' He noted, as potentially helpful to his intentions, the arrival in Bombay from Pune of an agent of Jaswant Rao Holkar and Amrit Rao. 'It may be of importance to keep the ruling party (in Pune) in suspense as long as possible concerning the intentions of the British government, and the arrival of the deputation may be useful in quickening the mind of the Peshwa and bringing him to a prompt decision.'[18]

Together Duncan and Close interviewed Raghunath Rao in Bombay on 8 December, 1802. Raghunath Rao began by stating that he was 'charged by the Peshwa to renew the application for the succour of two native battalions.' He reported Baji Rao as still wishing to move to Bassein; he was protected by 2000 troops of his own. Duncan and Close questioned Raghunath Rao on the intentions of the Peshwa, and received 'the most solemn assurances that His Highness continued to adhere firmly to his written agreement... with the view that the proposed general defensive alliance should be concluded and carried fully into effect.' He reported that the Peshwa was anxious to arrange at once for the transfer of territory to the Company. Duncan, on the authority of the instructions received from Calcutta, told Raghunath Rao that the Peshwa would be protected by British troops, and was told that this would confirm Baji Rao in his intention to travel to Salsette. Close asked whether all those of importance with Baji Rao agreed with the request that had been made. He received this confirmation, for what it was worth. Raghunath Rao considered that Baji Rao would be safe at Bassein, and need not move to Bombay.

At this point the second of the sets of instructions arrived from Fort William, Calcutta. Close now decided that to furnish Baji Rao with a garrison at Bassein might 'be viewed by (Jaswant Rao) Holkar as an act of opposition' and could incite him to start hostilities. He therefore proposed to Raghunath Rao that there should be a Company force at Salsette, which was within Company territory, opposite Bassein. Turning to the substance of a possible negotiation between them, Close asked Raghunath Rao the nature of the communications passing between Baji Rao and Daulat Rao Sindia. Specifically, he wished to know whether Baji Rao 'had taken any steps to obtain the consent of Sindia to any permanent arrangement of friendship which his present exigency might induce him to conclude with the British government.' Raghunath Rao replied that representatives of both Sindia and Kashi Rao Holkar (the rival candidate for the Holkar inheritance, supported by both Baji Rao and Sindia) had approved the request of Baji Rao for protection by the Company. Both were allegedly aware that cession of territory by the Peshwa to the Company was likely to form part of any treaty settlement. Obviously feeling that these replies were disingenuous, Close enquired about 'the degree of hope' that Baji Rao had of confirmation by Sindia of what had been agreed. He received the reply that Baji Rao had no anxiety on this score, because 'Sindia's government being extensive and difficult to manage, required the whole of his attention ... (and) Holkar was become so formidable as to make it the interest of Sindia to assent to the cooperation of the British troops for his destruction.' Close then asked whether a British approach to Sindia would be consistent with the wishes of the Peshwa, since an attempt to reconcile him to the British concept of a general defensive system might fail. Again the response was optimistic; should Sindia 'unexpectedly manifest a contrary disposition, (Raghunath Rao) conceived that Sindia and Holkar should be allowed to continue the contest which would probably lead, without much delay, to a posture of affairs favourable to the advance of British troops to Pune.'[19]

In writing to Richard Wellesley, Close commented that he still believed that Holkar was 'bent upon making a new Peshwa' and would oppose any power, that is either Sindia or the Company, that assisted Baji Rao. He expected Sindia to await reinforcement from his northern brigades stationed in the Agra-Delhi region before marching south from Ujjain. If the Company, in the setting of a restoration of Baji Rao, had to oppose Holkar, a force of four regiments of European infantry and 12 native infantry battalions would be required. He recommended that Baji Rao should remain on the coast until his capital had been recaptured.[20]

Both Raghunath Rao and Barry Close moved to Bassein, where the Peshwa was encamped on his own territory but secure because of a British force at Salsette. On 18 December 1802 a full day was spent in negotiating a draft treaty, clause by clause, with Raghunath Rao consulting Baji Rao frequently. Eventually the entire wording proposed by Close was accepted, with two minor changes, and the two returned to Bombay to consider the schedule of territories to be ceded. These Raghunath Rao wished to be near the 'Toombuddra' in southern Maharashtra, where the writ of Baji Rao as Peshwa ran only with limitations. Close, on the advice of Duncan, wished more of the cession to be in Gujarat, an area in which the Bombay government was anxious to expand the commercial and political sway of the Company.[21]

At this point a further set of instructions arrived from Fort William, Calcutta; these raised the question of seeking compensation from Baji Rao for the prospective expense of his restoration by British troops. To raise this issue Close saw as likely to cause a setback to the entire negotiation, and, therefore, he wrote asking if this requirement could be set aside. He later determined to conclude the treaty without any such provision, knowing that the treaty settlement as a whole was subject to ratification by Richard Wellesley. In reporting on the progress made, Close noted the anxiety of the Peshwa to preserve his relations with both Daulat Rao Sindia and also with the claimant, Kashi Rao Holkar. These relationships overlaid any possibility of reconciliation with Jaswant Rao Holkar, to whom the Peshwa had a 'rooted enmity'.

> 'Unfortunately (Jaswant Rao) Holkar's demands of the Peshwa bear strongly against Sindia, and are absolutely destructive of the pretensions of Kashi Rao Holkar, who has always been acknowledged and patronized both by Sindia and by the Peshwa as the head of the family. To reconcile Sindia therefore to the present treaty and at the same time to require him to make concessions to Jaswant Rao Holkar may be attended with difficulty'.

Close outlined some of the possible courses of action open to Jaswant Rao Holkar, giving a listing of possible plundering expeditions south and east from Pune. 'If nothing particular occurs therefore to further Holkar's designs his embarrassments may increase to such a degree as to induce him to relax his demands on the Peshwa, and thus lessen the obstacles which at present apparently oppose the project of bringing him to an amicable accommodation.'

At the same time, there were reports from Pune that Jaswant Rao Holkar and Amrit Rao had appointed a *killedar* for the Bassein area, and that this official was moving there with a detachment of troops. Close ensured that this news reached Baji Rao, in the hope of stimulating his sense of insecurity. Those of the entourage of the Peshwa who were unaware of the negotiation in progress again urged Baji Rao to rely on the prospective help of Daulat Rao Sindia. It was in this atmosphere that the discussion of the proposed schedule of territories was resumed at Bassein. Close was concerned at the degree of influence of those urging Baji Rao to rely on Sindia. There was evidence of direct contact between them. He was now anxious 'to close the negotiation'. On the last day of 1802, he achieved this. He attended Baji Rao to consider the schedule; one of two drafts was accepted, and the treaty was signed 'a few moments before the commencement of the new year.'[22]

The terms of the Treaty of Bassein must be summarised. They were to be much discussed during 1803. It was in form a general defensive alliance, though one between very unequal partners. Both Peshwa Baji Rao and the East India Company agreed that in the event of 'unprovoked hostility or aggression against either' the parties would consult and take 'such further measures as the case shall appear to demand.' The central feature of the subsidiary alliance system, the cession of territory in return for the protection of the Company, was contained in the third and fourth articles. Peshwa Baji Rao undertook to receive and the Company to furnish a permanent subsidiary force of not less than 6000 regular troops. At the same time Peshwa Baji Rao had undertaken to cede territory to the value of Rs 26 lakhs. This territory was listed in the Treaty, although the scheme of cession was subsequently varied. The most important restriction on the use to which the subsidiary force could be put was that it might not be employed 'against any of the principal branches of the Maratha Empire.' The Peshwa undertook not to retain within his territory the nationals of any European country at war with Britain. Disputes between the Nizam of Hyderabad and Peshwa Baji Rao should be the subject of arbitration by the Company. Peshwa Baji Rao also undertook 'neither to commence nor to pursue in future any negotiations with any other power whatever without giving previous notice and entering into mutual consultations.'

The setting for the British contest with the Marathas had been created.

NOTES

Material for this chapter has been found in a range of sources. Almost every letter here quoted can be found in the Parliamentary Paper printed in 1804 of which the full title page reads 'Bengal also Fort St. George and Bombay Papers/Presented to the House of Commons/Pursuant to their order of 7 May last/From the East India Company/Relative to the Mahratta War in 1803/Printed by Order of the House of Commons 5 and 22 June 1804.' Parliamentary Papers at this period are not numbered, although in some series this volume has been given the number Sessional Papers 1803/4 xii. It is here referred to as SP. As this work is comparatively rare, alternative references are given where appropriate to the modern Poona Residency Correspondence.

1. Addington-RW 9,27,28 Sep 02 Add Mss 37308 f 367,371,373,375.
2. Sanad 25 Oct 02 PRC x 32: Close-Clive 25 Oct 02 Home Misc 466 p.43: Close-Duncan 25 Oct 02 SP p.341.
3. Close-J A Kirkpatrick 25 Oct 02 Mss Eur F 228/76.
4. Close Mem 1 Nov 02 SP p.345.
5. Malcolm-Duncan 5 Nov 02 SP p.347.
6. Close-Duncan 5, 9 Nov 02 pp.351, 355: Duncan Minute 9 Nov 02.
7. Close-GG 9,13 Nov 02 SP pp.356,359.
8. J A Kirkpatrick-Stevenson, Close 3 Nov 02 Mss Eur F 228/76 Home Misc 617 p.41: J A Kirkpatrick-Malcolm 17 Nov 02 Mss Eur F 228/58.
9. Clive-RW 9 Nov 02 Home Misc 466 p.39.
10. Close-GG 13 Nov 02 SP p.359.

11. Close-Duncan 22 Nov 02: Mem 22 Nov 02 SP p.367.

12. Edmonstone-Close 16 Nov 02 PRC x 45.

13. Edmonstone-Collins 17 Nov 02 Add Mss 13601 f 42: RW-Duncan 16 Nov 02 SP p.379.

14. Edmonstone-Close 22 Nov 02 SP p.64

15. Edmonstone-Close 29 Nov 02 SP p.66

16. Edmonstone-Collins 29 Nov 02 PRC ix 135.

17. Close-GG 28 Nov 02 SP p.376.

18. Close-GG 7 Dec 02 SP p.380.

19. Close-GG 10 Dec 02 SP p.384: Duncan Minute 10 Dec 02 SP p.381 PRC vii 32 Close-GG 12 Dec 02 SP p.388.

20. Close-GG 23 Dec 02 SP p.397

21. Close-GG 30 Dec 02 SP p.395.

22. Close-GG 2 Jan 02 SP p.403.

23. Treaty of Bassein 31 Dec 02 Martin iii 627 PRC x 258.

3

The Road to Poona
(January – May 1803)

Once the Treaty of Bassein had been concluded, it was possible to consider the form of polity which Richard Wellesley had been anxious to create. In the first instance, the Company wished to restore Peshwa Baji Rao to his capital city. This required the removal of Jaswant Rao Holkar from his present position. At the same time it might be possible to offer to the other Maratha rulers, although perhaps not to Jaswant Rao Holkar, a position within the subsidiary alliance system which Richard Wellesley saw as the controlling structure which would permit the British Company to manage diplomacy throughout India.

Despite the total refusal of Peshwa Baji Rao to permit any negotiation with Jaswant Rao Holkar, the withdrawal from Pune of Holkar took place, caused primarily by his financial difficulties but also by his associated failure to create an alternative Peshwa. Partly aided by conciliation of the southern *jagirdars*, the subordinate rulers in southern Maharashtra nominally ruled by the Peshwa, a detachment of Company forces commanded by Arthur Wellesley was able to move rapidly to Pune without encountering opposition. Following this, Baji Rao moved from Bassein to Pune, and was restored to his throne on 13 May 1803.

But the final element in the British political strategy went awry. No meaningful negotiation with Daulat Rao Sindia or with Raghuji Bhonsle took place. Impatient to resolve the restructuring of Maratha politics in the limited timeframe of his political mandate from London, in June 1803 Richard Wellesley delegated political and military authority to his brother Arthur Wellesley. The younger brother chose, as was almost inevitable in the circumstances and as was also probably foreseen by the Governor-General, to transfer the contest from the *darbar* negotiating tent to the battlefield. This set in motion not only the forces of the Company in the Deccan but also those in northern India, where a major threat to Daulat Rao Sindia had been created. Hostilities, initiated in the Deccan, but following in the Ganges–Jumna Doab, achieved part of the aim of the strategy, but also foiled it. A British position in the Maratha polity had indeed been created, but because of the perceived need for haste, the achievement of 1803 was incomplete.

The initial analysis of Richard Wellesley of the events within the Maratha confederacy can be seen in his instructions to Barry Close in November and December 1802. He also set out in December 1802, to the Directors of the East India Company in their Secret Committee, the objectives that he had set himself. When he knew of the *sanad* of cession of territory of 25 October, but not of the conclusion of the Treaty of Bassein, Richard Wellesley wrote to the Secret Committee that the crisis afforded 'the most favourable opportunity for the complete establishment of the British power in the Maratha empire, without the hazard of involving us in a contest with any party.' At the same time he withdrew the resignation as Governor-General which he had tendered to London.

Early in the new year Richard Wellesley wrote to Josiah Webbe in Madras, a former Secretary to the Governor there, to whom he felt obligated because of previous valuable services, and because he had been vindictively removed from a post by the Court of Directors, promising him appointment to a Residency with Raghuji Bhonsle at Nagpur. He indicated that apart from one contingent eventuality, he had determined to stay as Governor-General for another year, stressing that he had 'no intention to make war' and adding that he expected and intended to accomplish all his views at Pune peaceably. He hoped to secure 'by negotiation the basis of a general and lasting pacification of India.' To the Secret Committee of the Court of Directors in London, Richard Wellesley noted that all the principal parties concerned, Peshwa Baji Rao, Daulat Rao Sindia and Jaswant Rao Holkar, had sought the intervention of the British Company, and contended that it was necessary either to persist in the efforts to restore Peshwa Baji Rao to his authority, or 'abandon all hope ... of concluding with any of the Maratha states those defensive engagements which are essential to the complete consolidation of the British empire in India and to the future tranquillity of Hindustan.' He believed that this could be achieved 'by means of amicable negotiation.'[1]

From Fort St George, Madras, Webbe kept Arthur Wellesley in Mysore informed of the rapidly moving situation in the Maratha territories. By 7 January 1803 the conclusion of the Treaty of Bassein was known, Webbe believing that Baji Rao was sincere in its negotiation. Reports from Pune suggested that

> 'the original object of Jaswant Rao Holkar was certainly to have established his permanent authority by making Peshwa Baji Rao a pageant, by inducing Amrit Rao to be his dewan, and by retaining the sole command of the army. After the flight of Peshwa Baji Rao he seems to have intended the same thing by constituting the son of Amrit Rao as the new Peshwa.'

Webbe reported that Amrit Rao had refused to accept this elevation because of 'fear of his immediate deposition and disgrace.' By mid-January Webbe learnt from a confidential source in London that Richard Wellesley would be asked to stay in India for another year. Webbe considered that following the conclusion of the Treaty of Bassein and the 'preparations on the Toombuddra' an 'amicable negotiation' with Jaswant Rao Holkar would be possible. It seemed probable that Richard Wellesley would travel to Madras at the end of January to be nearer the centre of the negotiations with the Maratha powers. Webbe reported Richard Wellesley as 'sanguine in his expectation of accomplishing all his objects at Pune by negotiation' and as wishing it 'to be understood that he has no intention of war.'[2]

In explaining to Lake, Commander-in-Chief of all forces in India but stationed in Oudh, his hopes of achieving an alliance with Peshwa Baji Rao 'under the pacific acquiescence if not with the cordial consent and to the general satisfaction of all parties' Richard Wellesley indicated that he was 'inclined to believe that Sindia will act a neutral, at least, if not an amicable part.' He left it to the discretion of Lake to determine whether he should command the forces that would comprise the northern threat to Daulat Rao Sindia or join the army being assembled north of Mysore. Richard Wellesley gave it as his view that there was 'no probability of any important contest in the Deccan.' John Malcolm, briefly back in Calcutta after his journey to Bombay, before news of the signature of the Treaty of Bassein had arrived at Fort William, predicted to Lake that

> 'Holkar, though vain of his late success, is alarmed at Sindia and is by no means prepared to enter upon so unequal a contest as that with which he has been threatened if he refuses acquiescence to any arrangement which is supported by the Company and the Nizam. Sindia, however adverse to the establishment of a British force at Pune, feels too sensibly the danger to which his northern territory would be exposed to hazard a rupture with the English government.'

There was a clear need, in Malcolm's view, to demonstrate Company military force; this would ensure a peaceful outcome. Hostilities were unlikely, but if they came, Malcolm suggested to Lake, 'one short campaign would for ever dissipate the terror with which Indian politicians in England are accustomed to contemplate the power of the Maratha nation.'[3]

British policy towards the Marathas, subsequent to the signature of the Treaty of Bassein, continued to be directed by Barry Close as Resident with Peshwa Baji Rao, working within the general directive from Richard Wellesley of November 1802. It was Close who ordered forward troops from the Madras Presidency and from the British subsidiary force stationed with the Nizam of Hyderabad and who determined the timing and content of negotiation with Jaswant Rao Holkar and with Daulat Rao Sindia.

In controlling the course of policy in early 1803 Close would seem to have made three assumptions, each of them justified in the event. He expected, firstly, that there would be some measure of support for Peshwa Baji Rao among his own feudatories in southern Maharashtra. In this he did not rely on the simplistic optimism of a court in exile, he believed that the southern *jagirdars* would have interested motives for seeking to secure the approval of Peshwa Baji Rao and of the British Company. It followed that when the detachment soon to be placed under the command of Arthur Wellesley moved forward into Maratha territory, it would meet with little opposition. Secondly, Close assumed that Daulat Rao Sindia and Jaswant Rao Holkar would not readily combine against the British Company. This assumption was also made in Calcutta, despite the later protestations to the Secret Committee in London of the willingness to undertake hostilities if necessary against the combination of the two Maratha rulers. There were two reasons for the confidence that this union would not occur. One, the geographic distance between the forces of the two Maratha chiefs, but more important, second, the depth of the personal rift between them. Even the new situation of the Treaty of Bassein, and the consequent association of Peshwa Baji Rao and the East India Company, would not quickly lead Daulat Rao Sindia and Jaswant Rao Holkar to compose their differences. The third assumption was that Holkar would withdraw peaceably from Pune. What he had hoped to secure by military operations before Pune in October 1802 had, as Webbe had noted, eluded him; it was the person of Peshwa Baji Rao.

During this time Barry Close gained further experience of the difficulty of working with Peshwa Baji Rao. He was reminded of the unrelenting hatred of Baji Rao for both his half-brother Amrit Rao and for Jaswant Rao Holkar. This enhanced the difficulty of the attempt by the Company to insinuate mediation into the disputes of the Maratha confederacy. Close knew that the attitude of the Peshwa to his new alliance was at the least constrained, and perhaps disingenuous. Peshwa Baji Rao was, for example, anxious to do nothing that might discourage Daulat Rao Sindia from moving to Pune. In this way he might still secure a return to his own capital freed from obligation to the British Company. Even if Sindia failed in an attempt to aid Peshwa Baji Rao, he would have been weakened by conflict with Jaswant Rao Holkar. Perhaps most important, Close once again found, as had been the case in the previous year, that faced with a decision, Baji Rao took refuge in delay, hoping perhaps that the rapidly shifting political scene would bring a new variation in the pattern in which the course of action to be followed would be clearer. This last characteristic worked to the advantage of the British; had Peshwa Baji Rao been more active, he could have attempted to manoeuvre the Company in his own interest, but for such a venture he was far too indolent.

The authority of Peshwa Baji Rao over both the major feudatories of the Maratha empire, and the lesser rulers of southern Maharashtra had been lost, as John Malcolm was to put it nearly two years later 'because the different chiefs and *jagirdars* were so well trenched in ancient customs, hereditary rights and prescriptive claims, as always to be able to evade the orders and disappoint the views of their legitimate superiors.'[4]

The British Company could deal with Baji Rao either as one Maratha chief among many, holding forts and lands nominally on grant from the Raja of Satara, or as 'exercising the authority he derives from his station as the first civil officer of the Maratha government over the different branches and chiefs of that empire.' The capacity in which Baji Rao had signed the Treaty of Bassein was in a real sense not for the British to determine. A British assertion carried with it no guarantee that the major Maratha chiefs would view the Treaty as an alliance with the head of the confederacy. The determinant of the significance of the Treaty would be the actions of Jaswant Rao Holkar, Daulat Rao Sindia, and Raghuji Bhonsle.

It was perhaps appreciation of this that led Richard Wellesley in early February to modify significantly the earlier statement of the direction of his policy to the Secret Committee of the Court of Directors, arguing that 'the complete operation' of the Treaty of Bassein was 'still subject to doubt.' It had always been evident, the Secret Committee were now told, that the major Maratha chiefs were 'averse to an alliance between the British government and the sovereign power of the Maratha empire.' It followed that

'knowledge of our arrangement with the Peshwa may induce Daulat Rao Sindia and Holkar to compromise their differences and to offer to the Peshwa proposals for restoring his Highness to the *masnad* of Pune. In such an event, it is not my intention to attempt to compel the Peshwa to adhere to the faith of his engagements, at the hazard of involving the Company in a war with the combined Maratha states. If however, the majority of the Maratha *jagirdars* and chieftains subject to the authority of his Highness should concur on the restoration, I shall consider it my duty to proceed, without regard to any partial opposition on the part of Sindia or Holkar, either singly or united.'

Meanwhile steps were taken, both to attempt to conciliate Jaswant Rao Holkar and also to preempt the two major Maratha rulers in any actions to aid Peshwa Baji Rao. This would avert the danger of a combination that would stand in the path of the restoration of the Peshwa by British action alone.

In early January, directly after the signature of the Treaty by Peshwa Baji Rao and before he knew whether it would be ratified by Richard Wellesley—as was the outcome in the event—Barry Close reported that Jaswant Rao Holkar was rumoured to have quarrelled with Amrit Rao in Pune. The presumption of the Company 'politicals' was that the centre of this quarrel was the inability of Amrit Rao to seize the resources of Pune and its surrounding districts to a degree which placated the insistent demands for plunder of the forces of Jaswant Rao Holkar. In February, Amrit Rao wrote to the Governor of Bombay, and although nothing came of this approach, this was a further indication that Jaswant Rao Holkar was in difficulties and that he was 'probably apprehensive that his demands on the Peshwa' were 'such as cannot be complied with.'

At the same time Close reported that the resource difficulties of Jaswant Rao Holkar were probably insuperable. 'From the territory north of Pune he can derive nothing, as he has made it a desert, and to attempt to penetrate to the southward for subsistence for his numerous cavalry and banditti ... would involve him in serious opposition.'

Close had believed in December that pressure for further plunder would lead Jaswant Rao Holkar southwards into the territory of the British Company or that of its ally the Nizam of Hyderabad. The assemblage of military power that Jaswant Rao Holkar commanded at Pune was formidable, despite a near mutinous condition brought on by lack of resources. In an intelligence statement from Pune which Barry Close sent to Arthur Wellesley at this time, it was given as 56,000 cavalry 15,900 infantry and 157 guns of various calibres.[5]

The content of any negotiation that could be opened with Jaswant Rao Holkar had, at the least, to be within the knowledge of Peshwa Baji Rao, even if not approved by him. In mid-February Close discussed the demands made by Jaswant Rao Holkar of the Peshwa with the principal minister of Peshwa Baji Rao, Raghunath Rao. The minister explained that Baji Rao saw Jaswant Rao Holkar as a rebel. As Peshwa he would not, therefore, send orders to Daulat Rao Sindia, who alone could meet them, to satisfy any of the demands of Jaswant Rao Holkar. Further, Baji Rao wished to preserve his relationship with Daulat Rao Sindia.

In a long discussion with Peshwa Baji Rao himself in early March, Barry Close pressed the case for negotiation with Jaswant Rao Holkar, but with total lack of success. Instructions from Fort William had suggested that an attempt should be made to reconcile

Peshwa Baji Rao and Jaswant Rao Holkar, although it was accepted that the claims made by Holkar were 'utterly inadmissible.' Adjusted terms were to be prepared, worked out by Barry Close in conjunction with Peshwa Baji Rao, combining 'firmness and concession.' An offer to pay to Jaswant Rao Holkar a considerable sum, to be advanced by the Peshwa on the basis of a guaranteed loan from the Bombay Government, should be considered, together with 'the grant of a fort, with a jagir' by which 'the tranquillity of the Deccan would be cheaply purchased.' Jaswant Rao Holkar was to be warned against 'any opposition to the arrangements which have been made for the restoration of the Peshwa to the *masnad* of Pune.' If these terms were rejected by Jaswant Rao Holkar, 'the allied forces of the Company, the Peshwa and the Nizam' were to be employed 'to compel his submission.'[6]

When these instructions from Fort William reached him, Close first delayed their application and then essentially modified them. He reported to Richard Wellesley on 6 March that he proposed to defer any approach to Peshwa Baji Rao on these lines until he knew more of the movements of the detachment to be commanded by Arthur Wellesley that was to enter Maratha territory from the south. Peshwa Baji Rao maintained his total refusal to permit any approach to Jaswant Rao Holkar. Barry Close was able to do no more than write to Jaswant Rao Holkar informing him that the British Company was about to give effect to the Treaty of Bassein by restoring the Peshwa, and offering him British mediation in his disputes with the other members of the Maratha confederacy, although without any undertaking on the terms of such mediation.

It is perhaps questionable whether a genuine opportunity to conciliate Jaswant Rao Holkar had been lost, although some of the group of political officers certainly felt that this was the case. While Barry Close could scarcely have been certain that Jaswant Rao Holkar was about to withdraw from Pune, he could reasonably forecast that the need for plunder would force some move, and that even aside from the objections of Peshwa Baji Rao to negotiations of any kind, the demands of Jaswant Rao Holkar would have been difficult to resolve.[7]

In November 1802 Richard Wellesley had directed Collins to return as Resident with Daulat Rao Sindia. Sindia had written to Calcutta stating that he was moving to the Deccan with the intention of 'arranging the disordered affairs of that quarter.' He expressed the hope that any negotiation with Peshwa Baji Rao would be 'in concert and concurrence' with him. To this letter Richard Wellesley had replied in very general terms, saying that no British action would be taken contrary to the 'obligations of reciprocal attachment' and adding that the purpose of resuming the presence of the British Resident at his court was to concert means of restoring peace to the Deccan.[8]

The first interview of the resumed Residency with Daulat Rao Sindia took place a few miles from Burhanpur on 11 March, 1803. Collins reported the fact but not the content of the Treaty of Bassein, and the intention of the Company to restore Peshwa Baji Rao, 'not doubting but that these measures would meet with the entire approbation and strenuous support of the principal Maratha chieftains.' He added that his own visit was intended to propose British mediation in the disputes between Daulat Rao Sindia and Jaswant Rao Holkar, and to offer admission to the defensive guarantee structure to Sindia. Collins, to quote his own report to Richard Wellesley, set out the proposals which he was deputed to make as first, that of concerting the most effectual means of restoring and securing tranquillity in the Deccan, secondly, that of offering the mediation of the British government to achieve a reconciliation between Daulat Rao Sindia and Jaswant Rao Holkar, and third, the making of an offer of 'the benefits of the general defensive alliance on terms similar to those recently concluded with Peshwa Baji Rao.' The reply that Collins received was that time was required to consider these matters. The Resident claimed to have detected a difference between the personal attitude of Daulat Rao Sindia and that of his ministers, to whom Sindia was in debt and from whom he could have been rescued by an alliance with the Company. The Resident reported movements of envoys from Jaswant Rao Holkar to Daulat Rao Sindia and from Daulat Rao Sindia to Peshwa Baji Rao, although not the content of these negotiations.[9]

After pressure to secure it, Collins was able to hold a second discussion with Daulat Rao Sindia on 24 March. In this he stated that he detected that the *darbar* seemed by no means to favour the suggestions of Richard Wellesley, that it appeared that Daulat Rao Sindia 'entertained designs incompatible with the relations of friendship,' and that it could, therefore, be inferred that 'this court was dissatisfied with the part which the English had taken in the

late disturbances that had arisen in the Maratha empire.' Collins
added that 'the declared intention of creating a new Peshwa' and
'the ambitious aim of Jaswant Rao Holkar to possess himself of the
Naibship (the command of all Maratha forces) had been frustrated
only by the military preparations of the British government, consequent upon the defensive alliance lately concluded by the Peshwa.'
He challenged Daulat Rao Sindia 'to disclose to me his real intentions.'

After the ministers of Daulat Rao Sindia had attempted to argue
that Peshwa Baji Rao should have consulted Sindia before concluding the Treaty of Bassein, Collins secured an intervention in the
discussion from the Maharaja, a declaration that 'he had no intention whatever to obstruct the completion of the arrangements lately
concluded.' Daulat Rao Sindia then directly asked the Resident the
terms of the Treaty, which were not formally known to him,
although they must have been the subject of reasonably accurate
newswriter surmise. Collins undertook to explain the content 'if
the Maharaja would enter into a discussion of the different articles
of the Treaty with me, for the purpose of becoming a member of
the general defensive alliance.' This approach was prevented by the
ministers of Sindia and in writing to Richard Wellesley Collins
correctly forecast that they would continue this obstruction, with
the result that Peshwa Baji Rao would be restored solely by the
actions of the British government.[10]

The preoccupation of Barry Close at the court of Peshwa Baji
Rao at Bassein was certainly military advance, not negotiation with
members of the Maratha confederacy. He wished to ensure that it
was the British Company alone that replaced Peshwa Baji Rao on
his throne and in his capital, and this objective he achieved. The
letters that he had sent from Pune late in the previous October,
followed as they had been by confirmatory instructions from Calcutta, now paid formidable political dividends. At the end of
January, Close had stressed to the Governor of Madras the urgent
need for the subsidiary force at Hyderabad 'in the greatest strength
possible' to 'be advanced to the western frontier of the Nizam so
as to menace Pune.' At about the same time, instructions from
Calcutta were received in Madras which ordered the forward movement of at least part of the detachment of Company troops already
assembled near Harihar in northern Mysore. The timing of the

crossing of the boundary of Maratha territory was to be determined by Barry Close.

The immediate aim of the detachment was to march north as far as Miraj, where it was hoped that Peshwa Baji Rao would join it, and there to link with the subsidiary force from Hyderabad. The responsibility for the coordination of military movement and political negotiation also remained with Close.[11]

In territory ceded to the Company from Mysore in 1799, the measures which were to lead to the restoration of Peshwa Baji Rao to his *masnad* were in train. After rather more than a month of intensive logistic preparation, Arthur Wellesley had written on the first day of the new year to Barry Close at Bassein. Assuming that the objective would be to march to Pune, he forecast that it would be the first days of March before the detachment, which at that time he assumed would be commanded by Stuart, the Commander in Chief, Madras, would be ready to cross into Maratha territory. He detailed a possible route, and continued 'I do not think that you ought to look out for us at Pune before the end of April.'

But such timing was dependent on the most favourable of assumptions, namely that the *jagirdars* of southern Maharashtra would compose their differences, and warfare between them would not obstruct the movement of the Company detachment and its following logistic convoys. 'The countries on the other side of the Toombuddra are in a sad state of disorder. The heads of districts and of villages have seized the supreme authority, and have raised troops, and are carrying on against each other a petty warfare.'

That the difficulties which the detachment would have to face in its northward journey were to be as much political as logistic had been evident at the beginning of December. In discussion with a representative of Goklah, the son of the Maratha commander with whom Arthur Wellesley had cooperated in the pursuit of Dhondiah Vagh in 1800, the *vakil* had been anxious to enter into a negotiation which would have safeguarded the right of Goklah to enter Company territory with his troops if he found himself under threat from Jaswant Rao Holkar. After reference to Madras, Arthur Wellesley was advised to reply that there could be no admission of armed men into Company territory. From this encounter, and others which followed, Arthur Wellesley was able to begin to build up a picture of the relationships between the southern *jagirdars*, and prepare himself for the task of handling them. The objective would

be so to proceed that those that felt a loyalty to Peshwa Baji Rao
would advance with him towards Pune, and that during the passage
of the Company detachment there would be no hazard of renewed
hostilities which could endanger the movement of supplies.[12]

Arthur Wellesley had also turned his attention to the need to
create a depot 'on the coast opposite to the island of Bombay.' This
he proposed, subject to the views of Stuart, to suggest to the
Governor of Bombay. Three weeks later Arthur Wellesley set out
his ideas to Duncan at Bombay, and initiated a correspondence
which went fully into the supply needs of a detachment deployed
on the Deccan plain above the western Ghats to the east of Bombay.
The depot should be within easy reach by water from Bombay, and
capable of being defended. The supplies required were those for
the feeding and safeguarding of European and Indian troops;
further military stores would be required only if the detachment
was involved in fighting before it reached Pune.[13]

In the first days of March both Stuart, Commander-in-Chief, Fort
St. George, and Arthur Wellesley, were in the 'ceded districts' that
is Mysore territory which had been transferred to Company control
by the Partition Treaty of 1799. In response to a request from Stuart,
Arthur Wellesley set out a possible order of battle of a detachment
'not only of sufficient strength to defend itself, but also to give
confidence to, and keep together, the Peshwa's party in the state.'
It should have a regiment of European dragoons and three regiments
of native cavalry, one of European infantry and six battalions of native
infantry, artillery and pioneers. To this would be added cavalry
provided by the Raja of Mysore and by the Maratha *jagirdars*.

> 'If you should take command of it yourself, (Arthur Wellesley
> added in writing to Stuart) 'I hope you will do me the favour to
> allow me to accompany you in any capacity whatever ....If you
> should not think proper to take command of this detachment
> yourself, and... you should be pleased to entrust it to me, I shall
> be infinitely gratified, and shall do everything in my power to
> forward your views.'

An operational command could rarely have been solicited in so
courtly a manner.[14]

The following day Arthur Wellesley was able to report to Barry
Close that the outcome was that 'everything ends, at last, with my
going forward with a detachment, and the main body of the army

is to remain on the frontier with a view to its defence or to giving support to the advanced division if it should be necessary.'[15]

The earlier instructions to the Government of Madras sent from Fort William were the basis of the detailed directive now issued to Arthur Wellesley by Stuart. The commander of the detachment was to 'encourage the southern *jagirdars* to declare in favour of the Peshwa's cause,' to advance to Miraj and effect a junction with Peshwa Baji Rao, the Hyderabad subsidiary force and an element of the army of the Nizam of Hyderabad, and finally 'to proceed eventually to Pune and establish an order of things in that capital favourable to the return of the Peshwa and to the attainment of the ends of the late Treaty.' In the conciliation of the southern *jagirdars*, specific commitments were to be avoided. The intention was clear; a rapid advance and junction with the Peshwa and the forces moving from Hyderabad which would frustrate any attempt of the major Maratha rulers to come to the assistance of Peshwa Baji Rao.

> 'If the majority of the southern *jagirdars*, and the sentiments of the body of the people, are found to declare in favour of the restoration of Peshwa Baji Rao, the British detachment ought to persevere in the endeavours to reestablish his authority... should the detachment during the prosecution of that endeavour encounter the hostility of any individual *jagirdar* ... they are to employ every practical means to overcome his opposition.'

But this authority to 'compel... submission' was to apply only if hostility was encountered; the principle of the policy of Richard Wellesley, as Stuart correctly interpreted it, was to avoid war.[16]

After deciding in late January 1803 that he could not himself move to Madras, as both Arthur Wellesley and Clive, the Governor of Madras, had suggested, Richard Wellesley had determined to send John Malcolm, ostensibly as Resident at Mysore, but in reality as an envoy at large to assist in the political issues that would arise as the British detachment advanced into Maratha territory. Josiah Webbe discussed these questions with John Malcolm, once again and reported to Arthur Wellesley that 'everything seems to be favourable to Lord Wellesley's plan for the attainment of his objects without war. There is no reason to apprehend a confederacy of the Maratha states, and there is little reason to expect a union of Daulat Rao Sindia and Jaswant Rao Holkar.'

Webbe saw it as in the interest of Daulat Rao Sindia that Jaswant Rao Holkar should be destroyed by the British Company 'but I think that our natural policy is to adjust the claims of Jaswant Rao Holkar if possible by our mediation, in order that the Holkar family may be preserved as rival and counterpoise to Daulat Rao Sindia in the northern parts of the Maratha empire.' At about the same time Richard Wellesley urged Clive to stay as Governor of Madras and await the arrival of his still unknown successor, since 'the result of weak or wicked counsels at Fort St. George might affect the whole system of our political relations with the native powers in the peninsula, and expose our arms to disgrace and even to destruction, and leave our most important interests at the mercy of France on the eve of a returning war.'[17]

Arthur Wellesley crossed into Maratha territory on 11 March. After two days he wrote to his brother the Governor-General expressing optimism at the political prospects: 'all your plans will be carried into execution'. As the detachment moved forward, forces of Jaswant Rao Holkar, commanded by Mir Khan and Futteh Singh Mania, fell back. At the same time, Arthur Wellesley and John Malcolm learnt of the intrigues and contests between the 'southern *jagirdars*', the group of lesser feudatories in southern Maharashtra. The detachment made good progress. By 23 March Arthur Wellesley was able to report that he hoped to reach Miraj by 5 April. He now began to be concerned about Peshwa Baji Rao joining his detachment. Both Arthur Wellesley and John Malcolm considered that it would be appropriate for Peshwa Baji Rao to join them at Miraj, and move northwards with the detachment to Pune.

On 30 March in Bassein, Barry Close had a five hour conference with Peshwa Baji Rao, in which as he reported to Richard Wellesley, he

'had the mortification to find his Highness oppose every point that I urged with the same obstinacy that I experienced from him on the occasion when I used all my efforts to obtain his compliance with your Lordship's desire that he should offer some terms of accommodation to Jaswant Rao Holkar.'

Close reported that 'no urgency of manner on my part, nor any arguments which I found it possible to apply ... made any apparent impression.' Peshwa Baji Rao refused to join the Company detachment. It was true that Baji Rao disliked sea travel, and that his religious scruples prevented his taking food at sea, but Barry Close considered this, and an alleged shortage of equipment, were merely excuses. Baji Rao feared 'to join the army in a situation in which it may possibly have occasion to repel opposition.'[18]

By the first days of April, Arthur Wellesley knew that Jaswant Rao Holkar was withdrawing from Pune northwards towards Ahmednagar. He was now confident that he would soon be able to link his own detachment in its movements with that advanced from Hyderabad, consisting of Company units and some elements of the army of the Nizam. He now felt able to forecast that the detachment would arrive at Pune on 23 or 24 April, as it did, and to urge upon Barry Close the speedy return of Peshwa Baji Rao to his capital, after the arrival of Company troops, through the passes of the western Ghats.[19]

The detachment reached Akluj on 15 April; it was now close to the forces, Company and those of the Nizam, which had been moved from Hyderabad. A British infantry unit was transferred to the detachment commanded by Colonel Stevenson. Arthur Wellesley set himself to state fully to Richard Wellesley the political and military situation which had been created by the junction of the two Company detachments.

'I have been joined by some of the southern *jagirdars,* and of the officers of the Peshwa who quitted him by his desire at Mhar after he had fled from Pune (in November, 1802) but there are many of both descriptions still absent.... In all it is easy to observe.... not only a want of attachment and zeal, but a detestation of his person and an apprehension of his power, founded upon a long series of mutual injuries.'

Arthur Wellesley noted that the extent to which these feudatories would be prepared to assist Baji Rao in his new-found alliance with the British Company would 'depend much upon the Peshwa' and 'upon the manner in which the new treaty will work.' He explained to the Governor-General that he expected Holkar and the forces he had deployed south of Pune to fall back. Arthur Wellesley then turned to his central concern, 'a confederacy of the greater Maratha powers.'

'The question whether the supposed confederacy will be formed, and whether we shall have to contend with it ought to be brought to a decision as soon as possible.

firstly, because if we are to have a war, we shall carry it on with great advantage during the rainy season

secondly because we are ready, and the supposed enemy is not, and every day's delay after this time is an unnecessary increase of expense to us and an advantage to them

thirdly because we shall immediately ascertain the views and intentions of the Peshwa regarding the alliance in general, and we shall leave no time for intrigues among the *jagirdars* in his and our interest

fourthly because nothing but our determined and early opposition to the confederacy can save us from it, supposing it to exist. To withdraw from our engagements with the Peshwa will rather accelerate its attack, with the addition of the Peshwa's force.'

Arthur Wellesley recommended that the Peshwa should urge Sindia to move north of the Narbada. This perhaps showed a lack of appreciation of the limited authority of Baji Rao. Pressure should also be brought to bear upon Perron in the northern territories, and on the Raja of Berar. Such a 'system of menace', Arthur Wellesley believed, would 'put a stop to the negotiations for the formation of the confederacy', but if such deterrence did not serve to avert hostilities, 'the impression which will put an end to the contest ... must be made from the northern frontier of Bengal.'

Arthur Wellesley significantly added that John Malcolm had explained to him why Richard Wellesley was 'anxious to bring these questions to a decision as soon as possible.' This was a reference to the realisation by Richard Wellesley that the Ministers of the government of Addington were not willing to give support against the Court of Directors, and that the end of the Governor-Generalship was perhaps in sight. Arthur Wellesley spoke of this as a factor 'which must be conclusive to every friend of yours.'

Barry Close, Arthur Wellesley found, did not believe that 'the supposed confederacy' was about to be formed. John Malcolm at this time commented to Webbe at Madras that

'no effectual steps have yet been taken to break the threatened combination. All that I have seen since I entered this country convinces me of the necessity of some very considerable sacrifices being made to conciliate Jaswant Rao Holkar, but I fear the time is passed and we have now to depend more on our own spirit and firmness than on any chance of reconciling either Jaswant Rao Holkar or Daulat Rao Sindia to our plans.'[20]

As a means of frightening Peshwa Baji Rao, Amrit Rao had threatened the firing of Pune on the approach of Company forces or those loyal to the Peshwa, and these messages had been passed by Close to Arthur Wellesley. When he was within one extremely long forced march from Pune, knowing that Amrit Rao was still in the city, Arthur Wellesley pressed onwards over difficult ghat conditions and entered it, virtually as Amrit Rao left. By 21 April, Arthur Wellesley and John Malcolm were dating their letters from the capital city of Peshwa Baji Rao. 'The combined chiefs, of whom we have heard so much, have allowed us to come quietly and take our station at this place. They have not yet made peace among themselves, much less have they agreed to attack us, or on any particular plan of attack.'

Arthur Wellesley found the role of political adviser to his brother suited his literary style: 'In all great actions there is risk, which the little minds of those who form their judgement of yours will readily perceive ... but their remarks ought not to give you a moment's uneasiness.' John Malcolm, writing to Fort William at the same time, pointed out the advantages that would follow from a reconciliation with Amrit Rao, a possibility opened by a courteous exchange of letters with Arthur Wellesley directly after the occupation of Pune.[21]

During the next few days, Barry Close was chiefly concerned at the markedly dilatory journey of Peshwa Baji Rao from Bassein to Pune, noting to Arthur Wellesley from Kalyan on 27 April that 'you can conquer a kingdom under the most menacing circumstances in less time than I can move the Peshwa to re-accept his crown ... until he shows himself at Pune it will not be possible for me to direct his attention to the different important points that you have stated for adjustment.'

Peshwa Baji Rao was not finally reinstated in his capital city until 13 May. While it might indeed be the case, as John Malcolm wrote, that the Company 'faced no difficulties but what arise from the personal character of Peshwa Baji Rao', these now became of moment.

'Our first step must be to establish an influence with and over the Peshwa, for until that great point is effected we tread on hollow ground. We have ample means of making what arrangement we choose, but it is difficult to reconcile the weak, perverse and obstinate men with whom we have to deal with the ways of truth policy and wisdom.'

To Edmonstone Malcolm noted that he feared 'much difficulty from the weakness and depravity' of Peshwa Baji Rao adding that 'we have no children's play in hand and must devise means of directing his councils or of our rendering ourselves independent of their operation.' This stated the essence of the issue of relations with Peshwa Baji Rao. It was in a real sense never resolved, endless hours of *darbar* discussion producing belated acceptance of the inevitable, and effective government melting away because of an inability to appoint responsible ministers or to give them any delegation.[22]

Although there had seemed no immediate danger from the confederation to the north, and Arthur Wellesley had expressed the view of each of the members of the informal triumvirate when he stated that he expected 'much bad temper and many threats' but no hostilities, there was an expectation in early May that a southward thrust might be attempted. Collins as Resident with Daulat Rao Sindia reported that he believed that Jaswant Rao Holkar had received reassurances that he would have restored to him his family lands, that Raghuji Bhonsle of Berar was entering his tents to march towards Sindia and that Sindia himself planned to march towards Berar. All this would suggest that the Maratha chiefs were at the point of composing their differences and might march through the territories of the Nizam of Hyderabad north of the Godavari towards Pune. At about the same time Jaswant Rao Holkar entered Hyderabad territory near Aurangabad and secured extensive funding, possibly assisted in this by the treachery of a subordinate feudatory of the Nizam.

Barry Close was certainly inclined to put these reports together and from them to forecast a dash to Pune perhaps by the combined major Maratha chiefs 'in fourteen or fifteen marches.' This could be achieved before the monsoon flood waters filled the Godavari in mid-June. He, therefore, recommended that the main Madras Company army, which had been left far to the south in Company territory north of Mysore, should move to Hyderabad. Arthur Wellesley took a less alarmist view of the position, and did not believe that there was an immediate prospect of an alliance between Jaswant Rao Holkar and Daulat Rao Sindia. He wrote to the Resident with Sindia to tell him that this was his view, adding that he believed that these false reports were circulated to frighten the court of the Nizam of Hyderabad. He considered his own force as fully equal to that of Daulat Rao Sindia in the field, and the detachment from Hyderabad commanded by Colonel Stevenson as adequate for the immediate defence of the territory of the Nizam. He did not recommend a move of the main Company army to Hyderabad, although at a later point he did propose a movement northwards to a position from which either Hyderabad or Pune could be reached quickly, and from which the southern *jagirdars* would be intimidated.[23]

By the first days of May 1803, the statement that Arthur Wellesley had prepared at Akluj on 15 April had reached Fort William. It was at once clear that it coincided to a marked degree with the analysis of events which Richard Wellesley had formed. There had always been the intention to put pressure on Daulat Rao Sindia from the Ganges-Jumna valley. Draft instructions to the two Residents, Barry Close with Peshwa Baji Rao and Collins with Daulat Rao Sindia, which had evidently already been prepared and kept ready until a decision was taken, were now issued. Arthur Wellesley also received a hint at this time that he would be sent further instructions, although these were delayed in the event.[24]

The instructions now sent from Fort William, Calcutta, at first in summary form, and later elaborated, took almost three weeks to travel to both Residents. Daulat Rao Sindia was to be told that was no occasion for him to be encamped south of the Narbada unless it was his intention to attempt to upset the arrangement that had been reached between Peshwa Baji Rao and the British Company enacted in the Treaty of Bassein, or to reestablish at Pune the ascendancy that he had exercised there for some years before 1802. It was further to be explained to Daulat Rao Sindia that Peshwa Baji Rao had been fully justified in turning to the British Company for aid, and that his own security had been increased by the move of British troops northwards to Pune. Only if Daulat Rao Sindia withdrew northwards across the Narbada could he avoid the loss of the advantages that he could derive from the system of subsidiary alliance which was again to be offered to him, in the context of explaining the terms of the Treaty of Bassein to him. He was also to be asked to be explicit in his explanation of the 'nature of his negotiations with the Raja of Berar' and warned that any attack on the territory of the Nizam of Hyderabad would be an act of hostility against the British Company.[25]

While these instructions were crossing the Deccan, Daulat Rao Sindia continued to act in a way which, at the least, justified the suspicions of Barry Close rather than the optimism of Arthur Wellesley. At his *darbar* the Resident Collins entered into a dispute over the theoretical right of Daulat Rao Sindia to collect *chauth*, the legalised protection money which the Maratha collected from other rulers in central and northern India. A demand from Sindia coincided with an enforced contribution on Aurangabad made by Jaswant Rao Holkar. The *darbar* justified their contention that these exactions were in order in a manner so insulting that Collins threatened to leave camp and end his embassy, although in the event he did not do so. In a private letter to Arthur Wellesley, Collins expressed total scepticism of the prospects of persuading the *darbar* of Daulat Rao Sindia that there were advantages for Sindia in the subsidiary alliance system. Collins remained convinced that a confederation between the three Maratha rulers had been achieved.[26]

Arthur Wellesley took the alarm of Barry Close at the prospect of a military initiative by Daulat Rao Sindia sufficiently seriously to consider movement northwards of both his own detachment and that commanded by Colonel Stevenson. 'This moment is critical; the rivers will fill in about a month and it appears to me that Daulat Rao Sindia if he intends hostilities has marched in this hurry to establish himself in some post of consequence or to make a dash at Hyderabad so as to get back across the Godavari before the river will fill.'

This was to assume greater capacity for action than was natural to Daulat Rao Sindia. Arthur Wellesley also suggested to the Resident that Daulat Rao Sindia was no longer being invited by Peshwa Baji Rao to visit Pune. In a direct hint to Calcutta that wide delegated political authority was becoming urgent, Arthur Wellesley noted, 'we are playing a little at cross purposes here.... We ought to have some authority to settle matters with all these chiefs under some general instructions ... the state of affairs varies daily and before orders can come from Bengal on any question the circumstances

that ought to guide the decision have entirely changed.' As will be
seen, was the first suggestion on these lines, which ultimately
brought Arthur Wellesley the powers he sought.[27]

Barry Close, John Malcolm and Arthur Wellesley turned their
attention afresh to the immediate matters on which they had to
press Peshwa Baji Rao. They were concerned that the Peshwa
should write to Daulat Rao Sindia to ensure than he was under no
illusion that his presence at Pune would be welcome. Further, the
Peshwa had still to fulfil his obligations under the Treaty of Bassein
to provide troops to meet the purposes of the alliance. This could
really be achieved in one way only, the conciliation by Baji Rao of
the southern *jagirdars* who had moved northwards with Arthur
Wellesley. In an extended audience on 14 May, Peshwa Baji Rao
seemed to accept these needs, although the first was evaded for
some time, and probably counteracted by secret messages in an
opposite sense, and the second was delayed for more than a month.
Hoping that either revised instructions or delegated political authority
was on its way to him from Calcutta, Arthur Wellesley deferred
sending significant instructions to the Resident with Daulat Rao
Sindia, although he suggested that a reminder of the scale of the
military presence of the British Company would be appropriate.[28]

An armed confrontation between the Company on the one hand,
and Daulat Rao Sindia and Raghuji Bhonsle on the other seemed
imminent. The resultant tension was to remain unresolved for two
months.

NOTES

The convention followed is that references are not given for letters
written by Arthur Wellesley. These letters can be found in the
various editions of his despatches, including the Supplementary
Despatches, and also to some extent in the Poona Residency
Correspondence series. References to all other letters are given;
they can be found in the Wellington Papers, cited as WP, the Poona
Residency Correspondence, the published Despatches of Richard
Wellesley, and the Richard Wellesley papers in the British Library.

1. RW-Sec Ctee 24 Dec 02 Martin iii 3: RW-Webbe 7 Jan 03 Add Mss 13622
   f.9.

2. Webbe-AW 7,18 Jan 03 WP 1/135.

3. RW-Lake 7 Jan 03 Martin iii 28: Malcolm-Lake 11 Jan 03 Kaye Life i 202.

4. Malcolm-Edmonstone 31 Jan 05 NUL Bentinck Mss Pw Jb 32 f.162.

5. Close-RW 2 Jan 03 PRC x 59: Close -RW 11 Feb 03 Home Misc 616 p.143: Intelligence from Pune 7 Feb 03 WP 3/3/45.

6. Edmonstone-Close 11 Feb 03 PRC x 79.

7. Close-RW 6 Mar 03 PRC ix 151.

8. Sindia-RW rec 13 Dec 02 PRC ix 137: RW-Sindia 14 Jan 03 PRC ix 139.

9. Collins-GG 12 Mar 03 PRC ix 152.

10. Collins-GG 25 Mar 03 PRC ix 162.

11. Close to Clive 26 Jan 03 Home Misc 616 p.113.

12. AW-Stuart 4 Dec 02 AW-Clive 19 Dec 02.

13. AW-Duncan 20 Jan 03.

14. AW-Stuart 3 Mar 03.

15. AW-Close 4 Mar 03.

16. Stuart-AW 9 Mar 03 Grwd (1844) i 345 PRC x 81

17. RW-Clive 4 Apr 03 Add Mss 13622 f 10: Webbe-AW 10 Mar 03 WP 3/3/93.

18. Close-GG 31 Mar 03 Home Misc 616 p.279.

19. AW-Close 30 Mar 03.

20. AW-RW 15 Apr 03:AW-Close 16 Apr 03: Malcolm-Webbe 8 Apr 03 A Mss 13746 f.140.

21. AW-RW 21 Apr 03: Malcolm-Houghton 21 Apr 03 A Mss 13746 f 144: Malcolm-Edmonstone 21 Apr 03 "Life" i 215.

22. Malcolm-Shawe 25 Apr 03 A Mss 13746 f 148: Malcolm-Edmonstone 1 May 03 "Life" 1 216.

23. AW-Stuart 27 Apr 03: Collins-GG 25 Apr 03 PRC ix 184: Close-AW 2 May 03 PRC ix 194: AW-Collins 2 May 03 SD iv 68: AW-Close 3 May 03: AW-Stuart 3 May 03 PRC ix 193.

24. Shawe-Malcolm 5 May 03 (letter misdated in Mss) A Mss 13602 f.4.

25. Edmonstone-Collins 5 May 03 PRC ix 198 Martin iii 93.

26. Collins-GG 30 Apr 03 2,4 May 03 PRC ix 188, 191, 195: Collins-AW 7 May 03 WP 3/3/53.

27. AW-Collins 9,10 May 03 SD iv 73, 74: AW-Stevenson 9 May 03: AW-Stuart 10 May 03: AW-RW 10 May 03.

28. Close Mem 11 May 03 PRC vii 75: Malcolm-Shawe 16 May 03 A Mss 13746 f.156: Close-GG 21 May 03 PRC x 101: Close-Balaji Kunjar 18,20 May 03 PRC vii 80,81; AW-Collins 18 May 03.

4

Confrontation
(June, July 1803)

By early June 1803, it was clear to the group of military and political officers in the northern Deccan that the British Company forces, whose presence had safeguarded the restoration of Peshwa Baji Rao to his capital, now faced a wider threat, that of a potential Maratha confederacy. This was the danger to which Arthur Wellesley had directed the attention of his brother the Governor-General in the letter that he had written to him from Akluj in mid-April. The membership of this potentially hostile confederacy was still uncertain: various of the Maratha chiefs might elect to join it. Further, the intentions of the confederacy were unclear, and it was still possible that the offer of subsidiary alliance which Richard Wellesley was prepared to extend might be accepted.

A critical point in the attempted dialogue with Daulat Rao Sindia, the most significant of the major Maratha rulers, was the interview with him that the Company Resident Collins held on 28 May. At this *darbar* meeting the content of the Treaty of Bassein was stated in detail, and the Resident secured from Sindia confirmation, for what it was worth, that he did not consider the terms of the treaty were in any way prejudicial to his interests. Closely following instructions that had been sent to him by the Fort William Secretariat in early May, and which he had just received, Collins then commented in open *darbar* that he presumed that Sindia was in negotiation with Raghuji Bhonsle of Berar, who was about to join him with his army in the upper Purna valley. He further stated that Sindia had also concluded an agreement with Jaswant Rao Holkar, and that he had stated an intention to visit Baji Rao in Pune, accompanied by the Raja of Berar.

Collins added that taken together these three assumptions, of which the second, that of an alliance with Jaswant Rao Holkar, was at this stage surmise, could lead to suspicions of 'designs adverse to the interest of the British government'. The proposed point of meeting of the two armies suggested confederation with the intention of invasion of the territories of the Nizam, and the Peshwa, or the alteration of the arrangements made between the British Company and Peshwa Baji Rao at Bassein.

One of the Ministers of Sindia then informed Collins that he would receive no satisfaction on the points that he had raised until after a full discussion with Raghuji Bhonsle, and was at once reminded by Collins that the proposed meeting 'was in itself a sufficient cause to excite the suspicions' of the British government. Collins added that Peshwa Baji Rao was fully entitled to use British power to secure his restoration, and pressed hard for an immediate explanation of the conduct of Sindia. Once it became clear that this was going to be refused, Collins warned that precautionary measures would have to be taken at the Company frontiers, and that the creation of a Maratha confederacy against the British would lead to hostilities. The warning was specific, and covered both an advance to Pune and an attack on the territories of the Nizam, since the most direct route to Pune from the Ajanta passes passed through Hyderabad territory. Collins urged Sindia 'to remove all my doubts and suspicions by an immediate and candid avowal of his intentions'. This Sindia refused to do, saying only that after the discussion with the Raja of Berar Collins would 'be informed whether it was peace or war', these words being delivered 'with much seeming composure'. A great deal was made out at this *darbar* exchange of the contention that Sindia had received an invitation from Peshwa Baji Rao to visit Pune. In a private letter to Arthur Wellesley Collins commented that 'although the Maharajah made so stout a reply, I cannot believe that his ministers will venture to involve him in a war.'[1]

Barry Close, John Malcolm and Arthur Wellesley at Pune received word of this *darbar* discussion, which had taken place near Burhanpur, by 4 June, 1803. There was clear concern at the fact that Daulat Rao Sindia had delayed giving to Collins a definite reply, Arthur Wellesley even suggesting to Collins that the answer he had been given 'might justify an immediate attack upon the possession of Sindia.' He noted that Sindia was forcing the continued and costly deployment of British forces, at precisely the time when news from England of 11 March suggested that the renewal of war with France was imminent. To the Governor-General, Arthur Wellesley commented on 4 June that 'as I think it possible that the Raja of Berar and Sindia may never meet, I have urged the Colonel to press Sindia to name a day on which he will explain his intentions, and if Sindia should decline to name a day he should fix one for him, beyond which in my opinion he ought not to remain in his camp.' If Collins received a positive response from Sindia, Arthur Wellesley proposed that a redeployment of forces would be required that would take account, among other dangers, of a possible attempted return of the French to Pondicherry. This attempt was made in June 1803, but failed. Once again, Arthur Wellesley lamented to Calcutta that there were not 'powers here to act at once'. Reference to Fort William, Calcutta involved a delay of six weeks, since despatches took an average of three weeks to be carried between the Deccan and Calcutta via Hyderabad.[2]

Arthur Wellesley also left his brother in no doubt of his views on the worthless alliance with Peshwa Baji Rao. The Peshwa had

'broken the treaty by not producing an army ... he trusts none of his ministers, and pretends to do his own business, although his time is much taken up by religious ceremonies and his pleasures and he is very undecided. These faults in his character, added to a slowness natural to every Maratha negotiation, render hopeless the conclusion of any important transaction.'

To Barry Close, Arthur Wellesley added that if means could not be found of determining whether Baji Rao was in secret correspondence with Daulat Rao Sindia and Raghuji Bhonsle, the treaty with him required revision. Close in response welcomed the pressure that Arthur Wellesley had placed

'on the necessity of our still urging Daulat Rao Sindia for a decided reply. The aim of his *darbar* is undoubtedly to trifle away the period of the monsoon, during which his army shut in between the rivers must be entirely helpless and deprives us, in the event of a rupture, of attacking immediately his northern possessions and laying siege to Ahmednagar on the rising of the rivers.'[3]

Two days later John Malcolm sent to Arthur Wellesley a letter written by Merrick Shawe in Fort William a month earlier, which had recorded the very favourable reaction of Richard Wellesley to the letter written from Akluj on 15 April, 1803. The analysis there given of the threat of a Maratha confederacy had been seen in Calcutta as giving 'a masterly review of the state of our interest and of the present posture of affairs with the Maratha empire, together with a most able opinion with regard to the policy conduct and military operations which it may be proper to adopt.' It had led to the transmission in the first days of May of the instructions, prepared some time earlier, which Collins had used in the interview of 28 May 1803. Arthur Wellesley could, therefore, be confident in early June that his analysis of political interests in relation to the presumed alliance was shared in Calcutta.[4]

For the next few days the anxieties of the young Major General were strictly military. There had been no reinforcement of his detachment by the southern jagirdars, with whom he had dealt, as far as possible without formal negotiations, on the way north to Pune. He needed the support of Maratha horsemen if he was to operate, with his own necessarily slower moving force with artillery and infantry elements, in the face of the *silledar* and *pindari* horsemen of Sindia and Bhonsle. The refusal of the southern *jagirdars* to move to join his detachment could be attributed to the deliberate procrastination of Peshwa Baji Rao. 'There is something to prevent our having a Maratha army in the field besides (the Peshwa's) incapacity for business.' This reinforcement was needed, either to give 'such strength as would probably prevent hostilities or to ensure success in those hostilities if unavoidable'. Arthur Wellesley reminded Barry Close that it was on the assumption of 'a community of interests' with the Peshwa that the front of military power had been created against, contingently, the confederacy of Daulat Rao Sindia, Raghuji Bhonsle and Jaswant Rao Holkar. If there was to be no contribution to this front of deployed power, perhaps the point had been reached at which the 'mode form and object of our negotiations' should be altered. 'The alliance in its present form, and with the present Peshwa, will never answer.' Arthur Wellesley added that had he been free to choose, his 'efforts would be directed to withdrawing from it with honour and safety.' The informal triumvirate would do well, he now suggested, to consider this matter, while awaiting what he had now for the second time sought from Calcutta, namely 'powers on the spot to settle everything regarding these Maratha affairs.' [5]

Arthur Wellesley considered that the detachment was ill-prepared to meet the enhanced danger which it now faced. It was supplied by an extended line of communication which reached back into the territory of the Company north of Mysore, and depended in large measure on the continuous movement of large trains of draught bullocks moving military supplies and bullion as well as those belonging to the *banjaras* who made their livelihood by selling supplies to armies. Unsuitable feeding and the change to monsoon conditions had caused such heavy mortality amongst these animals that this seemed likely to imperil the safety of the army.

'We got a tolerable quantity of forage yesterday,' Arthur Wellesley wrote to Barry Close from the Goor river on 9 June 1803

'but in the evening there was a fall of rain, by which we lost numbers of cattle, as well belonging to the *banjaras* as to the public departments. The cattle are so weak, in consequence of the lack of forage near Pune, and the bad quality of what they get, that they are unable to stand the rain. It is difficult to decide what to do; we cannot march, and we cannot halt in the same place, because we soon destroy the little forage that we find.' [6]

John Malcolm and Barry Close, both in Pune at this time, needed no reminder that it was only on the basis of a more effective alliance with Baji Rao that a successful challenge to Sindia and Bhonsle could be made, or that the threat from the proposed assemblage of military power was weakened by the absence of Maratha horse. As John Malcolm explained to Merrick Shawe in Calcutta, he had stayed in Pune to help Barry Close 'push through this impracticable *darbar* some arrangements which are indispensable to the success of our affairs.' They were considering, as an extreme measure, but one to which they might well be forced, 'by guaranteeing certain lands to the principal jagirdars to form a separate interest in the empire, which will hereafter be found as formidable to the Peshwa as to his enemies.'

Both John Malcolm and Barry Close saw a discussion with Baji
Rao at this time as satisfactory; it had 'added to the evidence we
already possess of his being firm to his engagements'. Baji Rao
denied having written to Sindia and Bhonsle asking them to come
to Pune, and agreed to ask them not to do this. At the same time
the two political officers attempted to move forward the reconciliation of Peshwa Baji Rao and the southern jagirdars, without which
there would be no Maratha reinforcement of the detachment
commanded by Arthur Wellesley.[7]

Writing in Pune in mid-June, John Malcolm reviewed the courses
of action which were open. If satisfactory undertakings from the
two Maratha rulers—of the type which Collins had been instructed
to attempt to secure—were forthcoming, it would suffice for the
Company to take defensive measures against a possible return
southward of Jaswant Rao Holkar. But if the threat of a southward
movement of the armies of Daulat Rao Sindia and Raghuji Bhonsle
of Berar were real

> 'little or no aid is to be looked for from the Peshwa, whose
> weakness, timidity and irresolution will prevent his making any
> exertions of a friendly or of a hostile nature. All that is to be
> expected from him is a neutral inaction which, if it does not
> forward, will not be likely to counteract any of our measures....
> If we place any dependence whatever on the aid of this court,
> we shall be liable to constant disappointment; we ought not to
> engage in hostilities unless we are prepared to take their weight
> on our shoulders ... I have lost all faith, God knows I never had
> much, in this court.'

The conduct of the Peshwa would justify a withdrawal from the
alliance with him, but such a reversal would expose the territory of
the Nizam to Maratha attack, and perhaps also that of the Company.
Further it might encourage the French to attempt an alliance with
the Marathas.[8]

With these views Arthur Wellesley, writing to Malcolm on 20 and
22 June, 1803, was in agreement, although he discounted the
danger of an alliance of the French and the Marathas.

> 'Until the question of the confederacy is decided, we must
> stick to our ground in this country: otherwise the Nizam and we
> eventually suffer ... but as soon as there shall be no threat of the

confederacy, either by the withdrawing of Sindia or from the success of the war, it is my opinion that we ought entirely to new model the alliance, or to withdraw from it.'

The restoration of the nominal head of the Maratha confederacy had given the Company no authority over the Marathas; 'We have been mistaken entirely regarding the constitution of the Maratha empire.' There had been some support from the southern jagirdars, who hoped for an improvement in their conditions of tenure as a result of Company mediation. But for that 'we should have had a treaty with a cypher, bearing the name of Peshwa, without a particle of power.' He added that he felt that the danger of an alliance between the French and the Marathas could be overstated. 'The French on their arrival would want equipments, which would cost money, or money to secure them: and there is not a Maratha in the whole country, from the Peshwa to the lowest horseman, who has a shilling and who would not require assistance from them.' There was no doubt about the nature of the alliance with Baji Rao. 'Has he not daily communications with Sindia's *darbar*, and even with Holkar, of which the British Resident has no knowledge whatever?... The matter may drag on for some time longer ... the truth is that they are all shaking, and if the allies (the southern *jagirdars*) had come out of Pune with me, there would be no war.' These doubts were not stated to Fort William. 'I have not written to the Governor–General for a length of time. I do not like to communicate to him my sentiments of the Peshwa, nor do I wish to deceive him. I agree with you that strong measures are to be taken, but how are they to be carried into execution?'

Acute supply difficulties remained the reason why 'strong measures' could not be taken. These, as Close was told on 23 June,

'will be a useful lesson to governments and to us all; first to avoid entering into a treaty with a prince, the only principle of whose conduct is insincerity, and next to avoid, if possible, to enter upon a campaign at a distance of 700 miles from our own resources, not only *not* having the government of the country on our side, but in the shape of a friend, our worst enemy.' [9]

Meanwhile, in the upper Purna valley some one hundred miles north, Collins was unable to bring the two Maratha rulers to a clear statement of their intentions. Indeed the junction of the two courts

and armies itself became the latest in a series of expedient excuses
that could be used to justify further postponement of the continued
request. This assemblage of Maratha military force was a gain which
Sindia would wish to exploit, and he evidently hoped that contrary
to immediate appearances, Jaswant Rao Holkar could be persuaded
to join the confederacy. The two Maratha rulers met on 4 June 1803.
The Raja of Berar was accompanied by a force of 20,000 good
cavalry, ten battalions of infantry, and thirty-two pieces of artillery.
Writing to Arthur Wellesley that day Collins was still hopeful of an
'amicable accommodation' and of bringing the *darbar* of Sindia 'to
a proper sense of its danger.' Three days later he commented to
Barry Close that the Peshwa had not explicitly forbidden Sindia to
travel to Pune, as the Company politicals had asked. Seriously
unwell, with a fever 'attended by gouty symptoms' Collins defended himself to Arthur Wellesley on 9 June against the implied charge
that he had not been stern enough with Daulat Rao Sindia. He had
quoted the words of the Governor-General to explain 'what the
Maharajah had to expect should this explanation be withheld.' He
felt that he could not have 'pushed my importunities further after
Sindia had declared that he could not then afford me the satisfaction I demanded, without a violation of the faith which he had
pledged to the Raja of Berar.' He added that 'this declaration on
his part left it to the discretion of our government to commence
immediate hostilities.' He would regard a refusal to explain intentions after the next discussions between Sindia and Raghuji as 'an
avowal of hostile designs.'[10]

Heavy monsoon rain now disrupted the negotiations, the dining
tent in Collins' encampment had three feet of water in it, and a
stream between the two Maratha armies could not be crossed.
When matters could be taken further, Collins sent a formal memorandum to Sindia reminding him of his promised reply, and explaining that a refusal or further delay would be taken as
confirmation of an intention 'to obstruct the completion of the
Treaty of Bassein, either by means of his own power, or in conjunction with Raghuji Bhonsle and Jaswant Rao Holkar.' If his request
could not be granted, Collins asked for an escort and supplies, as
he wished to leave the camp of Sindia at once and travel to
Aurangabad. Reporting on 12 June 1803 to Gerald Lake, commanding the Company forces poised against Sindia in Oudh, Collins

commented that 'this *darbar* wishes to amuse me until the Maharajah is joined by Jaswant Rao Holkar.'[11]

But Collins did not leave. The stream separating him from the camp of the Raja of Berar subsided, and he was able to send his *munshi* to seek an explanation of Maratha intention. Raghuji Bhonsle contended that there could be no reply to the British request until a meeting had taken place not only with Jaswant Rao Holkar but also with the Peshwa. The *munshi* explained to Raghuji Bhonsle the British demand that Daulat Rao Sindia retire north of the Narbada, and added that 'General Wellesley according to the wish of the Peshwa had marched to this quarter at the head of the united forces of the Company and the Peshwa for the purpose, among others, of chastising Holkar.' To this Raghuji Bhonsle replied 'do not meddle with Holkar, he is united with me.' As Collins put it to the Governor-General on 22 June, Raghuji was evidently 'greatly inflated with the idea of being the head of a powerful confederacy.' Collins added that he had decided that to delay his departure would not prevent any military response that might have been planned, 'while on the other hand the greater my forbearance on the present occasion the more unjustifiable would the proceedings of this *darbar* appear in the event of war.' Collins suggested that Jaswant Rao Holkar could be taken out of the projected confederacy by conciliation by Peshwa Baji Rao, a policy already dismissed by Barry Close as impracticable at the beginning of the year, although John Malcolm was to recommend it again within a few days.[12]

Meanwhile, in camp about twenty miles from Ahmednagar, Arthur Wellesley believing that 'a few days will ... bring to a decision the question of peace or war' directed Colonel Stevenson on 14 June 1803 to move the Hyderabad subsidiary force forward. He was not, however, to move 'to a great distance from Aurungabad ... before I can cross the Godavari and give you support.' His own position had to be south of the Godavari until it was possible to capture Ahmednagar, which was 'full of everything we want'. Messengers from the north led him to believe that Jaswant Rao Holkar intended to cross both the Tapti and the Narbada moving northwards away from Daulat Rao Sindia and Raghuji Bhonsle; if this was so, Arthur Wellesley felt he could forecast on 19 June to Stuart, the Commander-in-Chief Madras, that 'there will be no confederacy'.[13]

Arthur Wellesley decided to write afresh to Collins on 29 June, stating firmly that the instructions from Richard Wellesley to which the Resident was working had been overtaken by events. News from Europe now suggested that hostilities between France and Britain were about to be renewed. The ineffectiveness of the alliance with Peshwa Baji Rao had been demonstrated. But it was still important to avert war with the Maratha rulers if possible. He reminded Collins that the supposed alliance between Daulat Rao Sindia and Jaswant Rao Holkar was prospective and uncertain: 'they hope by their threats to frighten us or our allies, and to induce us to abandon our situation at Pune.' Arthur Wellesley recommended that Collins should give Sindia a time limit of three days within which his declaration should be made; if the reply given by Sindia showed a real intention to preserve peace it should be accompanied by a withdrawal of forces. For the Company to withdraw from the alliance with Peshwa Baji Rao would show a want of self-confidence. What was needed to secure the withdrawal of the two Maratha rulers was to increase their sense of the danger in which they placed themselves.[14]

John Malcolm, after an interview in the company of Barry Close with Raghunath Rao, the principal minister of Peshwa Baji Rao, now left Pune to join Arthur Wellesley in camp. After emergency measures the worst of the supply difficulties of the detachment were now over. In a second memorandum written at the end of June, Malcolm surveyed again the dilemma in which the Company politicals found themselves. Writing in the belief that the issue of peace or war would be soon resolved, he stressed the importance of a prompt attack upon both Ahmednagar and Broach. The British could not now 'withdraw with either honour or security from the contest with which it is threatened.' This contest was now a separate issue from that of the conduct of Peshwa Baji Rao, where, if necessary, 'British interests should be secured from injury, if the urgency of the case demanded it, by a total departure from a treaty the most essential articles of which the Peshwa has already violated.' The total failure of Malcolm and Close in *darbar* discussion on 23 June to secure any acceptance of the need to conciliate Amrit Rao had been decisive in determining the view which John Malcolm now took of the alliance. Peshwa Baji Rao was clearly determined to act on principles 'incompatible with the obligations of friendship' and which were 'at variance with all political wisdom and

which render all plans of cooperation in war ... wholly impracticable.' The Company should now set itself to secure settlements with
both Amrit Rao and Jaswant Rao Holkar.[15]

Malcolm suggested that Amrit Rao should be offered districts
already ceded to the Company under the Treaty of Bassein; it should
be possible to handle Amrit Rao in such a way that he would not
intrigue with any of the three principal Maratha chieftains. Such an
action might well alarm Peshwa Baji Rao, or

> 'excite his jealousy to such a pitch that might make him
> secretly disaffected to the alliance, perhaps lead him to intrigue
> with Sindia or Bhonsle, or possibly impel him to the still greater
> extreme of flying from Pune. I have contemplated all these
> events, and I am satisfied that none of them would be attended
> with any effects which could counterbalance for a moment the
> solid advantages to the British interests which must accrue from
> the adoption of the plan I have suggested.'

British interests would receive 'as little injury from the Peshwa's
declared disaffection as they have hitherto received benefit from
his professed attachment.' Noting to Merrick Shawe in Calcutta on
4 July, 1803 that this analysis of the steps necessary in the event of
hostilities if 'the Peshwa continues obstinate' had been seen by both
Barry Close and Arthur Wellesley, Malcolm added that there had
been earlier hints of the prospect of extensive delegated political
authority; he hoped that this would soon arrive.[16]

On 8 July Arthur Wellesley decided, despite his earlier reluctance
to do so, to write to the Governor-General:

> 'We, who were ready on 4th June, have lost that month and part
> of this for our operations; and unless Colonel Collins has attended
> to a second representation which I made to him in the end of June,
> we are as far from our point as we were in the month of May. The
> Colonel has gone on a false notion from the beginning. He has
> supposed that peace was concluded between Holkar and Sindia,
> because Sindia's ministers have told him so. Under this notion
> he has been timid, and has afforded them time to conclude the
> peace, and to intrigue, which is all that they desire.'[17]

Barry Close now proposed a more positive threat to the two
Maratha rulers. Writing to Arthur Wellesley on 10 July, in terms

closely following the reasoning of John Malcolm, he argued that it was evident that the motive of Sindia 'in all his evasions and falsehoods is to gain time in order to have the means of commencing hostilities under conditions more favourable than he could possibly do at present.' Close urged that the British could attack both Broach and Ahmednagar while the rivers remained at monsoon levels. If this were not done, Ahmednagar when reinforced would subsequently become the base from which Sindia could threaten Pune once again.

The reason for the prolonged indecision of Sindia was, as Barry Close saw it, the fact that 'his darling scheme of the confederacy is not brought to maturity.' While Sindia was gaining time for this purpose, he was also being edged forward towards the Ajanta pass by his anxiety to relieve Ahmednagar 'and finally forming in force upon that post'. If this analysis was correct, it was essential not to let Sindia 'work out his hostile and wily scheme to the imminent danger of our Indian possessions.' Barry Close, therefore, recommended that Arthur Wellesley should write to both Sindia, and Bhonsle, insisting that there be no further advance towards the territory of the Nizam of Hyderabad, and that there should be an imposed time limit after which both Maratha rulers should withdraw from their present position. If this were not honoured by the two Maratha rulers, Company offensive operations should be initiated, against Ahmednagar by the detachment commanded by Arthur Wellesley, and by that commanded by Stevenson in a way which would engage the Marathas 'before they can have time to draw out their whole force on this side of the Ajanta pass.'[18]

Certainly, in the camp of Daulat Rao Sindia about twenty miles north of the pass, Collins was unable to bring to an end what Barry Close, John Malcolm and Arthur Wellesley now considered was merely a sequence of evasion by Sindia and Bhonsle. In discussion on 1 July, Collins had complained directly to Sindia to this effect, receiving in return 'a long discourse' on the need for consultation between the various rulers of the Maratha empire, but also a refusal at that stage to confirm that Sindia did not intend to oppose the arrangements concluded in the Treaty of Bassein. The discussion was resumed with both Sindia and Bhonsle on 4 July, with Collins insisting on 'the right of the Peshwa to contract engagements with the English without consulting with any of the Maratha rulers' and the Marathas contending that they required an explanation of the

Treaty of Bassein from the Peshwa himself, but affirming that they did not intend to advance towards Pune or ascend the Ajanta pass. Collins sought more, that 'Sindia should recross the Narbada and the Bhonsle repair to Nagpur,' but this he was unable to secure.[19]

On 9 July both Sindia and Bhonsle undertook, in letters to Richard Wellesley given to Collins, that they would not obstruct the Treaty of Bassein. There was a proviso, that the British and the Peshwa should not obstruct an agreement which had allegedly existed for a long time, although they could not find a copy of it, that dealt with consultation between members of the Maratha confederacy. Collins decided to ask both Barry Close and Arthur Wellesley, given that Sindia had refused to cross the Narbada, whether there was any other 'unequivocal proof' that the Marathas could give of an intention not to oppose the implementation of the Treaty of Bassein. Collins himself remained persuaded that the two Maratha rulers would 'not retire with their armies until they have had an interview with Jaswant Rao Holkar.' That there was continued effort to secure this confederacy was confirmed by news of the release of Khande Rao Holkar, a nephew of Jaswant Rao Holkar who had been imprisoned by Daulat Rao Sindia. This was certainly an act of attempted reconciliation between Daulat Rao Sindia and Jaswant Rao Holkar, evidently achieved by Bhonsle, but it had surely come far too late. It was not destined now to alter the evident purpose of Jaswant Rao Holkar, which was to withdraw far to the north. Once this had been done, he could not quickly involve himself again in the confrontation.[20]

By 11 July, when Arthur Wellesley had seen the report of the *darbar* meeting of 4 July, he suggested to Collins that the Maratha rulers might be prepared to 'withdraw to their own capitals' if given some indication of a possible British withdrawal.

> 'I certainly propose to repass the Bhima myself and to order Colonel Stevenson to repass the Godavari as soon as I find that these chiefs commence their march towards their own territory, and I shall break up the army in this quarter as soon as I shall be convinced that they no longer threaten the territory of the Peshwa or of the Nizam, and are settled, the one to the north of the Narbada and the other at Nagpur.'

Three days later, writing again to Collins, Arthur Wellesley drew on the reasoning of the recent letter from Barry Close. For Sindia and Bhonsle 'the advantage of delay is theirs ... they have made their pacific declarations in order to gain time ... their real intentions are to be known only from their actions.' Collins was to deliver a letter from Arthur Wellesley to Sindia, in which he was bluntly told that there was no occasion for the position of his army on the borders of the territory of the Nizam of Hyderabad. If he did not withdraw, Arthur Wellesley stated his intention to attack 'in consequence of the advantageous position of the Company's armies.' At the same time Barry Close wrote to Collins pointing out that the two Maratha rulers were 'stirring heaven and earth to draw Holkar into their plans' and attempting to keep the British 'in a state of fallacious hope and dangerous inaction.' The assurances which had been given in the letters to Richard Wellesley were conditional in character and were rendered nugatory 'by the petty shifts and shameful evasions' which the two Maratha rulers had practised.[21]

Arthur Wellesley had not included a time limit in his letter to Sindia; he explained to Close on 17 July 1803 that this was to give him the choice of the timing of opening of hostilities and to permit alteration of his course of action, in the light of prospective instructions from Fort William, Calcutta. John Malcolm spoke for all three of them when he commented to Calcutta that the 'affair must be brought to an early crisis. We have, I fear, been duped by these chiefs.'[22]

On 18 July, as expected, means to resolve matters arrived in the form of new and virtually all embracing military and political authority delegated to Arthur Wellesley. There had been at least three hints that this was what the situation required; the first in March made by Malcolm to Stuart, the Commander-in-Chief, Madras, which may have been passed on to Calcutta, the second by Arthur Wellesley in early May that the group was 'playing at cross purposes' and the third in early June, when he had expressed the wish that 'there were powers here to act at once'. Once the possibility of Richard Wellesley moving nearer to the scene of action on the Deccan had been eliminated, as had been decided in late January, (this could have been done only at the cost of lengthening the line of command to the army in Oudh) there was a likelihood for Richard Wellesley to make but one choice. If there had to be a political agent at the head of the Deccan army, that agent must be Arthur Wellesley.

The decision to delegate authority in this way, Merrick Shawe afterwards told John Malcolm, had been delayed for a month because Barlow as senior member of Council and Edmonstone as head of the political secretariat had urged on Richard Wellesley the risk of 'jealousy among the Residents'. This may have been an ostensible reason: both Barlow and Edmonstone were quite sufficiently informed about the structure of the Company to realise that the extensive delegation of political and military authority which alone could meet the case would be unpopular in Leadenhall Street. But it is clear that Richard Wellesley had considered this step when the letter that Arthur Wellesley had written from Akluj had first arrived. Subject only to the superior military authority of both Lake and Stuart, Arthur Wellesley was now given military and political control of relations with the Maratha powers. He was authorised to negotiate with any of the Maratha chiefs to achieve the objects of the Treaty of Bassein or to mediate in their disputes with the Peshwa; 'provisional interference' in their internal affairs was in order if necessary. Authority reverted to Stuart if he were to move northwards to take command of the forces in the Deccan at present commanded by Arthur Wellesley, who was however recommended to Stuart as his adviser. The Residents at the courts of the country powers were reassured that there was no intention 'to preclude the exercise of the ordinary functions of official station.'[23]

What Richard Wellesley saw as the objectives that were to result from war with Sindia and Holkar, if such was to be the outcome, were set out in further instructions, sent to Arthur Wellesley in cypher and to be revealed by him only to Barry Close. Perhaps surprisingly, John Malcolm was not mentioned as authorised to be privy to these issues; if Arthur Wellesley kept his own counsel, this point became important later.

Arthur Wellesley was instructed to order Collins to demand an explanation of their position from the two Maratha chiefs, and if this proved unsatisfactory he was to order Collins to leave. In the military operations that might follow, the particular objectives were to be Sindia's park of artillery, all armaments of European construction, and military stores generally. Military action was to be pursued 'to the utmost extremity which may appear ... to promise success .... The actual seizure of the person of Daulat Rao Sindia or of Raghuji Bhonsle would be highly desirable.' But on the assumption that hostilities might not be carried to that extent, 'the objects most desirable in the event of any treaty' were the territories of Sindia to the north of a line joining Gohad to the northern boundaries of the Rajput state of Jaipur, all the maritime possessions of Sindia including Broach, all his possessions in Gujarat, and all those south of the Narbada. From Bhonsle Richard Wellesley wished to secure Cuttack, the province as well as the town, and some land to the west of the Wardha.[24]

Shortly after he received these delegated powers, Arthur Wellesley set out fully to Richard Wellesley, in a letter of 24 July, 1803, the political setting in which the challenge to the two Maratha rulers would have to be made.

> 'The difficulties under which the force of the British government labours at the present moment, and which give the greatest encouragement to the confederate chiefs are, the state of weakness and confusion of the Peshwa's government, the general unsettled and ruinous state of the country, and the wavering disposition of the majority of the southern *jagirdars*, who preserve alone the appearance of relations of fidelity towards the Peshwa.'

A further 'principal inducement' to war was the state of the territories of the Nizam of Hyderabad, whose death was imminent. These factors were all inconveniences, but their consequences could be borne 'if we can strike such a blow during the rains as will give us the superiority, and keep our rear in tranquillity.'[25]

When the combined military and political authority arrived, Arthur Wellesley wrote at once to Collins saying that he was willing to negotiate with Daulat Rao Sindia and Raghuji Bhonsle only when they were at their normal positions. Collins was to 'call upon them to retire' and if they refused he was to leave their camp, and inform Stevenson that he had done so. If Collins left, Stevenson was to move his detachment as near to the Ajanta pass as possible.[26]

Collins meanwhile had received the earlier letter from Arthur Wellesley and the prepared memorandum to be given to Daulat Rao Sindia. A day later he received his copy of the despatch which gave the extensive delegated powers to Arthur Wellesley. He now forecast a change of tone from the two Maratha rulers. But the result of a long discussion with Raghuji Bonsle, held by the *munshi* employed by Collins on 21 July, was a reversion to the contention that the two Maratha rulers were entitled to an assurance from

Peshwa Baji Rao, in addition to that offered by the British Government, about the effects of the Treaty of Bassein, and that there had
to be further consultation with Daulat Rao Sindia.[27]

Looking ahead to the likely refusal by Daulat Rao Sindia to give the
undertaking which Arthur Wellesley required, Collins commented

> 'were I to consult my own feelings, I should not hesitate to
> quit the court of Daulat Rao Sindia the moment he refused, or
> evaded compliance with your requisition. But I really conceive that
> I am not at liberty to adopt this measure until it be sanctioned by you
> ... it appears that I have not the discretionary power of leaving
> this *darbar*. God knows I have not the least desire to remain
> with Daulat Rao Sindia from any private considerations, my
> health being very indifferent , and my expenses far exceeding all
> the allowances which I receive from the Honourable Company.'[28]

Collins now sent to both Maratha rulers a note requesting
withdrawal from the frontier of the territory of the Nizam to their
normal positions: refusal would be seen as proof of the insincerity
of their earlier declarations that they accepted that the Treaty of
Bassein was not contrary to their interests. At a discussion in the
court of Daulat Rao Sindia on 25 July, Collins urged the acceptance
of the demands of Arthur Wellesley. He received four points in
reply, that Daulat Rao Sindia and Raghuji Bhonsle were within their
own territories, that they had promised not to march to Pune, that
they required assurance of the peaceful intentions of Peshwa Baji
Rao, and that they could not move until they had completed their
negotiations with Jaswant Rao Holkar. Collins responded; the
position of the Maratha armies threatened the territory of the
Company and its allies, agents could be sent to the Peshwa Baji Rao
at Pune after withdrawal, and it would be easier to negotiate with
Jaswant Rao Holkar, who was himself far to the north beyond the
Narbada, after a move northwards. Collins finally agreed to a delay
in receiving a reply until 28 July.[29]

At the same time, in a private letter Collins agreed with the
optimism expressed by Arthur Wellesley earlier that

> 'If there be truth in a Maratha court we shall now have peace.
> To confess my real sentiments, I have no doubt but that Daulat
> Rao Sindia and his confidential minister Jadu Rao would will-
> ingly retire from the Nizam's frontier, although I do not believe

that the Maharajah would at present be prevailed on to recross the Narbada. However, as the greatest part of his infantry has been detached to Hindustan and as.... Ambaji Inglia also will shortly repair thither with a detachment of cavalry, I do not conceive any danger could be apprehended from Daulat Rao Sindia's continuance in the Deccan, provided that the Bhonsle will return to Nagpur. But on this last head I am rather doubtful having some notion that Raghuji had entertained a latent hope of being elevated to the *masnad* of Pune. However he must now see the folly of attempting to dethrone Baji Rao, if he ever indulged such an idea, of which I have no proof.'[30]

Collins had an interview with Daulat Rao Sindia on 29 July, 1803. This carried matters a little further. He reported that no new arguments were advanced and he was asked to delay his departure. This Collins refused to do, since being 'satisfied that this court only wanted to gain time for some particular purpose of its own, I should be deemed inexcusable were I to suffer myself to be further amused.' Collins wrote to Raghuji Bhonsle explaining why he was leaving. Prevented by heavy rain from leaving at once, although he had sent his heavy baggage on the road to the Ajanta pass, he attended a final discussion with both Daulat Rao Sindia and Raghuji Bhonsle on 31 July 'in the fullest *darbar* that I have yet seen.' A discussion which lasted more than four hours, with 'much disagreeable altercation' covered little more than a haggle over variant schemes of timed withdrawal. These Collins rejected, although he finally consented to send one to Arthur Wellesley, if given in writing. The proposal was stated differently in writing and Collins determined to leave the Maratha camp. Monsoon conditions prevented him from doing this until the morning of 3 August. Late that day he wrote to Stevenson and to Richard Wellesley from a position immediately to the north of the Ajanta pass, but within the frontier of the Nizam of Hyderabad.[31]

Arthur Wellesley and John Malcolm had waited for the outcome of this prolonged negotiation in camp a few miles from Ahmednagar. To Merrick Shawe in Calcutta, Malcolm commented that a peaceful settlement would be possible only on the 'tacit admission on the part of the Raja of Berar and Daulat Rao Sindia of our superior strength.' After a further delay, ('a few hours more suspense will exhaust all my patience') it was possible for Malcolm to report to Close that 'the General will move the first fair moment.' In a more extended comment to Fort William, Calcutta, Malcolm added that the Company

'still have great advantages but the whole of this question should have been brought to an issue two months ago. If it had, we would most likely have had no war for I do not believe it is Sindia's or Bhonsle's wish to engage in one. But the delays and trifling we have admitted have persuaded these chiefs that we are as adverse to extremities as they are, and nothing but the voice of our cannon will now convince them to the contrary.'[32]

In a final letter to Daulat Rao Sindia, clearly seen as that in which the breakdown of negotiations was accepted and justified, Arthur Wellesley informed him that the final proposition suggested was inadmissible. This was partly because of the ambiguity of the term 'normal stations.' The proposition was that the Company should 'withdraw to Madras Seringapatam and Bombay the troops which had been assembled for the purpose of repelling their aggressions' while the two Maratha chiefs 'should keep their troops united in the neighbourhood of the Nizam's frontier, and in readiness to take advantage of the absence of the troops of the British government and its allies, to carry into execution their hostile designs.' Arthur Wellesley, or perhaps John Malcolm writing for him, concluded with a flourish; 'you must stand the consequences of the measures which I find myself obliged to adopt, in order to repel your aggressions. I offered you peace on terms of equality, and honourable to all parties. You have chosen war, and are responsible for all consequences.'[33]

It is legitimate to question how far the British Company, and Arthur Wellesley in particular, were right in taking the view that the responsibility for conflict was entirely that of Daulat Rao Sindia and Raghuji Bhonsle. Certainly the two Maratha rulers had posted themselves, with their armies, in a position which indicated clearly that their intentions were at the least potentially hostile. But it is possible to contend that the negotiations with them, which Richard Wellesley had wished to initiate, had never taken place. The argument, although transferred to the battlefield, had merely been postponed. But the events of June and July 1803 had been an armed confrontation, from which a peaceful outcome was never likely.

Arthur Wellesley had been at the centre of a crisis that had elements both political and military. At the last, the decision between peace and war had been his.

NOTES

1. Collins GG 29 May 03, PRC ix 234 Martin iii 159. Collins-AW 30 May 03 WP 3/3/53

2. AW-RW, Collins 4 Jun 03.

3. AW-RW, Close 4 Jun 03 Close-AW 5 Jun 03 WP 3/3/45.

4. Shawe-Malcolm 5 May 03 Add Mss 13602 f 4: AW-Malcolm 6 Jun 03.

5. AW-Close 8 Jun 03.

6. AW-Close 9 Jun 03.

7. Malcolm-Shawe 5,10 Jun 03 Add Mss 13746 f.163,172; Close-Sec GG 10 Jun 03 Add Mss 13598 f.151.

8. Malcolm Mem 18 Jun 03 Add Mss 13746 f.182; Malcolm-AW 18 Jun 03 WP 3/3/70.

9. AW-Malcolm 20,22 Jun 03: AW-Close 23 Jun 03.

10. Collins-GG 3 Jun 03 PRC ix 258: Collins-AW 4,9 Jun 03 WP 3/3/53.

11. Collins-GG 12 Jun 03 PRC ix 262 Martin iii 170: Mem 12 Jun 03 PRC ix 264: Collins-Lake 12 Jun 03 Add Mss 13742 f.37.

12. Collins-GG 12,22 Jun 03 PRC ix 268, 283: Collins-AW 15,29 Jun 03 WP 3/3/53.

13. AW-Stevenson 14 Jun 03 AW-Stuart 19 Jun 03.

14. AW-Collins 29 Jan 03.

15. Malcolm Mem dated 28 Jun 03 in RW Mss and 4 Jul 03 in AW Mss WP 3/3/70 Add Mss 13746 f.196.

16. Malcolm-Shawe 4 Jul 03 Add Mss 13746 f.194.

17. AW-RW 8 Jul 03.

18. Close-AW 10 Jul 03 PRC ix 314.

19. Collins-GG 6 Jul 03 Martin iii 236: Collins-AW 8 Jul 03 WP 3/3/53: Collins-Close 9 Jul 03 PRC ix 313.

20. Collins-GG 9 Jul 03 PRC ix 310: Sindia, Bhonsle-GG 7 Jul 03 PRC ix 311, 312.

21. AW-Collins, Close 14 Jul 03: Close-Collins 15 Jul 03 PRC ix 335.

22. AW-Close, Collins 17 Jul 03: Malcolm-Shawe 17 Jul 03 Add Mss 13746 f.204.

23. Shawe-Malcolm 28 Jul 03 Add Mss 13602 f.29: RW-AW 26 Jun 03 Martin iii 149 PRC ix 291: Edmonstone-Close, Collins 27 Jun 03 PRC ix 295 Add Mss 13597 f.64.

24. RW-AW 27 Jun 03 Martin iii 153 PRC ix 291.

25. AW-RW 24 Jul 03.

26. AW-Collins 18 Jul 03 AW-Stevenson 18 Jul 03.

27. Collins-AW 22 Jul 03 WP 3/3/53.

28. Collins-AW 22 Jul 03 WP 3/3/53.

29. Collins AW 26 Jul 03 WP 3/3/53.

30. Collins-AW 26 Jul 03 WP 3/3/53.

31. Collins-AW 30 Jul 03 WP 3/3/53: Collins-Bhonsle 30 Jul 03 PRC ix 376: Collins-AW 1,3 Aug 03 WP 3/3/53: Collins-Stevenson 2 Aug 03 WP 3/3/84: Collins-GG 4 Aug 03 PRC ix 402.

32. Malcolm-Shawe 5,6 Aug 03 Add Mss 13746 f.223, 225.

33. AW-Sindia 6 Aug 03: Malcolm Mem 6 Aug 03 PRC ix 403.

5

The Sound of the Guns
(August–November 1803)

While awaiting the outcome of the armed confrontation of June
and July 1803, Arthur Wellesley had always been very clear as to his
first military objective. It was to seize Ahmednagar, a fortress
belonging to Daulat Rao Sindia and reportedly garrisoned by about
a thousand men. It was to this fortress that Barry Close had directed
his attention in the letters of mid-July. There was both a *pettah* or
outer defensive system and an inner fortress. After only one day's
delay, Arthur Wellesley launched an attack on the *pettah* with
relatively long-range artillery fire. It was then assaulted at a rush,
and this attack was quickly successful. In the following days there
were desultory negotiations with the commander of the fort, whose
mind was concentrated by a little further rather closer range
artillery fire. The garrison then surrendered, the *killedar* being
allowed to retain his private property.

Arthur Wellesley believed that the Marathas had placed extensive
military stores in Ahmednagar, some of which he desperately
required. Once the fortress had been secured, he had indeed found
within it the supplies he needed, although they were oddly located.
He could now advance across the Godavari in confidence that the
road to Pune was, to some degree, blocked by the capture of
Ahmednagar. He remained concerned that Jaswant Rao Holkar, if
he made any southern movement, might by-pass Pune and attempt
an attack on Company territory north of Mysore.[1]

Between the Godavari and 'the line of the ghats', that is the hills
that bounded the lands of the Nizam to the north, lay territory partly
in Maratha ownership and some of it currently under their military

occupation. But at the time of the capture of Ahmednagar by Arthur Wellesley the main group of forces of Daulat Rao Sindia and Raghuji Bhonsle were still in the Purna valley, south of Burhanpur, although they had moved fairly near to the Ajanta pass during the last days of negotiation with Collins, and there had been some southward movement of the *pindaris* at the time of the attack on Ahmednagar. The detachment commanded by Colonel Stevenson, the subsidiary force from Hyderabad reinforced by one unit, was already north of the Godavari. It now moved forward, the objective being to prevent the movement south of the line of hills of the Maratha *silledar* and *pindari* horse and the formed infantry brigades. Stevenson moved slowly to the northeast on 7 August 1803 from a camp near Aurangabad. On 10 August, nine miles from Aurangabad, he wrote to Arthur Wellesley, reporting that he had met Collins, the returning Company Resident with Daulat Rao Sindia. Collins gave to both Stevenson and Arthur Wellesley a listing of the forces of the two Maratha rulers. Collins had earlier given the forces available to Daulat Rao Sindia in the Deccan as 18,500 cavalry, a surprisingly small number, but perhaps to be explained by the irregular 'fringe' of plunderers, eleven regiments of infantry, 35 heavy guns and 17 field pieces. He listed the Raja of Berar as having 20,000 cavalry, 6,000 infantry, and 35 field pieces.[2]

Against these Maratha forces there were deployed in the Deccan the two detachments each containing Company units and each accompanied by lesser forces of the allies of the Company. The detachment directly commanded by Arthur Wellesley included some 1500 cavalry, the 19th Light Dragoons and three native cavalry units, about 4000 infantry, that is HM 74th and 86th and five native infantry units, about 1000 artillery and pioneer personnel and about 34 guns. It had with it 2000 Mysore cavalry and was eventually joined by about 3000 Maratha cavalry under two feudatories of Peshwa Baji Rao. The detachment commanded by Stevenson consisted of about 1000 native cavalry, and rather over 7000 infantry, six native units and the Scotch brigade, about 500 artillerymen and pioneers and about 20 guns, some of them of large calibre designed for siege operations. There were also units of the Nizam of Hyderabad, both infantry and cavalry, although of uncertain quality and loyalty.

In discussion with Stevenson on 10 August, Collins contended that the Ajanta pass, through which he had just travelled, was not practicable for guns and would prove difficult for loaded cattle. It is clear from later military movement, certainly of Arthur Wellesley and probably of Daulat Rao Sindia also, that this was not so. Stevenson was persuaded that it was unlikely that Sindia and Bhonsle would use the Ajanta, and since the two Maratha rulers were reported not to have completed the assembly of their cavalry—and there was at this stage no confirmation of their readiness to move their infantry and artillery into the Deccan through the line of hills—it seemed probable that he would be in good time to prevent any such attempt. If the infantry brigades of Daulat Rao Sindia and Raghuji Bhonsle were not being moved forward, it seemed probable that a Maratha predatory war would be attempted, entering the territory of the Nizam by a more easterly pass than the Ajanta, which would lead into 'a well cultivated, populous country' and one which had not been laid waste by Jaswant Rao Holkar the year before. There would be little inducement for the Marathas to seek one of the more westerly passes since the country to which they gave access 'had already been plundered'. Stevenson planned to place a detachment near the Ajanta pass, because he believed it could be adequately defended by a battalion, though he did not, in the event, do this.[3]

The later reaction of Arthur Wellesley to the suggestion that predatory war was in prospect, expressed in a letter to Collins of 15 August, was vigorous and, in the event, justified. 'The Marathas have long boasted that they would carry on a predatory war against us; they will find that mode of warfare not very practicable at the present... a system of predatory war must have some foundation in strength of some kind or other.' At this time Arthur Wellesley believed that the two Maratha rulers had sent their infantry northwards into Hindustan, although in fact some part of it had not been so moved, and were possibly planning not to utilise their brigades in the coming campaign on the Deccan. He commented that the Marathas 'must have little knowledge of human nature if they suppose that their lighter bodies will act.' While not discounting the consequences, especially for the inhabitants, of invasion by marauding horsemen—which he had earlier indicated to Stevenson that he did not expect the two detachments to be able totally to prevent—Arthur Wellesley recognised that the real contest would be with the formed infantry and artillery of the two Maratha rulers.

Collins, who had continued his march southwards, and was now encamped near Aurangabad, was still in touch with the camp of Daulat Rao Sindia. On 16 August, he wrote to Arthur Wellesley, commenting that he was in 'no doubt that Sindia heartily repents ere this not having complied with your requisition.' He asked that

'if Sindia be brought to proper sense of his danger by the capture of Ahmednagar, and in consequence make any overtures to me for the purpose of effecting a reconciliation with the British government, in what manner shall I answer him? Such an event is possible though improbable.'

Arthur Wellesley's reply was firm; while he wished to secure peace, 'we must proceed with caution, because I am afraid that we shall miss our object if we should appear too desirous to obtain it.' Collins was instructed to respond to any overture by reminding the two Maratha rulers that 'new pacific professions unaccompanied by facts will not persuade me that their intentions are sincere.' Clearly the experience of the protracted negotiations of June and July had left Arthur Wellesley in no mood for temporising. Collins responded that the General could

'be assured that I shall most carefully avoid giving Sindia any reason to believe that you are in the least desirous of peace, and should that chieftain write to me with a view of accommodating existing differences, my reply shall be exactly as you have suggested. But at present I have little hope of Sindia's adopting any measures of a pacific tendency, his pride being hurt at the loss of the impregnable fortress of Ahmednagar.'[5]

Arthur Wellesley was also at pains to remind Collins of the issue of timing that had been so central to his thinking during the two months of confrontation.

'You see the advantage which we derive from the commencement of hostilities during the season when the rivers are full. We have got possession of Sindia's only hold in the Deccan: he cannot receive assistance from Holkar, supposing that chief is inclined to assist him, and is confined by the Godavari in the execution of his plan of predatory war, supposing him capable of carrying it into execution. In the meantime I shall fill Ahmednagar with provisions, and when that is completed, all the Marathas in India will not be able to drive me from my position.'

Collins understood only too clearly this reference to the negotiations of June and July. 'I was always well aware of the advantages you would derive by commencing your military operations during the rainy monsoon... I thought it might be prudent to put the Maratha chieftains altogether in the wrong.'[6]

Collins was still receiving information about the movements of the forces of Sindia and Bhonsle. 'My newswriter still attends the camp of the Maharajah and my dak hircarrahs in that quarter have hitherto been permitted to remain unmolested at their usual stations.' On 16 August 1803 he reported that Sindia had moved near to Phardapur, a pass slightly to the east of that of Ajanta. Bhonsle was moving towards the Badauli pass further to the east, and was halfway towards it by the 17. Three days later Collins was able to report that both Maratha rulers were about sixteen miles from the Badauli pass. At that point his sources of information in the camp of Daulat Rao Sindia dried up. It was from Mohipat Ram, a major feudatory of the Nizam then in Aurangabad, that Collins learnt that Sindia, after moving towards the Badauli pass, had returned westwards to Phardapur, and that some of his cavalry had come quickly through a pass nearby. On 24 August Collins sent out four horsemen to ascertain the truth of these reports, but they could get no nearer than twenty miles to the Ajanta, and were pursued for many miles by *pindaris*. Collins hoped that when Arthur Wellesley reached Aurangabad, he would be able to 'quicken the measures' of the agents of the Nizam of Hyderabad 'who it seems are very tardy in furnishing supplies of grain.' Before Arthur Wellesley reached Aurangabad, Collins reported a conversation with Mohipat Ram in which he had urged him to arrange the storage of grain in the forts of the Nizam, and was told that there was no money to make the necessary purchases. The response from Arthur Wellesley of 28 August went to the heart of the matter: 'I will give the lakh of rupees required with pleasure, provided he (Mohipat Ram) will point out the places at which I can get the grain.'[7]

By 30 August 1803 Arthur Wellesley and his detachment had reached Aurangabad. The day would have been spent in discussion. To Mohipat Ram, Arthur Wellesley must have stressed the need for more active support from the servants and territories of the Nizam for the war against the Marathas. Collins was later able to report that Mohipat Ram had 'written to the different *zamindars* under his authority, directing them in the strongest terms to come to no sort of compromise with the Marathas, but to defend themselves to the last extremity relying in the meantime on being shortly relieved.' Time was to show the limited value of these instructions. Collins believed that Mohipat Ram was 'quite on the alert since his interview ... and will exert himself to the utmost for the good of the service.' But the task of urging the feudatories of the Nizam to the assemblage of supplies and to support of active hostilities against the Marathas was one to which Arthur Wellesley was to return later.

The long discussion between Collins and Arthur Wellesley was not recorded. Perhaps it was acrimonious; certainly Collins wrote directly afterwards to Richard Wellesley implying that he appreciated that it seemed unlikely that he would be further employed in a diplomatic capacity at least in the Deccan; Arthur Wellesley would almost certainly elect to rely on John Malcolm. The issue of the degree of pressure that Collins had put on Sindia and Bhonsle during the long period of negotiation from March to July 1803 must have arisen during the exchange. Arthur Wellesley was certainly confirmed during this meeting in his view that by the time he received his political authority, on 18 July, nothing could have averted hostilities with Daulat Rao Sindia and Raghuji Bhonsle. Guided in part by his discussions with Collins at Aurangabad, he saw Raghuji Bhonsle as the instigator of the conflict: 'war was inevitable and the Raja of Berar urged it on, in order to find a place for the subsistence of Sindia's and Holkar's troops, which must otherwise have entered his territories.' A few days later, when he hoped that it would be possible directly to threaten the territories of Raghuji Bhonsle, he mentioned to John Malcolm the considered view of Collins that the Raja of Berar was 'the only one of the three (major Maratha rulers) who cares one pin about his country, or has anything to lose by an invasion.' As will be seen, Arthur Wellesley had every intention of acting on this information. When four months later he was moving with his army in the territory of Raghuji Bhonsle, the degree of prosperity compared to other Maratha lands confirmed him in his assessment.[8]

Meanwhile Stevenson in the later part of August had moved eastwards from Phulambri. He reached Nygaum on 17 August,

crossing the area of the future battlefield of Assaye and was encamped eight miles west of Jaffirabad on the 19th. He reported that
both Maratha chiefs had been at the foot of the Badauli ghat the
previous evening and it was said in their camp that they were to
enter the territory of the Nizam of Hyderabad by that route. He
hoped that it would be possible to persuade Mohipat Ram to
provision the frontier forts, although he doubted whether 'his
influence extends far from Aurangabad.' He had ordered a small
detachment to advance carefully towards the ghat the following
morning. 'If on my arrival at Jaffirabad I find that there is any risk
in that position I shall not join... but the movement may create
delay in the movements of the enemy and perhaps change their
route.' Two days later, encamped east of Chickli 'about ten miles
south of the Badauli ghat and twenty four miles west of the
Lukhanwari ghat' he found that the Marathas had not moved and
were sending the nephew of Raghuji Bhonsle to Nagpur 'partly on
account of sickness and partly because they know that the English
troops are moving towards them.' By the morning of the 23rd
Stevenson knew that Sindia and Bhonsle had returned westward
and had not entered the eastern passes. They were now twenty
miles from the Ajanta pass.

'Their move to the eastward,' Stevenson now commented to
Arthur Wellesley, 'may have been intended to engage my attention
while their guns and infantry marched back to Burhanpur... having
effected that, they may have some future plans for ascending the
Ajanta.' He repeated his view that the passes to the eastward were
easier for ascent than those to the west and that the Marathas were
more likely to use them. Not only did these passes 'open immediately upon on a rich well cultivated country,' the Marathas would
also be aware that Arthur Wellesley had crossed the Godavari and
was 'entering upon the Ajanta road.' Stevenson evidently considered that the approach of the detachment commanded by Arthur
Wellesley towards Aurangabad would in itself safeguard the Ajanta
pass. He had just heard of a party of 5000 horses belonging to
Raghuji Bhonsle at a pass near to him to the east.

> 'Having heard yesterday morning that a party of the enemy's
> horse had appeared at Badauli ghat, I ordered two squadrons of
> native cavalry and 500 Mughal horse [forces of the Nizam of
> Hyderabad] to march there at daylight this morning to make an

observation on the Badauli fort and the road through the ghat. An officer has this instant returned and reports Badauli to be a common mud gurry and the road very easy and practicable for carriages. An officer and a party went east three or four miles into the country beyond the ghats but there were no remnants of the enemy camp which he had left in a northwesterly direction yesterday.'[9]

One march to the rear of Stevenson was an infantry brigade, part of his own detachment; this force he now ordered to withdraw on Jaffirabad 'as much to cover my supplies coming immediately from Aurangabad as to keep a watch over the western ghats.' On 24 August Stevenson reported that he was still planning to move westwards. By this time 'common report, as well as a letter that I have received from Raja Sukhruder' (another feudatory of the Nizam) had told him that Sindia and Bhonsle were 'pretty well advanced up the Ajanta ghat.' On 25 August Stevenson reported that he had moved from near the Badauli ghat to Dewalgaon. He had hoped to intercept the two Maratha rulers, after their ascent of the Ajanta and neighbouring passes, but 'as I am too late to effect that point, I must march on their left flank keeping them to the westward and taking any opportunity of attacking them whether by day or night.' Haliburton, commanding the brigade now withdrawn to Jaffirabad, considered that 'it may be necessary to advance his whole brigade towards Budnapur or advance to meet the grain. His force with this will form a chain to keep the enemy to the westward.... They are at present too far from me in a westerly direction for me to march right upon them.' Stevenson planned to move to Jaffirabad himself to 'keep on their left and press them southwards.'[10]

Stevenson marched 15 miles towards Jaffirabad on 26 August, presumably with cavalry and perhaps a single battalion, and reported that he had done this without serious interference from the *pindaris*, as had not been the case on the previous day. By 27 August he hoped to be encamped on the Jalna side of Jaffirabad. If an opportunity of an attack on the Marathas came, he would seize it, but he was also anxious to secure 'six thousand bullock loads of rice, for which I have made advances.' On 30 August Stevenson reported from Donegaum that the Marathas had marched in an easterly direction from Budnapur, having been repulsed from the town as it had an effective wall system and a vigorous *killedar*, had detached a force towards Paithan (Puttan) on the Godavari, and had been encamped the previous morning at Khalgaum six miles east of Jalna. The two Maratha rulers were now reported to be planning to move to Patri, on the Dunda, a feeder of the Godavari. Stevenson added that his own position appeared to him to be

'the best opportunity I shall have of getting the lakh of pagodas under charge of Lt Oliver and also three lakhs of rupees that I have now to expect is arrived at Aurangabad. I have therefore detached the 2nd Madras Native Infantry with three guns and the allies [cavalry of the Nizam of Hyderabad] with orders to proceed to Aurangabad and bring the treasure and the escort to join my detachment. To favour the march of the detachment I marched with my force in a southerly direction to Donegaum where I propose remaining until joined by my treasure if no particular information draws me from hence.'[11]

The detachment was two months in arrears of pay, so that the supply of bullion Stevenson was anxious to secure would have met its requirements for September and October. The cavalry of the Nizam of Hyderabad, that was being employed in escorting this move of bullion, was in itself six months in arrears of pay as reported by Collins two days later. Partly no doubt for that reason, as Collins correctly forecast, it could 'not be depended upon for actual service.'[12]

Leaving a small garrison in Aurangabad, infantry in the service of the Nizam of Hyderabad, formerly part of the French officered infantry disbanded in Hyderabad in November 1798, Arthur Wellesley had meanwhile, on 31 August 1803, marched east and south. He knew by now that the *silledar* and *pindari* cavalry of Daulat Rao Sindia and Raghuji Bhonsle had passed through the Ajanta line of hills that were the northern boundary of the territories of the Nizam of Hyderabad. It was soon rumoured that the Marathas planned a marauding expedition into the Hyderabad territory south of the Godavari. Arthur Wellesley now wished to use both detachments, his own and that commanded by Colonel Stevenson, to drive eastwards into the lands of Raghuji Bhonsle so as to 'give the Raja something to do in his own country.' He considered that he could not himself at once move eastward into Berar with his whole force because he was awaiting a reinforcement of a battalion bringing supplies and bullion with it; this had been travelling north from the Company territory in Mysore, through that of the Nizam of Hyderabad south of the Godavari. The alternative seemed to be to move forward with a light force, having placed baggage and heavy stores in a defended camp. This Arthur Wellesley recommended also to Stevenson. [13]

In the event this movement had to be countermanded, because of the threatened withdrawal of support by the Maratha cavalry commanded by Goklah and Appah Dessaye. Arthur Wellesley had literally to buy off this difficulty by undertaking responsibility for their pay. As he explained to Barry Close in Pune, he had no great expectation from the services of either of these two leaders of the Maratha horse, whose eventual presence with his detachment was the result of pressure placed upon them by Peshwa Baji Rao in June.

> 'Bad as they are, and weak as my expectations are from them, I must determine upon keeping them, at least for the present ... if they were to go, we should be surrounded in our camp and on our marches by *pindaris* and we should lose even the name of a body of cavalry... I must therefore determine to pay these chiefs myself.'

With this decision, unwelcome though it was on grounds of finance, Barry Close was in agreement:

> 'I am delighted to find that you are joined by Appah Dessaye. You must, my dear General, pay both him and Goklah. The Peshwa will be debited for the expense and the Gaekwar fund (land revenue income from the Gaekwar of Baroda) is good security. To be deprived of any of your present (Maratha) cavalry would be dreadful; you ought to have much more.' [14]

In place of the threatened movement into Berar by both detachments, Arthur Wellesley moved further south and east. By 3 September 1803 he had reached the Godavari at Rakshasubhuvam, Stevenson had captured Jalna, and Sindia and Bhonsle were at Partur. His own position, Arthur Wellesley believed, safeguarded the convoy of supplies which he was still awaiting, and would also serve to threaten the Marathas with a direct attack if they attempted to cross the Godavari river with boats, or with pursuit. The river had risen and fallen again; it had been full when he had ported his own detachment across it at Toka some six to ten days earlier.[15]

A day later it was clear that at least one brigade of Sindia's infantry had come south through the Ajanta pass. Two deserters from this brigade, known as that of the Begum Sumru, came into Aurangabad on 2 September 1803. They had 'thrown themselves on the clemency' of their countrymen, once they became aware of the prospect of hostilities against the Company. John Roach and George Blake had been artillerymen each in charge of a gun. They had 'left camp by permission' and immediately been robbed of all their possessions. On the second day after they had left their unit, they had heard 'a brisk and heavy cannonade for an hour and a half' presumably the preliminaries of the siege of Jalna by the detachment of Stevenson. They reported that two day's march behind their unit Colonel Pohlman was moving south with seven battalions of regular infantry and two battalions of matchlock men with five guns to a battalion of calibres from three to five pounds. Their own brigade had been moving at night, possibly to avoid observation.

Arthur Wellesley still hoped that the detachment commanded by Stevenson would be able to move into Berar. 'The Raja of Berar is at the heart of the confederacy. An invasion of his country would at all events make a seasonable diversion.' The first objective he wished to set this detachment, in fact quite a distant one, was the siege of Gawilghar, a major fortress of Raghuji Bhonsle many miles to the northeast in the Satpura range of hills north of the Purna valley. He evidently hoped subsequently to direct Stevenson to move onto Nagpur.[16]

Stevenson asked for further artillery and bullion, in addition to that already moving towards him, if he were to attempt a long march followed by the proposed siege. Meantime, both for the reasons that he had given to Arthur Wellesley relating to his supplies, and perhaps because he also feared the security of Aurangabad—which Arthur Wellesley had been prepared to accept was at hazard had he been forced to follow the Marathas southward—Stevenson had withdrawn south and westwards to Budnapur.

This move, which Arthur Wellesley would presumably not have endorsed if he had been able to comment, opened the way for an eventual unopposed junction of the Maratha brigades and artillery with the *silledar* and *pindari* horse. Arthur Wellesley now explained to the Governor–General that the cavalry of the Nizam, which might otherwise have helped to prevent this movement, were not 'true to the cause'. On the same day, he informed Stevenson that he did not feel able to assist his detachment in artillery, although he sent some ammunition, and 'a lakh of pagodas'. Writing to Malcolm on 6 September, he reported that Maratha *silledar* cavalry had attacked Stevenson's detachment on its march two days earlier, and that it had been necessary to use artillery fire to drive them off.[17]

By this time it was becoming clear that Daulat Rao Sindia and Raghuji Bhonsle had understood the fact that a marauding dash towards the capital city of the Nizam of Hyderabad that involved crossing the Godavari would lead to their pursuit by a British detachment. The two Maratha rulers moved their cavalry northwards, towards their infantry and artillery, now clear of the Ajanta pass. Arthur Wellesley hoped that the movement of the detachment (commanded by Stevenson) southwestwards to Budnapur would be seen by the Maratha rulers as a retreat and encourage them to attempt a general action. From the letters which he received from Stevenson at this time, one of which he received with annoyance and later described to John Malcolm as 'curious', Arthur Wellesley had to accept reluctantly that there was no immediate prospect of an attack on the territory of the Raja of Berar.[18]

All this had been closely observed by Barry Close in Pune who noted early in September that Arthur Wellesley had 'completely ... succeeded in giving the enemy a turn to the eastward.' If the brigade of the Begum Sumru had indeed come up the ghats that would be 'more heavy and tangible' and would aid Arthur Wellesley. Optimistically, Close also spoke of the 'young Nizam' being 'tolerably well prepared to meet them' if the two Maratha rulers were to advance towards Hyderabad; nothing could have been further from the truth. But the central concern of Close at Pune was to safeguard the transit of convoys forward to Ahmednagar and onward to the detachment. A group of banjaras with a thousand bullocks had nearly reached Ahmednagar on 2 September 1803, one lakh of pagodas was on its way from Harihar, supplies of rice were moving up the western Ghats from Panvel and would be sent forward. By late September Close could report that two and a half lakhs of rupees had been sent forward to Ahmednagar and that more would follow. Each of the two detachments would have required payment to the order of a lakh of rupees a month.[19]

In parallel to this reinforcement were the supplies from the 'ceded districts' north of Mysore and from Hyderabad. The positioning of Arthur Wellesley in the Godavari valley was not related solely to the threat of a predatory raid into the lands of the Nizam of Hyderabad south of the river, but also to the timing of the northern movement of these convoys. A major supply convoy, and an additional battalion, reached Arthur Wellesley some distance north of the Godavari on 18 September 1803. He was now free to plan a northward movement of both detachments, his own and that commanded by Stevenson. The two Maratha rulers had by now withdrawn their cavalry units to a position near Bakurdhan, near the Ajanta ghat. Their infantry and artillery units had perhaps never moved further south than this point. On 21 September Stevenson and Arthur Wellesley met near Budnapur about thirty miles south of the Maratha position. Together it was agreed that they should attempt to sweep the Maratha forces northwards towards the Tapti valley. The detachment under Stevenson was to move to the west of a lesser range of hills immediately to the north, that under Arthur Wellesley to the east. There were sections of narrow road; to have moved the two detachments by the same route would have caused delay, and risked a move of Maratha cavalry southwards. This decision to continue to operate as two detachments at this point would prove to be a fateful one.[20]

Both detachments moved north on 22 September. On the morning of the 23rd that commanded by Arthur Wellesley marched about twenty miles to Naulniah. Just as camp was being formed, word came that it was within six or eight miles of the Maratha position. Arthur Wellesley moved forward to investigate. After he had galloped some way northward, he would have seen an extended Maratha camp; in all some eight miles long from west to east, the combined forces of Daulat Rao Sindia and Raghuji Bhonsle, with the European officered infantry battalions of Daulat Rao Sindia on the Maratha left flank. Their position was to the west of a confluence of two rivers, the Kaitna and the Juah, each with quite steep banks in places. Reports at the time, which Arthur Wellesley later said that he accepted, were that the Marathas were preparing to leave their camp. The position of the British detachment would soon be known to the Marathas, whose *pindari* horse served as a constant screen and source of intelligence.

This was the crisis of the career of Arthur Wellesley in India; it was about noon on 23 September 1803. The decision that he then took was to attack with the detachment he commanded, although a message was to be sent to Stevenson, believed to be not more than eight miles away. Giving orders for the creation of a defended camp for the baggage, Arthur Wellesley resolved to cross the front of the Maratha force, ford the Kaitna, the nearer of the two rivers away to his right, deploy almost the whole of his detachment, although not the forces of his allies, on the ground between the Kaitna and the Juah to the west of their confluence, and attack the formed infantry brigades of Daulat Rao Sindia, and trust in the restricted ground to protect his small force from being overwhelmed by Maratha cavalry.

There were real elements of hazard in this plan. The British detachment would have faced annihilation if it suffered a reverse in the narrow plain between the two rivers. The prospect of rolling up the Maratha line, if it ever existed, soon vanished, because part of the Maratha infantry altered their position so that they faced eastward between the Kaitna and the fortified village of Assaye. Leaving the Mysore cavalry and that of Goklah and Appah Dessaye to its south, the detachment crossed the river and deployed facing the Marathas. Its artillery was limited in quantity, and was literally outgunned. The battle began with a misunderstanding of orders on the British right flank, where a mistaken attempt was made to move on the fortified village of Assaye. The predominance of Maratha artillery, marked across the whole line, was especially great here, and the attempt was a failure. Pressure from Maratha cavalry on a Kings and a native infantry unit on the right of the British line, endangered by this error, was relieved by a cavalry charge of the 19th Light Dragoons and two units of native cavalry. Fierce infantry fighting in the centre, aimed especially at the capture of Maratha artillery, made it possible eventually for the left and centre of the British infantry line to advance, wheel to the right and force the Maratha infantry against a second line of infantry, deployed parallel to the Juah. In this position the combined Maratha infantry line was assailed by a further British cavalry charge, although one which failed in its full effect. After a reverse British movement across the field of battle by a cavalry and an infantry unit, led personally by Arthur Wellesley—to recapture guns that had already been passed but which were again firing—the remnants of the Maratha infantry fled. The Maratha cavalry, despite their numbers, had played but a limited part in the battle.

It was a hard won victory. Of the total British force directly involved, which cannot have numbered more than 5000, over 400 were killed and over 1100 injured, more than 700 of them sufficiently seriously to be retained in the rudimentary hospital facilities, and over 100 of them to be likely stretcher cases a month later. The Marathas left 1200 dead on the field and were assumed to have suffered injuries of four times as many. The British captured 100 Maratha guns, and were impressed by their quality.

Assaye was an unexpected battle. It arose during a second attempted coordinated movement of the two detachments. The first had been an even more ambitious venture, envisaged a few days earlier, but abandoned almost at once, which would have involved placing the Ajanta line of hills between the two detachments. The movement northwards in two detachments while at close range to a massed Maratha force would always have been hazardous, and could have been disastrous in the event. To rely on swift communication between the two detachments, which had been operating separately for many months in territory where it was necessary to call on local guides—some of them newly hired—was to take a grave risk.

The standard analysis of the battle of Assaye has always followed the documentation created at the time by Arthur Wellesley. In this he saw the decision to continue to operate the two detachments as separate units as defensible and even inevitable. Yet the unexpected confrontation of the whole force of Daulat Rao Sindia and Raghuji Bhonsle by one of the two detachments, that commanded by Arthur Wellesley, represented a failure of intelligence.

It is not easy to reconstruct the intelligence resources that Arthur Wellesley would have had at his disposal in the campaign that led to the battle at Assaye. In a listing, possibly written in Calcutta in the following year by one of his chief assistants, Barclay, it appears that throughout the campaign Arthur Wellesley had one group of *hircarrachs* recruited in southern Maharashtra by Govind Rao, a former servant of Tipu Sultan of Mysore, another by 'a *hircarrah* named Rustam who had rendered particular service in Dhondiah's campaign and accompanied General Wellesley from Seringapatam' and a third a group sent in June 1803 from Pune by Colonel Barry

Close and evidently recruited near there. It was from this third group that Arthur Wellesley subsequently reported loss by desertion.

The matter is complicated by the use of the same term, *hircarrah*, to cover in addition to the groups just mentioned, 'guides' seized on the march, whose local knowledge may have been of higher quality, but where the danger of corruption and deliberate misinformation must have existed. If Arthur Wellesley did indeed hang a guide after Assaye, it may be assumed that the victim was of this latter class. Although he did not hesitate to impose the death penalty, for example on sepoys recaptured after desertion or detected in looting, he would hardly have ordered the execution of a member of a group selected for the work of intelligence gathering. But it could well have been in discussion with guides seized on the march that there occurred the confusion between the district of Bhokrdan and the town of the same name, that was in part responsible for the confrontation north of Naulniah of the detachment commanded by Arthur Wellesley with a prepared Maratha position. There is a hint that it was realised later that all was not well in the statement that 'after the battle of Assaye Colonel Stevenson sent six *hircarrahs*, Salabut Khan (a major feudatory of the Nizam of Hyderabad) sent four and Mohiput Rao sent four to the General. They were natives of Khandesh and Berar.'

But there is a further issue; if Stevenson was never more than eight miles distant from the detachment commanded by Arthur Wellesley, and received word of the Maratha position between the Kaitna and the Juah in the afternoon of 23 September, it is surprising that he did not reach that position until the evening of the 24th. Afterwards, Arthur Wellesley wrote of Stevenson having become 'entangled in a nullah' during the night, and therefore failing to reach Bakardhan, eight miles to the west of Assaye, the presumed position of the combined Maratha force, until eight in the morning of the 24. Arthur Wellesley was loyal to Stevenson, both at the time and later when his letters were published, and it is possible that he elected to conceal what happened.

It was Arthur Wellesley the political general who had taken the decision at noon on 23 September. There were powers nominally allied, at Pune and Hyderabad, as well as enemies, who had to be convinced that the British alliance had military validity. Arthur

Wellesley had seized the opportunity, to use his own words of 24 July to Richard Wellesley, to 'strike such a blow... as will give us the superiority.' Although the French-officered infantry of Daulat Rao Sindia was not destroyed at Assaye, part of it had been gravely weakened, not least by such a significant loss of artillery, and Sindia made a first tentative venture at peacemaking almost immediately afterwards. Raghuji Bhonsle was perhaps of tougher metal, and attempted a further southern predatory sortie within a month. A decision not to attack at noon on 23 September could have led later either to further northward pursuit of the two Maratha rulers by both detachments, or an attempted joint attack on the strong Maratha position on the Kaitna—if it had been retained, on the following day—perhaps at lesser cost. This had indeed been the original plan, although at a different location. Arthur Wellesley at least knew how much the outcome had been on a knife-edge, and that far from being a shrewd assessment with a high probability of success, the decision to attack had been a gamble for high stakes, justified by the potential political gain, but with a cost in human lives that stayed clear in his mind for a lifetime. He had forced matters by accepting the almost certain prospect of high casualties of both sepoys and Europeans, and for the latter at least there were no casualty replacements nearer than the ceded territories to the north of Mysore.

Reflecting on these matters in Pune, aided by the painstaking correspondence from the camp of Elphinstone, who forwarded a plan of the battle with a letter dated 26 September 1803, Barry Close and Edward Strachey developed their own analysis. Daulat Rao Sindia and Raghuji Bhonsle had seen their strength as that of their artillery and infantry, created a cavalry threat to Hyderabad and Pune to bring Arthur Wellesley forward and to cover the movement of their artillery and infantry southward through the Ajanta passes, and determined on a position where their advantage, in infantry and artillery, would be at its greatest.

'Daulat Rao Sindia never meant to pursue a predatory mode of warfare, for which indeed the greater part of his cavalry is not fitted ... in pressing through the pass with his cavalry, in circulating the reports that he did and running to the south of our troops, his real design was to draw off our attention from the passes by making us tenacious of Hyderabad and Pune, and afford leisure for his numerous infantry and cumbrous train to come uninterrupted and unnoticed through the ghats ... Daulat Rao Sindia had arranged to engage the united forces of the General and Colonel Stevenson.... The post he occupied seems to have been selected with the intention of using it for an action. It was particularly secure ... when the two British divisions separated, it does not appear that Daulat Rao Sindia made any movement to bring one of them separately to action, but keeping his ground at all hazards throughout as a lure [sought] to bring one of them into action.'

Barry Close wrote this in a private letter to Josiah Webbe at Madras. Strachey, writing in his private memorandum book on the same day, stated that he believed that on 22 and 23 September 1803, the Marathas 'gave rise to reports which induced the General to attack them with his division alone', when they were in such strength that 'they must have fought with great confidence and expectation of success.' Strachey considered that the decision taken at noon on 23 September to attack with one detachment only 'cannot but be pronounced hazardous' and when viewed against the potential consequences of defeat, 'extremely rash and injudicious'. His assessment concludes, in reference to Arthur Wellesley that ' no man in India but himself would have attempted it, and no man in India but himself could have executed it.' It was not until later that Strachey would have known that Arthur Wellesley had let slip to Elphinstone that he would have committed suicide had the venture failed.[21]

Late on 24th September, the detachment commanded by Stevenson arrived on the field of battle. Surgeons of both detachments were busy giving to the wounded the elementary medical services of those days, and after twenty-four hours Stevenson was sent north towards the Ajanta pass in pursuit of the Maratha forces. The Maratha infantry withdrew towards the Narbada. The area near the Ajanta pass was scattered with abandoned equipment and wounded Marathas. Arthur Wellesley was unable to place either the wounded of his detachment or the captured guns in a position of what seemed to him adequate security. This was because the *killedar* of Daulatabad, a fort belonging to the Nizam of Hyderabad near Aurangabad, some thirty miles to the south-west, refused to allow British use of the fortress. Arrangements were eventually made to place the wounded within the fortifications at Ajanta itself, after Stevenson had confirmed to Arthur Wellesley on 29 September that there was adequate accommodation within 'an octagon brick fort' and elsewhere to house them. To this setting they were moved northwards, and the improvised fortification strengthened with some of the captured guns, while other captured guns were moved southwards, eventually to Ahmednagar. At the same time artillery reinforcements were sought from Hyderabad; there could be no question of their arrival for some four weeks.[22]

The news of the fighting at Assaye reached in Pune within five days. On 28 September Barry Close sent to Richard Wellesley word that

'Khande Rao Rastiah who resides here has received a despatch this morning from a karkun belonging to him in General Arthur Wellesley's camp mentioning that four days since the armies of both sides met at the village of Dhygang in the parganah of Jalna at about noon. That a cannonade commenced which continued until near five in the evening when the General perceiving that he had no time to lose, charged the enemy's line and put them wholly to the rout taking fifteen pieces of cannon and the whole of their baggage, and that on the action being over General Arthur Wellesley encamped on the field and sent for his baggage which he had posted at some distance in the rear.'

To Arthur Wellesley Close wrote on the same day that 'we have had the happiness to hear that you have defeated the confederates and wait anxiously for a record of the event from your own pen.' At the same time Arthur Wellesley received the first indications of the victories of Gerald Lake in the north. Duncan at Bombay had forwarded to Close word from 'the soucars of Jynaghur.' The message was dated 9 September and certainly overstated the degree of the victories of the Company gained by that date. It read:

'The Hon. English Company eastern army having come, have taken Delhi Muttra and Agra and their flags are there displayed. On the part of Daulat Rao Sindia there is Perron. He was encamped with his army at Coel. The English army advanced upon which he fled and proceeded to Muttra, after that in a week more he sent a *vakil* and made his peace and has come in. In all this none of the ryots have been plundered and the English possession has been secure.'[23]

The message was confirmed to some degree by a letter from Musilapatam of 20 September which stated that Lake had defeated Perron and was pursuing him. Arthur Wellesley, therefore, knew by 1 October 1803 that the Company was beginning to make a formidable impact on the position of Perron in the Ganges-Jumna Doab.

Arthur Wellesley followed Stevenson northwards through the Ajanta pass, which was to be traversed three times in the next twenty days by his detachment, and turned to follow the cavalry of Daulat Rao Sindia and Raghuji Bhonsle westwards in the Tapti valley. A first tentative hint at peacemaking by Daulat Rao Sindia followed. In this an attempt was made to reopen the arguments about the departure of Collins from the camp of the two Maratha rulers in August, and to secure the visit of a British envoy. Arthur Wellesley wondered whether the objective was genuinely to begin a negotiation 'or to raise the spirit of the enemy's troops by showing a British officer in his camp, respecting whom it would be industriously reported that he had come to sue for peace.' He dealt firmly with the approach, and refused to send an envoy, while indicating a willingness to receive one.[24]

The surviving infantry of Daulat Rao Sindia had now concentrated on Burhanpur, while the cavalry of both Maratha rulers had taken two marches westwards along the Tapti valley and appeared by 8 October to be about to turn southwards from Khandesh; this could lead them once again to the Godavari valley, and even to Pune. There were unconfirmed reports that the two rulers had quarrelled and separated. Arthur Wellesley lamented that weakness of both Peshwa Baji Rao and the Nizam of Hyderabad prevented an immediate attack by both British detachments on the important fortress of Asirgarh: if this had been possible, he believed that it would 'put an end to the war.' He also noted that none of the forts of the Nizam of Hyderabad were

'sufficiently garrisoned. He has not a soldier in the country, except those belonging to the Company, and his *killedars* and amildars would readily pay the money they may have just to be allowed to sit quietly in their forts and towns. As for the Peshwa, he has possession of his palace at Pune and nothing more; and he spends the little money he receives either upon Brahmins or upon women, rather than give any to his troops, or even to his menial servants.'

Arthur Wellesley was confident he could now send Stevenson northwards from Ajanta to levy a contribution on Burhanpur. This had to be attempted, although contrary to Company practice, because of an acute shortage of money to pay the troops despite the movement of convoys northwards both from Hyderabad and from Pune. Stevenson was then to attack Asirgarh. Arthur Wellesley believed that two of the three infantry brigades that had fought at Assaye had suffered so badly that they were of limited value. Stevenson was specifically warned against exposing himself to Maratha artillery in the field. Arthur Wellesley was concerned that the effectiveness of the bombardment at Assaye could be repeated, if the Marathas could recover guns from Burhanpur or Asirgarh, although immediately after the battle he had commented to Close that he did not think 'anything with cannon will venture near us again.'[25]

After marching for three days southwards, starting on 9 October 1803, Arthur Wellesley was at Phulambri. He was conscious of his shortage of means of intelligence; 'the majority of my intelligence *hircarrahs* have either deserted or have been taken.' During the night of 15 October, reports reached him which convinced him that Daulat Rao Sindia and Raghuji Bhonsle planned to intervene in the operations of the detachment commanded by Stevenson in its operations against Burhanpur and Asirgarh. He was now reasonably confident that the Maratha forces had not penetrated southwards through the pass at the western end of the Ajanta range. He alerted Stevenson to the danger, explaining that he too would return northwards, paralleling the Maratha movement on the Ajanta road. Stevenson was to send forward into Burhanpur word of the offer by Richard Wellesley to match the pay of the officers of the infantry of Daulat Rao Sindia, if they left his service.[26]

By 18 October 1803, suffering from a severe attack of fever, Arthur Wellesley was once again dating his despatches from Ajanta. To enhance his support to Stevenson he again moved down the pass, this time to Phardapur. A further attempt at peace negotiations came in from the camp of Daulat Rao Sindia and was answered in the same way as its predecessor. By 23 October Arthur Wellesley knew that Stevenson had secured Burhanpur and captured Asirgarh by assault, and that Daulat Rao Sindia and Raghuji Bhonsle had certainly separated, the latter now planning a movement southward. A messenger brought in a letter from Stevenson to Stuart, the Madras Commander–in–Chief, and this Arthur Wellesley opened. It did not contain word of the capture of Asirgarh, but the messenger confirmed that he had been present in Burhanpur on 21 October when a salute had been ordered to celebrate the event. Later that day Arthur Wellesley knew from Stevenson himself that Asirgarh had been captured, and that the remnants of the infantry of Daulat Rao Sindia near Burhanpur had moved northwards towards the Narbada. Sixteen European officers and non-commissioned officers from the disciplined infantry had responded to the Governor-General's proclamation that offered them pay equivalent to that which they had received from Daulat Rao Sindia if they deserted. Stevenson was instructed to prepare to utilise the stores he found in Asirgarh in preparation for the siege of Gawlighar, the major fortress of Raghuji Bhonsle many miles to the east in the Satpura range that Arthur Wellesley had wished to attack in September. 'We have run the length of our tether against Daulat Rao Sindia,' Arthur Wellesley noted; 'he has nothing more to lose in the Deccan.'[27]

Arthur Wellesley again moved his detachment southwards, returning to Pahlood on 26 October and to Phulambri on 28 October. He continued to believe that Daulat Rao Sindia would soon seek peace, and perhaps Raghuji Bhonsle also, after a direct threat had been made to his own territories. Arthur Wellesley reported to Fort William, Calcutta:

> 'Since the battle of Assaye, I have been like a man who fights with one hand and defends himself with the other. With Colonel Stevenson's corps I have acted offensively, and have taken Asirgarh, and with my own I have covered his operations, and defended the territories of the Nizam and the Peshwa. In doing this I have made some terrible marches, but have been remarkably fortunate.'

The attempt to determine the order of battle of the formed brigades of Daulat Rao Sindia at Assaye continued. It had been

aided by the arrival at Pune of Stuart, a British officer who had
obtained his discharge from the first brigade of Daulat Rao Sindia,
known as Pohlman's, on 12 September. The first brigade had at
that time been encamped near Ajanta. Stuart had made his way
northwards to Burhanpur, and then southwards to Pune, being
'plundered of everything he had by the Bheels'. On 15 October
Close interviewed him, and set out a careful statement of location
of the brigades of Sindia, drawing on what Stuart had told him. He
drew from this the general conclusion, reported to Arthur
Wellesley, that

> 'you engaged all the infantry and guns which Sindia could
> collect, so that he must feel seriously the loss of his equipment.
> The brigades under Dudrenec and Brownrigg it would appear
> are off to Hindustan. At Ujjain there is nothing but the battalion
> under Baptiste and the one brigade forming at that capital, and
> at Burhanpur there can be nothing but the defeated infantry,
> by this time I suppose not very numerous.'

Arthur Wellesley put this, and the detailed interrogation report
which accompanied it, alongside an analysis attempted at Fort
William. He concluded that at Assaye 'the brigades engaged were
Pohlman's Dupont's and Begum Sumru's; in the whole sixteen
battalions,' and that there were only two brigades that had not been
engaged and were not destroyed 'excepting possibly one or two
battalions of Begum Sumru's and one of Pohlman's which were
sent off with the baggage at the commencement of the battle.'[28]
The immediate task was to counter the renewed southward
movement of Raghuji Bhonsle. He had separated from Daulat Rao
Sindia and 'passed through the hills which form the southern
boundary of Khandesh.' Arthur Wellesley moved in pursuit, eventually to positions southeast of Aurangabad, which he passed on
29 October. Writing to Stevenson during this southward movement, he lamented that it was not possible to 'take all the advantage
I could wish of our success, but the fact is that offensive operations
are not expected of us in this quarter ... matters are not as they
should be at Hyderabad and they cannot well be worse than they
are at Pune; it is therefore peculiarly incumbent upon me to act
with caution.' Two days later at Naundair Bari, southeast of Aurangabad, he reported that Raghuji Bhonsle had moved camp constantly

and that he did not 'despair of coming up with him.' He later mentioned to Close that he believed that it was only intelligence gained from 'the man who collects *chauth* at Aurangabad' that had enabled Raghuji Bhonsle to evade an action at this time. For the present Stevenson was to remain in the Purna valley and continue to watch the movements of Daulat Rao Sindia, but not to attempt to follow him.[29]

If Daulat Rao Sindia could be regarded as defeated in the Deccan, and Raghuji Bhonsle of Berar as about to retreat into his own territory, the territories now secure from immediate threat were those of the Nizam of Hyderabad, whose northern boundary was 'the line of the ghats', that is the Ajanta range. But the ineffectiveness of the government of Hyderabad remained. A theoretical power of command had been delegated by the Nizam of Hyderabad to Arthur Wellesley, an arrangement secured by James Kirkpatrick the Resident before both the outbreak of hostilities in July and the death of the Nizam. This authority placed the military officers of Hyderabad under the control of Arthur Wellesley, and had been confirmed on the accession of the new Nizam in August. This command authority proved worthless. Directly after the battle of Assaye, Arthur Wellesley set out fully to the Resident at Hyderabad the extent of the obstruction to his military movements. Apart from the unwillingness of the commander of Daulatabad to accept the wounded from the battle of Assaye, the *killedar* in Budnapur had fired on a supply convoy, and at several places duty had been levied on grain destined for the Company forces. Arthur Wellesley retained confidence in the capacity of the Resident at Hyderabad to achieve action at the court in accordance with Company needs, and this was justified in the orders subsequently received from Hyderabad which dismissed the *killedar* of Daulatabad, for whom Arthur Wellesley then sought clemency. Subsequently, the Resident reported that the Nizam had complained of intervention in the internal affairs of his country, and Arthur Wellesley had felt impelled to advise the Resident to abandon pressure on lesser matters and await growing appreciation by the Nizam of the benefits from the Company alliance. At a later date, the Resident was instructed from Fort William to protest in the strongest terms, and to seek confirmation that the 'young Nizam' appreciated the value of the alliance.[30]

At the beginning of November 1803, as the military effort turned from the effective campaign against Daulat Rao Sindia to that yet to be launched against the homeland of Raghuji Bhonsle, Arthur Wellesley repeated his concern at 'the total want of defence in this country'. A major supply convoy of 14,000 bullocks was endangered in the Godavari valley by a cavalry attack from Bhonsle, and had been saved by the disciplined response of three companies of a sepoy regiment from Madras and of the Mysore cavalry. On his return from the Ajanta to the area just to the north of the Godavari, Arthur Wellesley had found that 'all the amildars [loyal to the Nizam] were in treaty with the enemy to pay contributions.' There could be no clearer expression of lack of confidence in the alliance with the British Company. If there was not a marked enhancement in the degree of support from the government of the Nizam of Hyderabad at all levels, it would be necessary to 'confine the operations of the troops to a strict defensive.' To the Resident at Hyderabad, Arthur Wellesley emphasised that the issues of division of the territorial spoils of victory should not arise at this stage of the conflict. In any event, the temporary transfer of title of lands which had been the property of Daulat Rao Sindia near Burhanpur and Asirgarh would enable the Nizam, 'putting aside all considerations ... connected with the non-performance of his engagements' to benefit from their land revenue income.[31]

It was while faced with such hesitant support from a major ally of the Company that Arthur Wellesley set himself to threaten the Raja of Berar.

NOTES

1. AW-RW 12 Aug 03.

2. Stevenson-AW 10 Aug 03 WP 3/3/84: listing of the forces of Daulat Rao Sindia and Raghuji Bhonsle behind Collins-AW 25 Jul 03 PRC ix 353.

3. Stevenson-AW 10 Aug 03 WP 3/3/84.

4. AW-Collins 15, Aug 03: AW-Stevenson 18 Jul 03.

5. Collins-AW 16, 20 Aug 03 WP 3/3/53: AW-Collins 18 Aug 03.

6. AW-Collins 18 Aug 03 SD iv 158: Collins-AW 20 Aug 03 WP 3/3/53.

7. Collins-AW 16, 19, 24 27 Aug 03 WP 3/3/53: AW-Collins 28 Aug 03.

8. Collins-AW 31 Aug 03 WP 3/3/53: AW-Shawe 31 Aug 03: AW-Malcolm 6 Sep 03: Collins-GG 31 Aug 03 PRC x 13.
9. Stevenson-AW 19, 22, 23 Aug 03 WP 3/3/84.
10. Stevenson-AW 24, 25 Aug 03 WP 3/3/84.
11. Stevenson-AW 26 Aug 03 WP 3/3/84.
12. Stevenson-AW 30 Aug 03 WP 3/3/84: Collins-AW 2 Sep 03 WP 3/3/53.
13. AW-Stevenson 31 Aug 03.
14. AW-Close 1 Sep 03: Close–AW 4 Sep 03 WP 3/3/47.
15. AW-Kirkpatrick 3 Sep 03: AW-Stevenson 4 Sep 03.
16. Collins-AW and attached 'deposition' 2 Sep 03 WP 3/3/53: AW-Stevenson, Stuart, Shawe 4 Sep 03.
17. AW-RW 4 Sep 03: AW-Malcolm 6 Sep 03.
18. AW-Stevenson, Malcolm 12 Sep 03.
19. Close-AW 6, 7, 21 Sep 03 WP 3/3/47.
20. AW-RW 24 Sep 03: AW-Stuart 24 Sep 03: AW-Shawe 24 Sep 03.
21. Close-Webbe 6 Oct 03 PRC x 151: Strachey 6 Oct 03 IOR Mss Eur F 128/197.
22. AW-Shawe 28 Sep 03: AW-Stuart 29 Sep 03: Stevenson-AW 29 Sep 03: WP 3/3/84 Stevenson's description is paralleled in Jasper Nicoll's diary for 8 Oct 03 Mss Eur F 175/5 and in Maharashtra State Gazetteer Aurangabad District revised ed 1977 p. 835.
23. Close-GG 28 Sep 03 NUL Pw Jb 11 f.17: Close-AW 28 Sep 03 WP 3/3/47.
24. AW-Balaji Kunjar 5 Oct 03: AW-Close 5 Oct 03: AW-RW 6 Oct 03.
25. AW-Shawe 8 Oct 03.
26. AW-Close, Stevenson, Malcolm 11 Oct 33.
27. AW-Stuart 16 Oct 03: AW-Close 21 Oct 03: AW-Kirkpatrick 23 Oct 03: AW-Collins 23 Oct 03: AW-Stevenson 24 Oct 03: AW-Mohipat Ram 24 Oct 03: AW-RW 24 Oct 03.
28. Close-AW 15 Oct 03 WP 3/3/47: Close-GG 16 Oct 03 PRC x 154: summary of discussion with Stuart 15 Oct 03 PRC x 154 SNRR i 375: AW-Close 21 Oct 03: AW-Collins 23 Oct 03 SD iv 206: AW-Shawe 26 Oct 03.
29. AW-Stevenson 28, 31 Oct 03 (blanks in text inserted on surmise. In the copy in WP 3/3/84 the words are in cypher): AW-Close 31 Oct 03: AW-HW 24 Jan 04.
30. AW-Kirkpatrick 27, 28, 29 Sep 03, 7, 15, 25 Oct 03: Edmonstone-Kirkpatrick 25 Nov 03 WP 3/3/10.
31. AW-Kirkpatrick, RW 2 Nov 03.

6

Negotiations in the General's Tent
(November, December 1803)

It was in the military setting that has just been described, with the detachment commanded by Stevenson halting in the Purna valley, and his own moving north and eastwards from the Godavari valley towards the territory of the Raja of Berar, that Arthur Wellesley found himself faced with the prospect of peace negotiations. Since both Raghuji Bhonsle and Daulat Rao Sindia were in the Deccan, it had always been probable that, given the extensive political authority that Richard Wellesley had transferred in June, the responsibility of peace negotiation would fall on Arthur Wellesley. These fully recorded exchanges with *vakils* or agents of the two Maratha rulers were interspersed in the intervals of operations.

In June 1803, political authority had been delegated to Arthur Wellesley to declare war or make peace, with direction to attempt to 'destroy the military power of either or both chiefs.' The substantial territorial objectives had been set out. In early August, when the Fort William Secretariat must have realised the imminent probability was of Arthur Wellesley declaring war, they gave him further guidance. In the first place Arthur Wellesley was reminded of a necessary condition of any peace concluded in the Deccan, namely that treaties made by Gerald Lake and Graeme Mercer in Hindustan must be accepted by Daulat Rao Sindia, and that feudatories of Sindia who had chosen to transfer their allegiance and aid the British should not suffer on account of this. He was further advised that if Peshwa Baji Rao fled from Pune, a possibility which John Malcolm had mentioned in his memorandum of July, Amrit Rao should be appointed dewan; if this were done Baji Rao would soon tire 'of being carried about by Sindia as a pageant or instrument in his hands.' The best security for British predominance at Pune was 'the introduction of Amrit Rao, Moraba Furnavis Furkia and their party into authority.' Again possibly drawing on the notes of John Malcolm, Barlow as a senior member of Council at Fort William, stressed the advantages—if Jaswant Rao Holkar stayed neutral—of his being given a guarantee of his territories. On these points Richard Wellesley noted:

> 'We must establish an efficient government at Pune and I am inclined to think that it may be necessary to employ Amrit Rao in some mode. It appears also that Holkar must be conciliated. At all events, Amrit Rao and Jaswant Rao Holkar must be separated from Daulat Rao Sindia. The Peshwa must not be suffered to escape, and the government must be conducted in his name.'[1]

In mid-October, Barlow produced a fuller note, which was also annotated by Richard Wellesley. In the event, this became the latest expression of the views of Fort William on peace terms that was available to Arthur Wellesley when he found himself called upon to undertake negotiations. The requirements of a peace settlement—stated for the first time—included the exclusion (from the territories of both Daulat Rao Sindia and Raghuji Bhonsle) of Frenchmen and other Europeans, creation of frontiers between Berar and Cuttack on the east and Berar and Hyderabad on the west that would be 'compact and connected', that Daulat Rao Sindia should be deprived of territory south of the Tapti and in Gujarat, and that both courts should be required to receive a British Resident.

On a recapitulation of territorial requirements in the north, Richard Wellesley noted that 'the occupation of the right bank of the Jumna will secure the tranquillity as well as the safety of the whole Doab. Our garrisons must be Delhi, Muttra, Agra, Kalpi, and some position in Bundelkhand.'

On the issue of the confirmation of treaties signed with lesser rulers by British detachment commanders Richard Wellesley noted that 'an article of the treaty must provide for this, peace ought not to be delayed for the specification of every name.'

The procedural issue—that was to complicate the treaty settlements with both Maratha rulers—was stated in this manner to Arthur Wellesley for the first time. He had already appreciated it.[2]

While this guidance was still on its way to him, since it was possible that peace negotiations were imminent, Arthur Wellesley set out—in a long letter to Richard Wellesley—the terms on which he proposed to negotiate with Daulat Rao Sindia. In this letter he was taking into account the June instructions as well as the points made in the first note sent in August from the Fort William Secretariat. The territorial cession he proposed to seek from Daulat Rao Sindia was all lands north of Jodhpur and Jainagar, the forts of Broach and Ahmednagar, and lands south and east of the Ajanta hills. By other proposed provisions, Daulat Rao Sindia was to renounce all claims on the Nizam of Hyderabad and on the Rana of Gohad, to undertake that there would be no Europeans in his service, and that he would 'not molest the chiefs who may have assisted the British government in the war.'

Since this scheme of territorial cession went markedly less far than the June instructions in a significant area, namely the extent to which the Nizam of Hyderabad should benefit by the peace settlement, Arthur Wellesley explained why he proposed to act so. There were 'weighty objections' to an increase of territory on the northern frontier of Hyderabad such as would be involved if the Nizam were to secure Burhanpur and Asirgarh from the treaty settlement. More was involved here than the concern of Arthur Wellesley at the ineffectiveness of the government of the Nizam of Hyderabad. It could be held that it was in the British interest ' to preserve a part of the strength of Daulat Rao Sindia, to enable him to support himself against Jaswant Rao Holkar.' This was an early indication of an important difference of view on the scale of political defeat which should be inflicted on Daulat Rao Sindia.

There were two notable sub-themes in the discussion of the negotiations. In the first place, Arthur Wellesley clearly considered, and noted in letters to Fort William, that an attempt should be made 'to detach Daulat Rao Sindia from the confederacy' by offering him territorial compensation in Berar for his losses in Hindustan, provided he would join in the war against Raghuji Bhonsle. This was not taken further, since the *vakils* from Sindia, when they arrived, were by no means ready for negotiation, much less a reversal of alliances. At a later date, Richard Wellesley indicated that this was not an approach that he favoured. Arthur Wellesley also wished to use the territorial cession to the Nizam of Hyderabad that would result from the peace settlement as a bargaining counter to secure significant amendments to the treaty of defensive alliance with the Nizam, which would enable the Resident at Hyderabad to have the right to muster the troops of the Nizam, to impose a fine if their numbers were deficient, and to inspect the frontier forts to ensure that they were fully supplied. This suggestion led to a prolonged attempt, undertaken by the Resident at Hyderabad but ultimately a failure, to improve the readiness of the forces of the Nizam. [3]

Within a few days of writing in this sense, Arthur Wellesley received the second note from the Fort William Secretariat with annotations by Richard Wellesley. He was relieved and no longer concerned that his first thoughts 'would have been deemed tame.' He now questioned the advisability of forbidding the entry of Europeans into the military employ of the country powers, although he had earlier placed this in his own list of requirements. He now stated for the first time the view, much echoed later, that although the armies of Daulat Rao Sindia 'had actually been brought to a very favourable state of discipline, and his power had become formidable by the exertions of the European officers in his service,' these armies could have been more formidable had he carried on his operations 'in the manner of the original Marathas, only by means of cavalry.' The Marathas had come to feel that should their artillery and infantry be lost, defeat was inevitable, and while it was certainly the case that these gave the British 'a good object of attack,' predatory operations by cavalry could be a serious threat. There was no inconsistency here with his thought to Collins in August that predatory war required some basis in strength; the threat which he foresaw in a situation after a peace settlement was that to Company territory and that of its allies from marauding cavalry; it could not be countered at every point, and to attempt even more limited protection would be costly. [4]

The agent of Daulat Rao Sindia, Jaswant Rao Ghorpade, presented himself, and held a first discussion with Arthur Wellesley on 10 November. This was discursive, much time being spent on the events of July and August. Ghorpade was anxious to demonstrate that the break in relations and the onset of war had been due to the 'precipitate and violent conduct' of Collins as Resident with the court of Daulat Rao Sindia. Arthur Wellesley disputed this, significantly adding that Collins, far from having hurried away, had stayed much longer than he was authorised to do. As he pointed out to John Malcolm, 'all this preliminary anxiety about the cause of the war is very natural, as they well know that we shall found our claims to satisfaction and security on the fact that they were the aggressors.'

Ghorpade lacked authority to negotiate, other than a letter from Daulat Rao Sindia to Appah Dessaye saying that he was an agent, and Arthur Wellesley insisted on the provision of a clearer statement, although he noted in private letters that he had himself no written powers to act on behalf of either the Nizam of Hyderabad or Peshwa Baji Rao. He commented to Richard Wellesley that 'in proportion however as I gain experience of the Marathas I have more reason to be astonished at the low and unaccountable tricks which even the highest classes of them practise with a view however remote to forward their own interest.'

The negotiations were therefore delayed, although Arthur Wellesley believed that the credentials were already available. The distress to which Daulat Rao Sindia had been reduced seemed to make it probable that the mission of Ghorpade was 'intended to obtain peace.'[5]

Low and unaccountable tricks continued. On the following day, Appah Dessaye, commander of part of the Maratha cavalry sent forward from Pune after Arthur Wellesley had left the city, initiated a discussion in which he set out what he believed to be the terms which Daulat Rao Sindia would seek. He then spoke of the union of interests of Raghuji Bhonsle, Daulat Rao Sindia and Jaswant Rao Holkar, and contended that Sindia would negotiate for all three of them, and that if the terms were not agreed, Sindia would join with the British in enforcing their acceptance. Arthur Wellesley noted that the Company was not at war with Jaswant Rao Holkar, and would prefer to negotiate with Raghuji Bhonsle directly. To John Malcolm he commented that he would 'soon put a stop to this go-between style of going on through Appah Dessaye.'[6]

Arthur Wellesley asked, on 17 November, whether the authority to negotiate had been sent to Ghorpade, only to learn that matters were further delayed by an intrigue, in which the major chieftain of the Nizam of Hyderabad Mohipat Ram had played a part, by which a Moslem named Mir Muhammed Khan was to be the agent, with the possibility that concessions that would be demanded of Daulat Rao Sindia would be in the south and so would protect the continuing independence from the British of the Mughal Emperor in Delhi. There had been an earlier attempt in mid-October to arrange an embassy by this agent. Arthur Wellesley commented that 'all these intrigues and lies, backward and forward, will throw many difficulties in the way.' From Collins Arthur Wellesley already knew that Mir Muhammed Khan was the son of a confidential servant of Mahadaji Sindia anxious to 'reestablish...interest by forming a connection' but without 'the slightest influence with the Maharajah.'[7]

On 20 November, in an attempt to establish the position of Ghorpade, Arthur Wellesley challenged him directly, saying that he had letters from the *darbar* of Daulat Rao Sindia informing him that Ghorpade was an impostor and that no attention should be paid to 'any chief that did not produce the regular papers empowering him to act.' Ghorpade replied that he had a letter from Daulat Rao Sindia to Appah Dessaye and a letter from another agent of Sindia in the camp of Raghuji Bhonsle; both of these referred to his mission. He accepted that Arthur Wellesley was entitled to be totally suspicious of his position. In fact Arthur Wellesley was satisfied that the evidence available to him showed that the intentions of Ghorpade were genuine, and he allowed him to remain in his camp. Within two hours, as he later recounted to Richard Wellesley, he was brought a letter showing that the two agents, and Appah Dessaye, were empowered to discuss peace terms.[8]

Substantive discussions at last opened on the following day, 21 November. Elphinstone had, at the request of Arthur Wellesley, informed Appah Dessaye that he could not, as a commander of forces loyal to Peshwa Baji Rao, be an agent for Daulat Rao Sindia, and therefore could not be present. The other two empowered *vakils* stated that they were instructed to learn the wishes of Arthur Wellesley and to return with a British officer to the camp of Daulat Rao Sindia. To this Arthur Wellesley responded with a statement designed to establish that the war was one of aggression by Sindia and

'particularly noticed the conduct of Daulat Rao Sindia in first calling upon the British government to come forward to assist the Peshwa against Holkar, and afterwards his making peace with Holkar and sacrificing to him the vast territories which he had conquered from the Holkar family, only to induce him to become a part in the war against the British government.'

Arthur Wellesley added that 'the operations of the British troops had been most successful, the Maharajah had lost nearly the whole of his territories, and his government hung only by a thread.' The British government and those of its allies were entitled to compensation and security against attack in the future. Negotiations should properly take place in the British camp, since it was Daulat Rao Sindia who had 'much to ask from the British government.' Jaswant Rao Ghorpade responded by setting out the serious losses which Daulat Rao Sindia had sustained. He had been obliged to assemble large armies and had lost them; he had lost the territories which he had ceded to Jaswant Rao Holkar, but most of all he had lost his position at Pune. Arthur Wellesley agreed that these consequences had followed from the actions of Daulat Rao Sindia himself. He asked whether the *vakils* were empowered to enter into negotiations on the principle that the British and their allies were entitled to compensation for the injuries which they had received. The agents were not so empowered and Arthur Wellesley refused to indicate 'the extent of the compensation' until they were.[9]

Having accepted that there could be no negotiation on the terms of peace, the *vakils* sought an armistice. He had anticipated this request, Arthur Wellesley later explained to his brother. He first rejected any suggestion of a suspension of hostilities with Raghuji Bhonsle. The *vakils* showed Arthur Wellesley their secret instructions from Vithal Pant, the chief minister of Daulat Rao Sindia, from which it appeared that Sindia was greatly alarmed by the potential threat from a detachment commanded by Colonel Murray moving northwards on Dohad, and from the detachment commanded by Colonel Stevenson in the Purna valley. Daulat Rao Sindia wished to station himself at Burhanpur, an armistice having been concluded, while peace negotiations continued. Arthur Wellesley set out his conditions; an armistice would apply only to operations in the Deccan and in Gujarat, and Daulat Rao Sindia would have to move eastwards 'in the Berar country.' He refused to consider a suggestion that the armistice should be extended to northern India; he had no authority over the troops there, and could not communicate with Gerald Lake, the Commander-in-Chief in Hindustan, in less than six weeks. He proposed to set out the details of the proposed armistice.[10]

On the following day Arthur Wellesley stated the terms more fully. Daulat Rao Sindia was to move with his armies forty miles to the east of Elichpur. In Gujarat the British forces were not to advance beyond Dohad, nor was Sindia to approach it nearer than forty miles. Orders were sent to Stevenson that if Sindia attempted 'to pass to the westward' he was to be attacked. The suspension of hostilities was to be kept secret from the officers of the Nizam of Hyderabad, an intention which would have become increasingly difficult to sustain. The agreement required ratification by Daulat Rao Sindia within ten days.[11]

This armistice was a strange development, and it is not surprising that Arthur Wellesley was concerned to set out his justification for granting it, both to Stuart his Commander-in-Chief and also to his brother the Governor-General. He advanced four reasons for his action; he had no further capacity to injure Sindia, but Sindia might 'derange our plans against the Raja of Berar' either by turning on Stevenson when he was attacking Gawilghar or by diverting Arthur Wellesley from the threat he hoped to make, possibly against Nagpur itself. Further, Sindia had sent forces towards Gujarat where British forces were not sufficiently strong to withstand them, since Dohad was garrisoned by one battalion only. Finally 'by leaving the Raja of Berar out of the arrangement' the interests of the two Maratha rulers had been effectively separated and the confederacy dissolved. Arthur Wellesley was at pains to remind the Fort William Secretariat that he retained the right to end the cessation of hostilities at his discretion. A little later he noted that he considered the armistice so unfavourable to Daulat Rao Sindia that he doubted whether it would be ratified.[12]

The second element of the military threat which was designed to bring Raghuji Bhonsle to the negotiating tent was now put in place. Satisfied that the Raja of Berar had withdrawn from the Godavari valley, Arthur Wellesley advanced through the line of hills near Rajura, so that he was approaching the detachment commanded by Stevenson eastwards in the Purna valley. Four armies were now operating in the territories of the Raja of Berar, who quite possibly had initiated the war so as to divert marauding by his fellow Marathas from his own territory. Some of the limited siege artillery available was to be transferred to Stevenson. Without having determined to bring the two detachments together, Arthur Wellesley detailed the prospective movements that would bring him to the Purna, and so to a potential junction, by 27 November. [13]

Since mid-August, John Malcolm, who had in March 1803 moved forward with Arthur Wellesley from Mysore to assist in relations with the Maratha powers, had been recuperating at Bombay, after being forced by sickness to leave the army. By the end of October, he had left Pune on his return journey to camp, writing to Bentinck, the new Governor of Madras, from Walki on 23 November that

> 'from the present reduced state of the confederate chiefs there is I think reason to expect an early termination of hostilities, particularly if General Wellesley is able to carry into execution the plan which he has in contemplation of penetrating into the heart of Berar, as that operation must in all likelihood force Raghuji Bhonsle to consult his own preservation by concluding a separate peace, and his defection will completely leave Daulat Rao Sindia at the mercy of the British government.'

As the prospect of peace negotiations came nearer, Arthur Wellesley received the personal view of Malcolm on the terms to be offered; these views, because of his previous position, could be close to those of Richard Wellesley, although Richard Wellesley had not recommended that Malcolm should be privy to his political directive of late June 1803. Malcolm had seen the first letter to Fort William on peace terms, that of 11 November. He stressed the importance of keeping 'in the general arrangements, as distinct as circumstances would permit, the territory of the individual chiefs, in order that there may be an end to that clashing of authority and that mixture of power which constantly generates disputes.' He saw the most difficult part of the settlement as that of the scale of territorial cession to the Nizam of Hyderabad, who had 'certainly not fulfilled his engagements.' It would be important not to cede to the Nizam any Company territory to the south of the Tungabhadra. Peshwa Baji Rao would be ' the greatest gainer by the war...if he is restored to his former authority.' Malcolm wished to see the settlement varied significantly by increasing the subsidiary force at Hyderabad rather than by arranging for the mustering of the forces of the Nizam at Company discretion, and by setting the claim of Peshwa Baji Rao for *chauth* against the counter-claim of the Nizam of Hyderabad against the Peshwa for expense in his restoration.

In response, Arthur Wellesley noted that an equal division of the territorial spoils from the defeat of Sindia with the Nizam of Hyderabad, if followed by division of territory following the defeat of Raghuji Bhonsle, would eliminate the Nagpur state, which was 'inconsistent with the Governor General's idea of preserving all these Maratha states'. Increasing the subsidiary force at Hyderabad would not give the government of the Nizam the capacity 'to carry it through ordinary events'. If both organisation and logistics were not attended to, 'all will look well at Hyderabad, and in a despatch from the Resident to the Governor General, but really and at bottom all will continue to be weakness and confusion, and in the end the Nizam's government will fall to pieces.' Further, Malcolm had evidently not appreciated that the Maratha powers were continuing to demand *chauth* on the lands of the Nizam. The contribution was being paid 'and when Major Malcolm shall come here, he will know it.' It was not possible to secure as assets gained from Daulat Rao Sindia both Bundelkhand, an important barrier protecting Benares, and the Attavesi, the territory to the north of Chandore, and Arthur Wellesley was confident that faced with that choice, Richard Wellesley would elect to retain Bundelkhand. Arthur Wellesley did not lack self-confidence in his own judgement on the strategy of the peace settlement, but knowing that Malcolm would have sent his views to Fort William as well as circulated them to other political officers, he was anxious to demonstrate that there were counter-arguments to the objections which Malcolm had raised.[14]

The devious path of Amrit Rao now brought him afresh into the knot of political complexity within which the campaign had to be carried through. In August, before Malcolm had left the camp, a treaty concluded with a *vakil* of Amrit Rao—its content being kept secret from Peshwa Baji Rao—gave him a most extensive *jagir*. Amrit Rao having secured this agreement delayed moving his forces forward to join the British detachment. As Arthur Wellesley was to put it afterwards to his brother Henry, following ' the Maratha custom, after making this treaty (Amrit Rao) had waited to see which of the parties were likely to succeed in this war, and he had not decided this question in his own mind, till after the battle of Assaye and its consequence, the fall of Asirgarh.' After the withdrawal of Bhonsle from the Godavari valley, Amrit Rao determined that his future should indeed be that as an ally of the Company, and not as an independent Maratha ruler. He now moved to approach the detachment; a short time before Arthur Wellesley had believed that he was in negotiation with Raghuji Bhonsle.[15]

The importance of an effective relationship with Amrit Rao was no longer military; his forces of good quality, although of limited number, were now not of critical significance to the balance. What was of note was his political position. He had been the key figure, although reluctant, behind the alternative Peshwaship that had nearly been created in January, but he was also the victim of the hatred by Peshwa Baji Rao directed towards the able by the hopelessly incompetent. Although this was not a matter which could be resolved in the midst of a military campaign, to which the issues of a peace settlement were about to be added, Amrit Rao was seen by the Fort William Secretariat as the most eligible Maratha to be the chief minister to Baji Rao. For the present, all that could be attempted was to welcome him as he nominally placed himself under the orders of Arthur Wellesley. These forces played no active part in the campaign.[16]

Military matters again assumed centre stage. The central condition of the armistice agreement with Daulat Rao Sindia, concluded only days before,—that Sindia should move to the east of Elichpur by forty miles—had not been carried out. Before the detachments of Stevenson and Arthur Wellesley united on 28 November, the *vakils* of Daulat Rao Sindia, who were still in camp, begged Arthur Wellesley that the Company forces not attack the two Maratha rulers, but he refused to give this undertaking. 'I informed them repeatedly that there was no suspension of arms with Raghuji Bhonsle, and none with Daulat Rao Sindia till he should comply with the terms of his agreement, and that I should certainly attack the enemies of the Company wherever I should find them.' Daulat Rao Sindia was encamped at Sirsooli about four miles from the camp of Manu Bapu, the brother of Raghuji Bhonsle, who was encamped at Paterli. Late on 29 November the two British detachments approached the combined Maratha forces. As Arthur Wellesley moved forward to place the pickets of the infantry, he could see 'a long line of infantry cavalry and artillery regularly drawn up' immediately in front of the village of Argaum. Once again he was to be faced with an unexpected battle, although one which he must have realised was possible at the time that he created the armistice, the terms of which had not been honoured. Although it was late in the day, and the troops had marched a long distance, he was determined to attack at once.

The British force moved forward in column. They faced, from the Maratha right to left, the cavalry of Daulat Rao Sindia, infantry and artillery of Raghuji Bhonsle in the centre, and Bhonsle's cavalry to the left. The British forces were formed in two lines, with infantry in the first and cavalry in the second, including that of the Maratha forces loyal to Peshwa Baji Rao and that of the Nizam of Hyderabad. Part of the limited daylight remaining was lost by a panic in the native infantry which 'broke and ran off as soon as the cannonade commenced, although it was from a great distance and not to be compared with that at Assaye.' Arthur Wellesley rallied the two units and was able to 're-establish the battle.' It was within twenty minutes of sunset when a British cavalry charge was initiated. The whole Maratha line 'retired in disorder before our troops, leaving in our hands 38 pieces of cannon and all their artillery.' As Arthur Wellesley wrote his report to Richard Wellesley the following morning, the Mysore, Maratha and Hyderabad cavalry were again pursuing fugitives as they had by moonlight the previous evening. Casualties on the Company side here were far less than at Assaye.[17]

This was the setting of the first peace discussions with an accredited representative of Raghuji Bhosle. In a meeting held on the day after the battle of Argaum, Jaswant Rao Ramchandar attempted to argue that the movement of the army of the Raja of Berar to join that of Daulat Rao Sindia in the upper Purna valley in early June 1803 had been for the purpose of settling the dispute between Sindia and Jaswant Rao Holkar. This reconciliation had been necessary to preserve Berar from destruction by the other two Maratha chiefs. He also contended that Peshwa Baji Rao should not have concluded the Treaty of Bassein without consultation with the other members of the confederacy. Arthur Wellesley replied that it was Raghuji Bhonsle who had been 'the original cause of the war'. He again stated, as he had to the *vakils* of Daulat Rao Sindia, his view of the attempt to negotiate in the last days of July. He then 'recapitulated the injuries received from, and the various acts of aggression committed by the Raja, the losses sustained and the expenses incurred by the Company in the war... for all of which... compensation would be required as the price of peace.'

Arthur Wellesley then enquired from Jaswant Rao Ramchandar whether he had authority to negotiate on the basis of the right to compensation of the Company and its allies. As he had not, he was required to leave the British camp, a request for an armistice to last while he sought the necessary authority being decisively rejected.[18]

Negotiations with Daulat Rao Sindia were resumed at the same time. The two *vakils* brought the ratification of the armistice which had already been broken. When Arthur Wellesley sought from them confirmation that they were empowered to conduct peace discussions starting from the premise that the Company and its allies were entitled to compensation, the *vakils* asked what compensation would be involved. This was the circle into which Arthur Wellesley had resolved not to be drawn, and he insisted on seeing the instructions under which the *vakils* were working. When these were produced, he noted that they 'might be construed either one way or the other, as might be most convenient,' that this had been true also of the papers sent to him in late July. 'This want of sincerity and candour' had partly been the cause of hostilities. He added that if he did not receive the paper he required, he would be forced to ask the *vakils* to quit his camp and 'leave Daulat Rao Sindia to his fate'. 'There is no dealing with these Marathas unless they are treated in this manner,' Arthur Wellesley commented to Shawe in Fort William.[19]

The two Company detachments were now deploying for the siege of Gawilghar. After an interval of seven days, the *vakils* of Daulat Rao Sindia again asked for a discussion and produced a paper created in the *darbar*. This took the form of a counter-proposal setting out a simplified draft treaty which Arthur Wellesley was invited to accept.

> 'The first article stated that the British troops, having taken forts guns stores and property of all kinds from the Maharajah, a part of these were to be restored to him. The second article stated that in consideration of the first being agreed to, Daulat Rao Sindia would give the British government compensation for the expenses which they had incurred during the war. It then

recited the necessity to which he was reduced, and expressed a hope that the demand upon him would not be heavy.'

Arthur Wellesley made short work of this approach. He directly refused to consider any restoration of captured artillery; Daulat Rao Sindia was not without artillery, if he required additional guns to defend himself, he could cast them. Having enjoyed his moment of use of the prerogative of the victor, he then took the simplified draft as an indication of a willingness to negotiate compensation—in the sense in which he had earlier insisted upon it—and set out the terms of a possible peace settlement. In summary they followed the form of his letter to Richard Wellesley' 'the Company would require from Daulat Rao Sindia all his territories lying to the northward of those of the Rajahs of Jaipur Jodhpur and of the Rana of Gohad, the fort and territory of Broach, the fort and territory of Ahmednagar and the districts near the Godavari...'

Arthur Wellesley elaborated; treaties had been concluded with Jat and Rajput chiefs, which 'could not be departed from', the Nizam of Hyderabad required 'a distinct frontier,' the territories to the north were required to compensate the allies of the Company, who were feudatories of Daulat Rao Sindia who had accepted terms from the British in order to change allegiance, and to provide for the Mughal Emperor of Delhi. These terms, Arthur Wellesley added provocatively, would not much reduce the state of Daulat Rao Sindia, since Perron had never given Sindia any revenue and had become virtually independent. In response the *vakils* laid much emphasis on the significance of the position of Daulat Rao Sindia in relation to the Mughal Emperor; without that 'the Maharajah's state must fall'. By comparison the requirement that Daulat Rao Sindia should not retain the services of Frenchmen met with no difficulty; Daulat Rao Sindia, the *vakils* stated, 'had not the smallest wish ever to see a Frenchman again'. Arthur Wellesley refused an attempt by the *vakils* to negotiate on behalf of Raghuji Bhonsle.[20]

Three days later the negotiations were resumed. The central subject was the extensive territorial cession sought from Daulat Rao Sindia in Hindustan. On this the *vakils* pressed the suggestion that the territory to be devoted to the maintenance of the Mughal Emperor and of the subordinate rulers for whom the Company wished to provide should be retained by Daulat Rao Sindia and that he should be responsible for both. This Arthur Wellesley refused to consider, although he accepted an obligation to attempt a listing of the rulers concerned. He suggested that the *vakils* should provide him with a statement of the way in which the revenue in Hindustan had been collected. This request followed from the contention that the revenue in the area was divided three ways, between the Peshwa Baji Rao, Daulat Rao Sindia and Jaswant Rao Holkar. He reiterated the commitment in honour to the subordinate rulers who had signed agreements with the British Company. The delay in initiating peace negotiations, and the distances involved meant that he 'did not know the extent of their engagements, and therefore could not mention names. Much less could he mention the names of all the chiefs with whom engagements might be made before the officers authorised to make them would hear of the peace.' Writing to Fort William, Arthur Wellesley lamented his 'want of information regarding the proceedings of General Lake, even to the extent to which he has pushed his conquests, and of the country from which he has expelled the Marathas.'[21]

At the same time there was further discussion with the agent of Raghuji Bhonsle, whose fortress of Gawilghar was directly threatened. The agent, Jaswant Rao Ramchandar, brought letters of authority. The Raja of Berar agreed to give compensation to the British Company for the injuries which they had received, and therefore sought information on the terms which would be required. Arthur Wellesley stated them; cession of the province of Cuttack and the port of Balasore, linked by 'a convenient frontier' to other Company territory, cession to the Nizam of Hyderabad of territory which would extend his boundary towards the hills on which Gawilghar stood, and to the Wardha to the eastward, and renunciation of all claims within these territories. Jaswant Rao Ramchandar replied that acceptance of these demands would destroy the state of the Raja. He received the classic response that 'the Raja was a great politician, and ought to have calculated rather better his chances of success before he commenced the war, but...having commenced it, it was proper that he should suffer.'

Requests that Raghuji Bhonsle should agree to receive a British Resident and that the Raja should undertake not to employ Frenchmen or other Europeans were readily accepted, the agent contending that Bhonsle had never employed any Frenchmen. Ramchandar argued strongly that the British Company was seeking too much territory for the Nizam of Hyderabad. The Maratha rulers despised the military potential of Hyderabad, and were aware of the limited extent to which it had contributed to the British victories. Arthur Wellesley countered that the British would never fail 'the ancient ally of the Company.' He again refused to consider an armistice, warning that delay could be hurtful to the state of the Raja, and saying that he would insist on a hostage as a surety to the conclusion of the peace settlement; this in the event he did not do.[22]

Gawilghar had been an objective of Arthur Wellesley for at least three months; it had been in September, before the battle of Assaye and while both detachments were still near the Godavari that he had first commended it to the attention of Stevenson. The following month after the capture of Asirgarh, he had urged the movement of the military stores captured there for use in the siege of Gawilghar. He had also spoken of it as the necessary attack 'on the right flank' prior to a possible advance of both detachments into Hindustan. The fortress was rumoured to have the treasure of Raghuji Bhonsle within it. Contrary to Arthur Wellesley's normal contention that 'no Maratha has any money' rumour in this instance was soundly based, and a plate worth two and half lakhs of rupees was seized and subsequently set aside to be available for the payment of the detachments in January 1804. The fortress was also quite remarkably inaccessible; as Arthur Wellesley was afterwards to explain to Richard Wellesley:

> 'the fort of Gawilghar is situated in a range of mountains between the sources of the rivers Purna and Tapti. It stands on a lofty mountain in this range, and consists of one complete inner fort, which fronts to the south where the rock is most steep, and an outer fort, which covers the inner to the north-west and north. This outer fort has a third wall, which covers the approach to it from the north by the village of Labada. All these walls are strongly built and fortified by ramparts and towers.'

Arthur Wellesley went on to explain the road structure; the northern gate, where the ground was level with the fort, could be reached only by a road through the mountains. It took four days and 'a series of laborious services (for) the heavy ordnance and stores (to be) dragged by hand over mountains and through ravines...by roads which it had previously been necessary for the troops to make for themselves.' This labour was required to place a battery to the north of the fort, where alone it was possible to fire from a position which could do real damage to the walls.

At the same time preparation was made to create a diversion at the western approaches, from which the fort was far more difficult to access and from which artillery bombardment was virtually impossible. Once the effectiveness of the batteries created opposite the northern entrance to the fort was clear, it was possible to determine upon an attack on both approaches on the morning of 15 December. At modest loss, this was successful and the flag of the Company could be raised on the centre of the fort before midday. The forces defeated at Gawilghar were not solely its garrison but included elements of the disciplined infantry of Raghuji Bhonsle which had fled from the field at Argaon.[23]

When negotiations with the representatives of the Raja of Berar resumed immediately after the siege, the effect of the capture of Gawilghar was at once apparent, and matters were quickly resolved. An attempt was made, but not insisted upon, to secure the retention by Raghuji Bhonsle of the province of Cuttack. Jaswant Rao Ramchandar, the *vakil*, then tried to secure a marked reduction of the territorial cession to the Nizam of Hyderabad, Arthur Wellesley requiring either an annual land-revenue income of Rs 30 lakhs or the river Wardha as a boundary. It was agreed that the fort of Gawilghar should be restored to Raghuji Bhonsle after the completion of the peace settlement. As Arthur Wellesley had expected, the major difficulty arose over the clause in the proposed peace treaty which guaranteed the agreements reached with lesser feudatories in Cuttack. In an attempt to make this element in the settlement as palatable as possible, Arthur Wellesley spoke of the demand as being 'indispensable' but added that 'there was no intention to injure the Raja's state, and that he might rely with security on the honour of the British government, that no engagement should be entered into after it should be known that the peace had been concluded.' This promise covered matters which Arthur Wellesley was not in a position to control.[24]

Writing to his brother, Arthur Wellesley made clear the difficulty in which he found himself due to the lack of information for the treaty with Bhonsle, quite as much as that with Daulat Rao Sindia.

'I wished to be able to define more accurately the bounds of the cession of the province of Cuttack, but I had no information upon the subject. Lt Col Harcourt stated it as his opinion that it would be convenient if the districts of Sohnpur and Boad were ceded besides Cuttack, and Mr Melville his, that it would be convenient to add to the province of Cuttack countries which would have joined the northern circars with the province of Bundelkhand. But upon reference to the map, which is all the information which I could procure, I found that even the first would have increased the extent of the demands on that side to such a degree as to make it necessary to give up part of what I demanded on this side, or to risk the conclusion of the treaty altogether.'

A clause of the treaty was designed to meet this difficulty; it subsequently gave rise to controversy. It was an attempt to meet the conflicting requirements of a prompt restoration of peace and the securing of territorial ambitions.

To Stevenson, Arthur Wellesley explained that the treaty required ratification within eight days. Had it not been concluded, it had been his intention to press forward to Nagpur, while Stevenson threatened Narnullah, a further hill fortress, and subsequently, after breaking the suspension of hostilities with Daulat Rao Sindia, to have again turned northwards.[25]

Meanwhile, negotiations with the agents of Daulat Rao Sindia proceeded. On 12 December, just before the attack on Gawilghar, Arthur Wellesley had commented on the main difficulty. This was 'a want of information regarding the proceedings of General Lake, even to the extent to which he has pushed his conquests, and of the country from which he has expelled the Marathas and taken possession.' Within a few days he became more optimistic. 'I have no doubt but that...Daulat Rao Sindia will make his peace as soon as he can. Indeed, his *vakil* and I are agreed on the principal points, and we should have concluded a treaty some days ago, if I had received from Bengal any information whatever...I was therefore obliged to acknowledge my ignorance, and to ask the *vakil* for information of the state of the countries in Hindustan.' The letter from Richard Wellesley of 27 June had listed quite clearly 'the countries which the Governor-General wished to have' and Arthur Wellesley had quoted them. What he lacked was a listing of the subsidiary treaties which he assumed that Lake and Mercer had concluded.

When the agents of Daulat Rao Sindia were joined on 24 December by Vithal Pant, his chief minister, a discussion was initiated of the possibility that Daulat Rao Sindia might 'connect himself more closely with the Company...and establish an alliance.' Arthur Wellesley had been forewarned in earlier discussions with the agents of the concern of the *darbar* that Jaswant Rao Holkar was expected to turn against the northern territories of Daulat Rao Sindia.

'The *vakils*...disclosed a great apprehension of the power of Jaswant Rao Holkar and they almost expressed an expectation that Holkar would attack them, as soon as the peace with the Company should be settled. They said that in that case they must depend on the Company for assistance in money and troops.'

Arthur Wellesley emphasised to Vithal Pant that such an alliance could only be defensive in character. The irony of the request went deep. During the abortive attempt to form a total Maratha confederacy against the Company in June 1803—of which the British assumed that Raghuji Bhonsle had been the instigator—a treaty had been signed between Jaswant Rao Holkar and Daulat Rao Sindia, by which territory earlier seized by Sindia should be restored to Jaswant Rao Holkar. This treaty had not been honoured. The Company now found itself in the position of urging that an alliance that had been created against it should be implemented, so as to eliminate a potential source of conflict of a now proposed ally. Finally Arthur Wellesley secured a direct admission that the unfulfilled element of the treaty had been that Jaswant Rao Holkar should join in the attack on the British. This was public avowal for the first time in *darbar* discussion of the attempted confederacy of June 1803, of which at the time Arthur Wellesley had been most sceptical.[26]

When the Treaty of Bassein had been signed in the last moments of 1802, the main sphere of influence of the East India Company had lain to the south of the Tungabhadra and to the east of the Ganges-Jumna Doab. With the ratification of the Treaty of Sarji Arjangoan in February 1804 the military and political influence of the Company dominated the Deccan and stretched north to the Narbada. In Hindustan it reached southwards into central India as far as the Chambal.

The main elements in the diplomatic pattern remained the individual Maratha chieftains, but their position and mutual relationships had been greatly altered. Alone of the major Maratha chieftains, Jaswant Rao Holkar had given the British no opportunity to assess his military power and had remained aside from the conflict. Both Daulat Rao Sindia and Raghuji Bhonsle had suffered military defeat. They had then elected to seek and secure peace terms which had brought with them a heavy cost in loss of territory and prestige. It remained to be seen how far they were in fact reconciled to their changed position, and their new relationship with the Company. Of the former head of the Maratha confederacy there was little doubt; Peshwa Baji Rao was by character and inclination destined for the role which Richard Wellesley had seen for him in his informal notes of August, that of a 'pageant.'

The peace settlement which Arthur Wellesley had secured, based on the military achievements of 1803 both in Hindustan and the Deccan, contained within it elements of uncertainty, and the seeds of further *darbar* controversy. As other generals have discovered, Arthur Wellesley was to find that peace-making was too serious a matter to leave to politicians.

NOTES

1. RW-AW 27 Jun 03: Shawe-AW 3 Aug 03 A Mss 13,778 f.11 WP 3/3/7; Barlow Mem 3 Aug 03 annotated by RW A Mss 13,722 f.1 WP 3/3/5.

2. Barlow Mem 16 Oct A Mss 13,722 f. 27 WP 3/3/5: RW-AW 27 Oct 03 SD iv 187.

3. AW-RW 11 Nov 03.

4. AW-Shawe 18 Nov 03.

5. Conf 10 Nov 03 SD iv 221: AW-Malcolm 11 Nov 03: AW-RW 11 Nov 03.

6. Conf 11 Nov 03 SD iv 224: AW-Malcolm 13 Nov 03.

7. AW-Stuart, Stevenson 20 Nov 03: AW-Collins 23 Oct 03: Collins-AW 12 Nov 03 WP 3/3/53.

8. Conf 20 Nov 02 SD iv 226: AW-RW 24 Nov 03.

9. Conf 21 Nov 03 SD iv 228: PRC x 165.

10. Conf 21 Nov 03 SD iv 228: (this part of the recorded discussion is not included in the text printed at PRC x 165).

11. Suspension of hostilities 23 Nov 03: AW-Stevenson 22,23 Nov 03: AW-Stuart 23 Nov 03: AW-Shawe 23 Nov 03.

12. AW-Stuart, Shawe 23 Nov 03: AW-Stevenson 25 Nov 03.

13. AW-Stevenson 25 Nov 03.

14. Malcolm-Bentinck 23 Nov 03 Bentinck Mss PW Jb 32: Malcolm Mem undated, but about 18 Nov 03 WP 3/3/70: AW-Close 24 Nov 03: AW Mem 23 Nov 03 (not dated in WP 1/156) Shawe-Malcolm 9 Dec 03 A Mss 13602 f. 70.

15. AW-HW 24 Jan 04.

16. AW-Graham 6 Nov 03: AW-RW 13 Nov 03: AW-Close 27 Nov 03.

17. AW-RW 30 Nov 03.

18. AW-Shawe 2 Dec 03: Conf 30 Nov 03: SD iv 272 PRC x 180.

19. Conf 1 Dec 03 SD iv 239: AW-Shawe 2 Dec 03.

20. Conf 8 Dec 03 SD iv 241. (not printed in PRC x)

21. Conf 11 Dec 03 SD iv 246 (not printed in PRC x): AW-Shawe 12 Dec 03.

22. Conf 9 Dec 03 SD iv 277: PRC x 183.

23. AW-RW, Malcolm 15 Dec 03.

24. Conf 16 Dec 03 SD iv 281 PRC x 186.

25 AW-RW 17 Dec 03.

26. AW-Shawe 12 Dec 03: Conf 24,26 Dec 03 SD iv 251,254, PRC x 168, 171.

7

A hill-fort in the hands of a Maratha (January-April 1804)

The embassy of John Malcolm at the court of Daulat Rao Sindia, which lasted from January until the first days of May 1804, took place against the setting of a dispute over the content of the peace settlement of December 1803. Although the embassy appeared to begin on a positive note with the securing of the subsidiary alliance with Daulat Rao Sindia—which had always been the objective of Richard Wellesley—this achievement was an empty one, in part because Sindia elected not to accept the central feature of the subsidiary alliance, the presence at the capital of the country power of a Company army.

The freedom and frequency of the letter writing of John Malcolm, both to Arthur Wellesley and to others, makes it possible to reconstruct the embassy in detail. Malcolm joined the camp of Daulat Rao Sindia west of Burhanpur by 12 January. His health remained far from good. He had agreed that Arthur Wellesley should suggest to Richard Wellesley that it should be Malcolm who took to England, by sea from Bombay, the despatches describing the victories of 1803. But within a few days Malcolm was suggesting to Arthur Wellesley that he must leave for England, whether or not this duty was assigned to him, although in the event he did not do so. He also asked Arthur Wellesley to arrange that Strachey should be sent from Pune to assist him in his embassy, and that Josiah Webbe, travelling northwards from Mysore to serve as Resident at Nagpur, should be appointed rather as his relief with Sindia.[1]

The camp and army of Daulat Rao Sindia was in a deplorable condition, as Malcolm explained a little later. 'The distress in his camp is at present dreadful, numbers die daily from want, and I see no prospect of any speedy relief. The coarsest grains are selling for two seers the rupee, and at that advanced price are not yet to be had in any quantity.'

Daulat Rao Sindia did not have the means to pay his troops. Their arrears were 'neither paid nor put into any train of liquidation'. Sindia had lost most of the disciplined brigades in the campaigns both in Hindustan and the Deccan. Before 1803 they had enabled him to control both the *silledar* and *pagah* horse and the *pindaris* that had attached themselves to his armies. In an attempt to restore its shattered financial position, the court of Daulat Rao Sindia turned on the *pindaris*, seeking to extort from them some part of their plunder. It gained some slight respite in this way.[2]

As Arthur Wellesley and John Malcolm saw it, the first priority of the new embassy with Daulat Rao Sindia was to take up the attempt to create a subsidiary alliance. This certainly went with the wishes of Richard Wellesley. But the venture was to be made in the changed circumstances of military defeat. Malcolm outlined the dilemma to Shawe in Calcutta.

> 'Every part of his country that was productive has been taken from him (Daulat Rao Sindia) and I question much whether he will be able to maintain himself against (Jaswant Rao Holkar) his rival in Malwa even for a season unless he has our aid. Yet such is the mode of the Marathas that this court either is, or pretends to be, lukewarm about the defensive alliance.'

On the item on which Arthur Wellesley in his detailed instructions to John Malcolm foresaw difficulty, the stationing of a Company subsidiary force within the bounds of the territories of Daulat Rao Sindia, it was clear that there would be opposition. This requirement Malcolm contended was an essential, although following his instructions he offered as an alternative, the cession of territory north of Gujarat, to permit the protection against 'the sudden invasion of a powerful enemy', which could only be Jaswant Rao Holkar.[3]

In June and July 1803 political authority had been delegated by Richard Wellesley both to Gerald Lake in Hindustan and to Arthur Wellesley in the Deccan. In the south, because of the illness of John Malcolm, Arthur Wellesley had necessarily, apart from the help of Elphinstone, handled this political delegation alone. In the north

Lake had relied on Graeme Mercer as his political assistant. Both military officers had been given detailed instructions by Richard Wellesley on the extensive territorial objectives of the campaign against the Maratha powers. In these instructions the intention to vary significantly the political structure of northern India was very clear.

It had been markedly in the interest of the *vakils* and ministers of Daulat Rao Sindia not to discuss in camp in the Deccan in December 1803 points of detail of the proposed settlement in Hindustan. Doubtful points in the proposed settlement could possibly be varied to their advantage subsequently. Arthur Wellesley was negotiating the entire settlement with Daulat Rao Sindia and was therefore responsible for securing the gains of the extensive military operations led by Lake in Hindustan, as well as those of the Deccan campaign. Arthur Wellesley was clearly anxious to hurry the peace process. For this there could have been a number of reasons. Perhaps the first was his continuing concern, which he had expressed in April 1803 and which was destined soon to be reinforced by the study of letters of September 1803 from London, over the security of the political mandate on which the Governor-General was dependent. It is probable also that Arthur Wellesley believed that Daulat Rao Sindia was less than convinced of the validity of the defeat he had suffered, and might therefore attempt to resume hostilities. If Sindia were to do this, further military operations from the Deccan would be at very long range, dependent on lines of communication lengthened to an almost intolerable extent, and in territory, which it was becoming clear, had suffered severely from years of warfare.

A negotiated agreement requires the transfer to the negotiators of power to commit those ultimately responsible, and in December 1803 in the discussions between the Company and Daulat Rao Sindia this was less than total. Arthur Wellesley had indeed extensive political authority, but he had also received elaborate instructions already, and more were on the way. Fully to understand these required a detailed knowledge of Hindustan, which he lacked. On the side of Daulat Rao Sindia the representation had been that of a relatively senior figure at his court, possibly concerned about his own position there, and only in the last stages that of an acting chief minister. Given the preference for a speedy agreement, the outcome was a peace settlement in which a range of important issues were remitted to later negotiation. The subsequent attempt to resolve these matters played a major part in determining the climate in which relations between the Company and Daulat Rao Sindia were to evolve.

It was characteristic of the thoroughness of Arthur Wellesley that after what must have been many hours of discussion with John Malcolm on the Maratha policy that must follow the peace settlement, he gave him a detailed written analysis of the issues that would arise in the embassy at Burhanpur. He sent a copy to Richard Wellesley, where the messages he was trying to convey were almost certainly not fully appreciated.

Starting from the premise of permanent peace with Daulat Rao Sindia and making the assumption that Company hostilities with Jaswant Rao Holkar would be averted, Arthur Wellesley saw slight risk of a reconciliation between Daulat Rao Sindia and Jaswant Rao Holkar. It seemed more probable that the Company could find itself, having concluded an alliance with Daulat Rao Sindia, dragged into war with Jaswant Rao Holkar. He drew this conclusion from the evident anxiety shown by Vithal Pant at their first discussion in December for a Company alliance, clearly directed against Jaswant Rao Holkar.

Arthur Wellesley reminded John Malcolm of the agreement concluded between the two Maratha chiefs in June 1803, that by which Daulat Rao Sindia had agreed to restore disputed territory to Jaswant Rao Holkar, as he had not done, in return for a promise of joint hostilities against the Company, also not fulfilled. Arthur Wellesley had pressed for information about this treaty in the discussions in December; he considered that it should be accepted as a valid instrument, even though it was in form an offensive alliance against the Company. The treaty had to be accepted as constituting a 'register of the rights of the two parties.' Only if this were done would it be possible to honour the undertaking which he had himself given to Jaswant Rao Holkar of non-interference in his internal affairs, always provided that he refrained from attack on the Company or its allies. This was almost certainly to take too positive a view of the importance of an interim agreement in the endemic disputes between the major Maratha rulers.

Arthur Wellesley saw the central requirement to be the preservation of peace between Daulat Rao Sindia and Jaswant Rao Holkar.

'Sindia's military resources are nearly destroyed, those of Holkar are unimpaired. Daulat Rao Sindia has no abilities himself and has no person about him capable of managing his affairs. Jaswant Rao Holkar has the reputation of being an able man, and has certainly been a successful one. The consequence of the existence of tranquillity for a year or two years will be that Daulat Rao Sindia's government and his military resources will in some degree recover.... Jaswant Rao Holkar's will become worse than they are at present, as the certain consequence of tranquillity, to an overgrown army constituted as his is, must be its gradual dissolution.'

This was not how events were to move. The pride of Daulat Rao Sindia remained, but neither the resources nor the will to exercise military power. While it was possible that the position of Jaswant Rao Holkar was precarious if conditions of 'tranquillity' were to prevail, the powerful dynamic of greed for plunder rendered it far more probable that he would be forced to turn once again to brigandage, which the Company would regard as aggression.[4]

Both Arthur Wellesley and John Malcolm were making a basic assumption about the atmosphere at the court of Daulat Rao Sindia, namely that, to quote a later letter from Malcolm to Shawe, the Maratha ruler had 'been conciliated to friendship' and that this 'favourable impression' followed from 'a sense of the moderation with which victory was used'. A deliberate approach to the *darbar* of Daulat Rao Sindia in a tone of conciliation was attempted by Malcolm and supported by Arthur Wellesley. This influenced the later negotiation of the subsidiary alliance and played its part also in the approach of Arthur Wellesley and John Malcolm to the issues that arose in the margin of the peace settlement, more especially those relating to treaties with dependent chieftains in northern India. As will be seen, these matters were viewed in a totally different light at Fort William, where there was no sense of the importance of moderation in the use of victory. This difficulty began to emerge before the *darbar* consideration of the subsidiary alliance with Daulat Rao Sindia, and continued after it had been concluded.[5]

The area of controversy with the court of Daulat Rao Sindia following the treaty of Sarji Anjangaon was that of interrelation of two agreements concluded by Lake and Mercer. The first was with a Jat ruler known to the Company as the Rana of Gohud, a territory which included the fortress of Gwalior. The second agreement was that with Ambaji Inglia, the main representative in Hindustan of Daulat Rao Sindia.

The fort of Gwalior is a little less than one hundred miles south of the Jumna. It had fallen after the third battle of Panipat in 1761 into the hands of a Jat chief who became known as the Rana of Gohad, and was effectively independent. It was from him that Mahadaji Sindia captured the fort in 1779. To build up a barrier against Mahadaji Sindia, the Company concluded an agreement with the Rana, and the fort was recaptured from Mahadaji Sindia by the Company in 1780, and restored to the Rana. In the later peace settlement with Sindia, the Treaty of Salbai, while an attempt was made to retain it in the hands of the Rana, he was in the event left to his fate, and the fortress reverted to the possession of Mahadaji Sindia, who recaptured it in 1784.

The political objectives in Hindustan of the campaign of 1803 had never been modest; they were nothing less than the creation of an advanced political frontier for the Company, reaching south-wards and westwards beyond the Ganges-Jumna Doab. This full statement of political aims had been drafted on the premise that 'the supposed confederacy will vanish upon the approach of the British force' and that the Maratha rulers would be faced down by the front of Company power, but it was always far more probable that territorial gains of the order being sought would be achieved only following military operations.

One object sought in this political or more probably military confrontation was 'to form alliances with the Rajputs and other inferior states beyond the Jumna, for the purpose of excluding Daulat Rao Sindia from the northern districts of Hindustan.' This 'would establish a powerful barrier between our frontier and that of Daulat Rao Sindia by the intervention of the Rajput and other inferior states strengthened under our protection.' A series of negotiations with various subordinate rulers were therefore envis-aged, and these Richard Wellesley attempted to direct in detail. 'In the event of a war with Daulat Rao Sindia the security of the British possessions in the Doab against the future designs of that chief would seem to demand the total abolition of his authority and interference in the northwestern provinces of Hindustan.'[6]

Ambaji Inglia was one of the foremost of the chiefs of Daulat Rao Sindia. He had been the all-powerful agent of ' aulat Rao Sindia in Mewar for eight years, had absorbed a major part of the land revenue of the territory, and had amassed a personal fortune. In 1801 Ambaji Inglia was displaced by Perron, not only from the management of extensive territory, but also from control of the great forts of the Delhi-Agra region. He attempted secretly to urge Company pressure on Daulat Rao Sindia to discharge the French officers, and also sought a promise of asylum if he elected to leave the service of his ruler. There was no response at the time to these suggestions. The proposition that Daulat Rao Sindia should discharge the French officers in his service had been part of the scheme for a subsidiary alliance that Collins was instructed to put to Sindia in early 1802, in the event with total lack of success. In June 1802, when this embassy had failed and been withdrawn, there were again furtive indications that Ambaji Inglia still hoped for Company protection.[7]

In July 1803 the prospect of securing a transfer of allegiance by Ambaji Inglia was taken up again. While there was no doubt of the centrality of the concern of Richard Wellesley to acquire Gwalior, Lake and his political adviser Mercer, noted that it would be appropriate to avoid an early attack on Gwalior, since

> 'with most of the strong forts on this side of India belong tow Ambaji (Inglia) and his brother Kunroji. An attack on Gwalior would compel them to take an active part against us, whereas it is not impossible, adverting to the ill terms they are on with Daulat Rao Sindia and his minister, if unmolested they would remain quiet, and as they formerly wished to form an alliance with the British to guard themselves from the grasping ambition of Daulat Rao Sindia, they might be brought over to our interest.'[8]

Some while before Collins left the camp of Daulat Rao Sindia in the first days of August 1803, one of his agents was invited to attend secretly at Ambaji Inglia's tent at night. He was there told that Ambaji Inglia 'was now more desirous than ever of obtaining the protection of the British government, that he had been scandalously plundered by the ministers of the Maharajah and in consequence was endeavouring to get away to Hindustan (and) that on his arrival there in the event of a war between the English and

Daulat Rao Sindia, he would willingly consent to become tributary to the British.' The conditions of this transfer of allegiance, as Ambaji Inglia saw them, were 'that the districts which he now held should remain in his possession, that no money should be demanded from him by the English for the next two years ... (and) that should he require the assistance of a body of English troops it should be granted him free of all charges.' To this approach Collins replied through an intermediary with an undertaking both to preserve secrecy until Ambaji Inglia had returned to Hindustan, and to inform Richard Wellesley of this approach.[9]

In August 1803 Ambaji Inglia was once again appointed by Daulat Rao Sindia as his representative in Hindustan, in succession to Perron. Rumour at the time, recorded for example in an important pamphlet written in February 1804,[10] was that Ambaji Inglia had purchased this appointment by an extremely large gift to his ruler. Ambaji Inglia moved north during August, with cavalry and a substantial body of trained infantry, some of the brigades originally created by De Boigne. It was this well-publicised movement which had led Arthur Wellesley to suppose for a time that he might not be required to face the disciplined infantry of Sindia in the Deccan. The supersession of Perron by Ambaji Inglia was one of the factors which led the Frenchman to abandon the employ of Daulat Rao Sindia and withdraw into Company territory, as he did in the first days of September.

After the capture by Lake of Aligarh, Ambaji Inglia made an approach by an agent to the Persian Secretary to the Governor-General. This was later described by Richard Wellesley as 'a direct proposal ... to withdraw his allegiance to Daulat Rao Sindia and to become tributary under certain conditions.' The approach was made through the intermediary of a newswriter. Richard Wellesley commented on the interrelation of this negotiation with that which he wished to see undertaken with the Rana of Gohad. He believed it to be probable that Ambaji Inglia would be 'satisfied with a limited extent of territory under the terms of independence and of exemption from the payment of tribute or revenue.' He set out other conditions, making the assumption that Ambaji Inglia, having transferred Gwalior to the Company, would become an independent ruler, possibly of a limited area, bound by a subsidiary alliance.[11]

Following the publication of the terms under which the French officers serving Sindia could be pensioned by the Company, their withdrawal left to Ambaji Inglia, in addition to other forces, command of such portion of the disciplined infantry of Daulat Rao Sindia in Hindustan as survived the battle outside the walls of Agra. It was against these forces that Lake had fought the battle of Laswari on 1 November. During the midday interval that occurred in the battle, Ambaji Inglia attempted to negotiate with Lake the surrender of his guns in return for a safe conduct, but the gunners refused to give up the artillery and the negotiation came to naught. A few days after the battle, the agent of Ambaji Inglia sought terms from Lake and Mercer. The agent proposed that the territories of various rulers, including that of the Rana of Gohad, should be granted as if from Peshwa Baji Rao to Ambaji Inglia 'at the same revenue which was settled by Mahadaji Sindia', that the British should guarantee that no increase would be sought, that there should be no demand for the first two years while the advance was realised from the country, and that Ambaji Inglia should be considered a Company ally in the event of peace being concluded with Daulat Rao Sindia. [12]

The response from Mercer to this proposition was to set out far more restrictive terms. By these Ambaji Inglia would be required to 'relinquish whatever parts of Gwalior Gohad Bhondi Dholepur and other countries now in his possession, with the forts and the places in them, as the British Government may deem it expedient to give to the Rana of Gohad.... Ambaji Inglia would be free to maintain forts in the territory granted to him 'but he will deliver over the fortress of Gwalior without contest to the Company's troops, as a security for his friendship.' [13]

The negotiations faltered, but at Sirhindi on 16 December Lake was able to sign a treaty which transferred Gwalior to the Company. Ambaji Inglia signed on 22 December; he had agreed 'to deliver over without any delay or evasion to the Company's government the fortress of Gwalior with the districts undermentioned which have hitherto be held by him in farm with the forts situated in them whenever the officers of the Company's government may be deputed for the purpose of taking possession of them.' The treaty also stipulated that 'in the event of a peace being concluded between the Company and the Maratha states, the Company shall consider Ambaji Inglia included in the treaty as an ally of the Company.' The requirements of the instructions of Richard Wellesley to secure Gwalior had apparently been achieved.[14]

These dealings by the political officers of the Company in Hindustan were with Ambaji Inglia as an independent ruler. Ambaji Inglia was certainly regarded by the Marathas as a representative of Daulat Rao Sindia in Hindustan. The agreement which had been reached had to be reconciled with that with a Maratha whom the Company chose to regard as the Rana of Gohad, a territory which included the fortress of Gwalior and which had been seized by Mahadaji Sindia in 1783. The Rana of Gohad was stated in June 1803 to be

'reduced to poverty and to be destitute of resources or power. This chief however is said to retain considerable influence with the Jats. It is said that the Rana of Gohad is anxious to obtain the support of the British government. With our support he would probably be enabled to raise a considerable force, which might assist in opposing the march of Daulat Rao Sindia into Hindustan. The possession of the fortress of Gwalior by British troops would enable us to support the authority of the Rana in the country.'[15]

Mercer followed these instructions, opening relations with the former or supposed Rana of Gohad, advancing him money and securing the creation of a body of troops. Since the lands intended for the Rana of Gohad were within those managed for Daulat Rao Sindia by Ambaji Inglia, it was proposed at this stage to compensate Ambaji Inglia for the loss of Gohad and Gwalior by guaranteeing his possession of the remainder of the lands being managed by him. This the treaty of December 1803 with Ambaji Inglia appeared to have achieved, leaving the way clear for the Company to cede Gohad to its supposed or previous ruler, the Rana, in a treaty concluded late in January, while retaining in Company possession the fort and town of Gwalior. The treaty was signed at Beenah by Lake on 17 January 1804, by the Rana on 29 January, and ratified by Richard Wellesley in Fort William on 2 March.[16]

When in January 1804 a detachment sent forward by Lake sought to occupy Gwalior, its commandant refused to yield the fortress. It became clear later that this was on the orders of Ambaji Inglia himself; the fortress was nonetheless occupied after an agreement with the garrison on 4/5 February. Later instructions to Mercer were to inform Ambaji Inglia that the treaty signed with him less than two months before was rendered invalid by the action of the commandant of Gwalior.

In December 1803, Arthur Wellesley had explained to Fort William that he lacked information on the rulers with whom Lake and Mercer had concluded agreements. Although he would have received, perhaps by early September, copies of the instructions to Lake prepared in July, it was not until 30 January, one month after the treaty settlement, that he was aware of the nature of the concluded negotiation with Ambaji Inglia; it was a fortnight later that he learnt of its subsequent breakdown. In concluding the Treaty of Sarji Anjangaon in the last days of December, given his determination to reach a speedy peace settlement, he had necessarily to devise a method by which he could reconcile this requirement with his lack of information on the political negotiations that had been proceeding in Hindustan.

The method Arthur Wellesley chose was to deal in two articles in the treaty with the cession of territory by Daulat Rao Sindia, in the circumstances of his lack of detailed knowledge of Hindustan. By the second article, Daulat Rao Sindia was required to confirm that he had ceded to the Company and its allies

'All his forts, territories and rights in the Doab, or country situated between the Jumna and the Ganges, and all his forts territories rights and interests in the countries which are to the northward of those of the Rajas of Jaipur and Jodhpur and of the Rana of Gohad... Such countries formerly in the possession of the Maharajah situated between Jaipur and Jodhpur and to the southward of the former are to belong to the Maharajah.'

In using this formulation Arthur Wellesley was following the listing in his letter of 11 November to Richard Wellesley. He was regarding the lands of the Rana of Gohad as an existing territorial unit.

By article nine of the treaty, Daulat Rao Sindia confirmed 'certain treaties... with Rajas and others, heretofore feudatories' provided 'that none of the territories belonging to the Maharajah situated to the south of those of the Rajas of Jaipur and Jodhpur and the Rana of Gohad, of which revenues have been collected by him or his amildars, or have been applicable as saranjami to the payment of his troops are granted away by such treaties.'[17]

Meanwhile at Fort William in early December the elaborate and definitive guidance intended for Arthur Wellesley in his conclusion of the peace settlement with Daulat Rao Sindia was prepared. It was sent off from Calcutta in packets behind letters dated 9 and 11 December and began to reach Arthur Wellesley in camp on 13 January, fifteen days after the treaty with Daulat Rao Sindia had been concluded.

On territorial expansion in Hindustan the requirements of these Fort William instructions of December 1803 were that 'Daulat Rao Sindia's claims on the Rana of Gohad to be renounced. The Rana of Gohad to be independent of Daulat Rao Sindia and included in the treaty of peace as an ally of the British government. All territories now held by Ambaji (Inglia) to be ceded to the British government. Ambaji to be independent of Daulat Rao Sindia and to be included in the treaty of peace as an ally of the British government.' In supplementary notes sent at the same time Arthur Wellesley was instructed to secure for the Company territory to the northward of a line from Jodhpur to Behut, a town on the western extremity of Bundelkhand and referred specifically to Rennell's map.[18]

In camp on 13 or 14 January, deprived as he now was of the help of either John Malcolm or of Elphinstone, who he had appointed to be Resident with Raghuji Bhonsle, Arthur Wellesley listed the requirements, which the instructions from Calcutta had stated, against the treaty he had concluded. His purpose was to satisfy himself that every item had been covered. On the two political objectives just cited, he was confident that the first, that of a provision for the Rana of Gohad, was covered by article nine of the Treaty of Sarji Anjangaon. On the second, the requirement that 'all the territories now held by Ambaji' should be ceded to the Company, Arthur Wellesley concluded that this was 'in part' covered. He evidently appreciated that the territories of Ambaji Inglia, if such they were, could be held to be doubtfully ceded to the Company.[19]

At the same time, in the 'numerous and voluminous packets from Bengal' that Arthur Wellesley received on 13 January, he noted that at the time that they were prepared 'nothing has been concluded with any of the Rajas or other chiefs.' He wrongly surmised 'from the complexion of the negotiations' that none had been concluded. His first reading of part of the notes on the peace settlement that he had received led him to believe that he had made a better peace than the Governor-General could have expected. He significantly added 'the only doubt I have is about Ambaji'. As he looked more carefully at the papers the following day, he appreciated that it was 'the Governor-General's intention to restore the power of the Jats as a state at the expense of Daulat Rao Sindia; I did not know that their state had ever been destroyed.' He still hoped it would be possible to secure the independence of these territories by the interrelated operation of the two articles of the treaty of peace just cited, although he now felt it necessary to warn the Fort William Secretariat that he thought it 'very improbable that Daulat Rao Sindia would ever consent to declare these people independent of his government unless compelled thereto by necessity, such as the British government having made treaties with them.'[20]

From the camp of Daulat Rao Sindia near Burhanpur, Malcolm on 16 January reported to Arthur Wellesley that 'the munshi tells me that this *darbar* is in alarm about Ambaji Inglia and wished to know how far government would endorse his right to alienate Daulat Rao Sindia's territories which might be under his management.' At this first enquiry Malcolm was able simply to refer to the treaty wording. Two days later he admitted to Arthur Wellesley that he was not clear what lands could be regarded as belonging to Ambaji Inglia, or the nature of his tenure; on the one hand he understood that 'he rented or held in *saranjami* to the amount of near a crore' but against that the only land revenue schedule he had seen suggested that the possessions of Ambaji were very limited. Expressing to Merrick Shawe at Fort William his anxiety to learn of the opinion of Richard Wellesley of the peace treaty, he commented that he appreciated that 'the great point of difference is respecting the Rajas of Jodhpur, Jaipur and the Rana of Gohad and Ambaji Inglia—yet all those by the treaty are secured if they have concluded treaties or entered into any engagement...'[21]

The court at Burhanpur now learnt that the *pettah* or outer walled system of Gwalior was already in the hands of the Company, and begged Malcolm to write to Lake requesting that 'in the event of his taking the place' there should be no reduction of its military potential since Daulat Rao Sindia 'understood from the terms of the treaty that it must be returned to his authority'. On this Arthur Wellesley commented that

'as to Gwalior, the question is to whom did it belong, to the Rana of Gohad or to Daulat Rao Sindia? I think to the former. I know that our government considered it so and that under this consideration Gwalior was heretofore given over to the Rana of Gohad when we had taken it. If Gwalior belonged to Daulat Rao Sindia, it must be given up (by the Company) and I acknowledge that whether it did or did not I should be inclined to give it to him.'[22]

When, on the evening of 30 January, Arthur Wellesley received letters from Fort William of 7 January setting out some of the treaties which had been concluded with the Rajput rulers, and also that concluded with Ambaji Inglia, he was greatly relieved, although he now expected the Company to lose Gwalior. But for the moment he could be confident that his treaty settlement, the text of which had still not reached Fort William, would be accepted, and that his policy of conciliation of Daulat Rao Sindia was appreciated and even supported. His relief was related to the position he had taken in December, when in the discussion with the *vakils* of Daulat Rao Sindia he had attempted to reassure them that the ninth article would be interpreted in a way which would not deprive Sindia of territory to the southwards of the line selected as a boundary.[23]

On 10 February Arthur Wellesley received word which led him 'to judge that the treaty of peace will be approved' and that Richard Wellesley agreed with 'the general article regarding the treaties with the feudatories, instead of a particular article providing for the independence of each petty raja.' The information that now reached him, drafted on the assumption that the treaty settlement still lay in the future, was designed to enable him to 'define the territories to be permanently withdrawn from the authority of Daulat Rao Sindia.' Arthur Wellesley considered that he had already achieved this definition by the two articles in the peace treaty. Richard Wellesley appreciated that 'the treaty concluded with Ambaji will be disagreeable to Daulat Rao Sindia' but added that it seemed to him 'to be a measure of sound policy to confirm Ambaji in the possession of all the territory specified in that treaty.' It was perhaps the case, Richard Wellesley added, that the authority of Daulat Rao Sindia had never been exercised over some of these territories. The listing, he assured Arthur Wellesley, was 'rather intended for the purpose of apprising you of the general outline of the limits within which it is my desire to confine the power of Daulat Rao Sindia, than to form the grounds of any enumeration of districts in the treaty of peace.' Richard Wellesley indicated also that he realised that the peace settlement might well have been concluded by the time of the arrival of the detailed instructions of 11 December.[24]

Meanwhile, there was already doubt at the court of Daulat Rao Sindia about the loyalty of Ambaji Inglia, and Malcolm reported that the *darbar* would be

> 'half distracted to hear of the defection of Ambaji Inglia, on whose allegiance the Maharajah placed great dependence, and (the loss of) all the districts ceded or rather guaranteed to him to the south of the line of Gohad and Jaipur... It will be particularly unhappy if these engagements should clash with each other. I perfectly recollect the objections of the *vakils* to the ninth article, and am satisfied that they entertained at that period suspicions of Ambaji Inglia's proceedings, when they (foresaw?) the possibility of that wretch running off with half of Daulat Rao Sindia's possessions in Malwa.'

To this Arthur Wellesley could at first respond calmly; 'the treaty is clear, we are to receive nothing south of Jodhpur etc and all treaties made by us are to be confirmed no matter where the Rajas are, unless *saranjami* or *khas* lands should have been granted away by them.'[25]

Once Arthur Wellesley learnt of the decision of Richard Wellesley to treat the treaty with Ambaji Inglia as rendered void by the action of the commandant of Gwalior, he was, as he noted to Malcolm, freed 'from all anxiety about Ambaji Inglia.' But he doubted, and in this he was right, that Richard Wellesley would rest matters there. He now received the first news of the attempt of Ambaji Inglia to reenter the intrigue at the court of Daulat Rao Sindia, where his agent was joining in the contention to John Malcolm that the treaty settlement was being misinterpreted. Ambaji Inglia, he commented, was 'just like all the rest of the Marathas. I am not sorry for Gwalior either.'[26]

The transmission from the Deccan to Fort William of the treaty which Daulat Rao Sindia had signed, but which required the ratification of Richard Wellesley, was delayed in its journey across Berar and Hyderabad. The attempt to create a 'Hindustan dak', that is a system of runners northwards from Burhanpur across the territory of Daulat Rao Sindia to the positions of the Company army in Hindustan was also faced with difficulty. It was not until 7 February that word of the treaty of Sarji Anjangaon arrived at Fort William. At that stage the indication was indirect, since all that had arrived was the letter that Arthur Wellesley had written about the extent to which the treaty could be regarded as compatible with the instructions from Fort William. It was a letter from Hyderabad that had brought the first information to Calcutta of the acceptance by Sindia of the treaty of peace, and it was not until 13 February that from Graeme Mercer then at Gwalior, that the Fort William Secretariat obtained a copy of the treaty itself.[27]

Malcolm had meanwhile initiated a negotiation with the *darbar* of Daulat Rao Sindia of a subsidiary alliance treaty, sending both to Fort William and to Arthur Wellesley a proposed text. By 27 January he was able to discuss the proposed treaty informally with Kavalnyn, who was for some months in early 1804 the principal intermediary between the Resident and the court of Daulat Rao Sindia, and was gratified to find that they were in broad agreement on the elements of the agreement. The one item of difference was that which both Arthur Wellesley and John Malcolm had foreseen as that likely to generate controversy, the issue of the stationing of Company troops within the territory of Daulat Rao Sindia.

'There seems to be great objection to having the force in the Maharajah's territory' Malcolm reported

> 'I have explained the dangers which may result from their being at a distance, and at last to conciliate our difference suggested the only possible expedient which occurred, the Maharajah giving Dohad Godra and Champaneer in exchange for other territory in lieu of increase of forces... I told him I would endeavour to get him a regiment of Europeans as well.'

From such a position, once it was Company territory, the subsidiary force would be able to protect Ujjain, the capital of Daulat Rao Sindia, from 'the sudden invasion of a powerful enemy', that is from Jaswant Rao Holkar.

Although in suggesting this position for the subsidiary force, Malcolm was following the instructions of Arthur Wellesley, they had both moved away from the guidance of Richard Wellesley, who had remained anxious to secure not only a subsidiary treaty with Daulat Rao Sindia, but also the advantages to the Company in its policy towards the Marathas, of the positioning of a force in an advanced position. Richard Wellesley wished so to place the Company forces in the territory of Daulat Rao Sindia as to gain political influence throughout his territory, and beyond.

The combination of the military caution of Arthur Wellesley, who doubted the wisdom of placing several battalions of the Company's native infantry at an isolated location, far from other support, and the concern of John Malcolm to conciliate the *darbar* of Daulat Rao Sindia, combined to deprive Richard Wellesley of this prize, which would have had political consequences of note had the force been in position in mid-1804.[28]

A week later Malcolm reported fully on the situation at the court of Daulat Rao Sindia. The ruler left 'the administration of all public affairs in the hands of ministers' although it was evident that he was 'more deficient in application than in ability' and might soon realise the need for personal attention to his affairs 'as the only possible means by which he can hope to restore his dominions to a state of peace and prosperity.' Malcolm believed that the numbers of *silledar* horse in the service of Daulat Rao Sindia would decline because of the lack of means to pay their arrears in full.

> 'The consequences of the insubordinacy of the military and of the unsettled state of the civil administration of the government of Daulat Rao Sindia are ruinous to the dominions of that chief. Those who have military power direct it to the attainment of plunder, while those who have civil authority are exclusively engaged in schemes for the promotion of their own interests and make no efforts to restore the affairs of the state to order and prosperity, because they expect to derive no personal advantage from that object being effected.'

There could be no question of an immediate removal of the court and the army to Ujjain, in part because this would place Daulat Rao Sindia at risk from Jaswant Rao Holkar. Malcolm believed that anxiety of exposure to attack was the main driving force taking the *darbar* towards the conclusion of a subsidiary alliance.[29]

Following from the peace settlement, and because of the extensive territorial cessions made by Daulat Rao Sindia in Hindustan, it had been agreed that some of the major feudatories of Sindia who had held lands in jagir should either receive further lands in compensation, or be granted pensions. Malcolm opened discussions with the *darbar* on the way that this clause of the treaty should be implemented. The ministers of Sindia professed concern that these payments would affect the loyalty to Daulat Rao Sindia of the pensioned chiefs; this Malcolm countered by entering a clause in the *sanads* of appointment stating that the benefits would be forfeit if the holders were guilty of treachery to Sindia. Malcolm accepted from the *darbar* a list of the proposed pensioners, and secured the approval of Arthur Wellesley to the terms of the *sanad* of appointment. This practice, of the Company pensioning major feudatories or ministers of the country powers, was not unique to the court of Daulat Rao Sindia. In the event, pensions were awarded to a total of Rs. 15 lakhs. Malcolm was optimistic that this pensioning of major figures in the court of Daulat Rao Sindia would lessen the danger of a conflict between Sindia and the Company; 'it will gain us many friends at this *darbar*'.[30]

Steady progress was made in the agreement of the terms of the subsidiary alliance. The submission by Malcolm of a draft text at the end of January was countered by a draft characterised with the privately reported comment that 'so great a jumble of nonsense was never collected in a regular form.' Malcolm continued to be optimistic that by being 'firm and explicit' he would yet secure the treaty, and was finally able late on 27 February to report that he had received a copy of the treaty sealed by Daulat Rao Sindia. 'The temper of the Maharajah and his ministers is at this moment excellent, and they appear perfectly satisfied with the steps that have been taken.' A day later Malcolm could set out to Richard Wellesley the terms of the new alliance.

Malcolm began by stressing the jealousy of their independence with which the ministers of Daulat Rao Sindia had approached the negotiation. He had worked within the instruction from Arthur Wellesley 'to tranquillise the minds of this court'. He had felt bound to make concessions, and had varied the standard form of subsidiary alliance treaties, though he believed that 'the essential principles' remained unaffected. The treaty was a mutual defensive alliance. Malcolm had not secured the cession of the districts of Champaneer and Dohad as a location for the subsidiary force; it was rather to be stationed at a point to be determined by the

Company near to Sindia's frontier. There had been prolonged discussion on the article by which Daulat Rao Sindia had undertaken 'never to pursue any negotiation with any states or principal powers without giving previous notice and entering into mutual consultation.' Malcolm had been bound to resist the suggestion that this obligation should be reciprocal, and had finally prevailed. The subsidiary alliance treaty of Burhanpur of 27 February was subject to ratification by Richard Wellesley within seventy days.[31]

The successful conclusion of the subsidiary alliance treaty had not prevented continued dispute about the terms of the peace settlement. Malcolm explained to Shawe that 'every attempt was made during the negotiation of the late treaty to take advantage of our ignorance of the precise nature and situation of the extended possessions of Daulat Rao Sindia.' He added that although Arthur Wellesley had sought information from the *vakils* of Sindia, this had been withheld. 'The certain and great acquisitions which were gained by our taking advantage of the impressions of an hour of triumph were thought too important to be put at risk,' and in the event the pretexts for not providing the information had been accepted.

The lack of precision that had followed from this uncertainty had led to the formulation of the line Jodhpur-Jaipur-Gohad in the treaty. 'I had always supposed,' Malcolm added, 'that the Rana of Gohad was a chief in the possession of some small power previous to the war. I have lately heard that he was an exile from his country and has been so for many years.... I mention these points to show you in what ignorance the treaty with Daulat Rao Sindia was formed.' On the lands 'lately under Ambaji Inglia' he added that he suspected that the *darbar* 'means to contest that the Rana of Gohad had no possessions. If so the ministers will find that they have overreached themselves when they meant to deceive others.' Writing to Arthur Wellesley Malcolm noted that the arguments of the *darbar* of Daulat Rao Sindia could be countered 'and we have justice and possession both in our favour, and therefore this point will be settled.' But he now urged Arthur Wellesley for the first time that he should write 'fully and strongly' to Richard Wellesley. Gwalior should be restored to Sindia, whose government had 'now been reduced more than policy requires'.

At the same time Malcolm reported to Fort William that an agent of Ambaji Inglia had sought from him letters to the Commander-

134 THE MAKING OF ARTHUR WELLESLEY

in-Chief seeking the restoration of Gwalior, on the grounds that this fortress was still the possession of his master. The ministers of Daulat Rao Sindia, Malcolm learnt at the same time, had written to Ambaji Inglia confirming that the fortress was to remain in the possession of Sindia. Writing to Lake, the Commander-in-Chief, Malcolm noted that Ambaji Inglia had 'continued from the day of his return to Hindustan (in September 1803) to the day of the peace to afford Daulat Rao Sindia every assurance that could confirm that chief in his confidence in his fidelity and attachment.' Malcolm concluded his second letter to Shawe with a suggestion of the need for 'an impression of liberal proceeding' and the expressed hope that Richard Wellesley would 'reject the narrow suggestions of engineers and revenue officers who, overlooking altogether the state of the human mind, think nothing of consequence but the state of the fortifications and the state of the assessment.'[32]

The activities of the agent of Ambaji Inglia at the court of Daulat Rao Sindia were continued, and two days later Malcolm reported his contention, in the presence of Kavalnyn, the representative of Sindia, that 'the fort of Gwalior and the country of Gohad were not comprehended in the cessions made to the Company' and that 'there was no such person as the Rana of Gohad ... he had been dispossessed these thirty years.' Malcolm could respond only with an assurance that the treaty would be fairly and liberally interpreted by Richard Wellesley. To Shawe he added that 'the fort of Gwalior is an object of such importance in the eyes of this government that I hardly think that they would have made peace, reduced as they were, if it had been demanded.' As a justification for the liberal interpretation of the treaty which he hoped to learn had been selected in Fort William, he added 'I am not one of those who attach much consequence to a hill fort in the hands of a Maratha. It can never give such an advantage in a contest with the English nation, though it adds greatly to the menace of one Maratha power against another.'[33]

From Fort William Richard Wellesley explained to Lake the Commander-in-Chief his view of the terms of the ninth article of the treaty of Sarji Anjangaon of which he was now informed, and which he was about to ratify.

'Although the literal construction of that article would limit its operation to the treaties and engagements actually concluded by ... the date of the treaty of peace, the true intent and meaning and the just construction of that article must be considered to be to provide for the confirmation of all treaties and engagements concluded ... to the period of ... receipt of official information of the termination of hostilities.'

Turning at once to the occupation of lands ceded by the treaty with Ambaji Inglia, Richard Wellesley noted that the rights secured were not the subject of guarantee by Daulat Rao Sindia, and the lands did not revert to him 'by the violation of those engagements on the part of the chieftain by whom they were contracted.' The cession to the Company was therefore covered by the ninth article of the peace treaty, and the Company was free 'for political purposes to assign those territories to the Rana of Gohad'. Further, the Rana of Gohad was 'universally admitted to possess an hereditary right to those territories which have now been guaranteed to him.' Lake was therefore directly to occupy these lands 'for the purpose of transferring them to the possession of the Rana of Gohad,' avoiding, if it were possible, hostilities with Ambaji Inglia. The Resident with Daulat Rao Sindia was instructed to seek the acceptance by Sindia of a complete list of the subsidiary agreements secured by Lake and Mercer which could be regarded as covered by the ninth article.[34]

When Malcolm knew the terms of these instructions from Richard Wellesley to Lake, he commented that this plan was 'not consistent with good policy' and would 'soon oblige him to do his work over again'. The loss of the reputation of the Company for good faith would 'do the English government more harm than the loss of fifty Gwaliors.' Malcolm's own position would be destroyed; his previous arguments 'will now be considered as fudge ... I shall be assumed to be one who has directed his art to deceive them and as such can never possess either their regard or their confidence.' He again asked Arthur Wellesley to write to Calcutta 'if your sentiments coincide with mine.' Perhaps the right course would be for Malcolm to move quickly to Fort William. This 'would keep everything quiet here and might be productive of good.' He had become convinced that at the time of the peace settlement in December the *vakils* already knew of the agreement reached by Lake and Mercer with Ambaji Inglia, and that it would be broken.

These letters Arthur Wellesley received at Pune, which he had reached after a military reconnaissance in force, leading to what he subsequently called the battle of Munkaiseer, against a *pindari* force in the territory of the Nizam of Hyderabad south of the Godavari. He begged Malcolm to stay at the court of Daulat Rao Sindia 'till everything is settled'. Malcolm had earlier suggested that Arthur Wellesley should travel to Fort William 'to inform them of what is practicable'. In response Arthur Wellesley had agreed that he must soon leave the lands of Peshwa Baji Rao, with whom he was quarrelling over settlement of his country, but noted that he could not do so if there was to be a war with Jaswant Rao Holkar. By 3 March Arthur Wellesley knew that the treaty with Daulat Rao Sindia had been approved in Calcutta. He travelled from Pune to Bombay, receiving an address from the community speaking of the 'glorious and happy termination' of the war and of the 'happy union of military science and political skill' which he had shown. Arthur Wellesley noted in response the 'practical example of the moderation of the British counsels'. Within a few days, having received copies of some of the letters which Malcolm had been sending to Calcutta, amply reinforced by personal and frank letters addressed only to him, he was able to assess the position at the court of Daulat Rao Sindia and write urgently . to Richard Wellesley.[35]

Arthur Wellesley set himself to invite his brother to look afresh at his Maratha policy. A powerful and well-reasoned state-ment, taking into account the standing of Richard Wellesley with the government in London and the Court of Directors, it was a second instance of written brotherly advice during the Governor-Generalship. To Arthur Wellesley the parallel would have been with his letter from Akluj of April 1803; he would have hoped that this letter of March 1804 would be of equal effect. Of the conclusion of the subsidiary alliance with Daulat Rao Sindia which Malcolm had arranged, Arthur Wellesley commented to Richard Wellesley that 'this completes everything you wished for in this part of India.' He then pointed out the extent to which the prospects of peaceful relations with Daulat Rao Sindia turned on the agreement which had yet to be secured upon Gwalior. It would be unwise to assume too easily that Sindia had lost all resources or means of waging war. It was also possible to over-estimate the potential British influence upon the court.

But the central point was the standing of Richard Wellesley at home, and it was this that Arthur Wellesley stressed, because he well understood the concern of his brother to build a political career at home on the basis of his achievements in India. In that context, further hostilities would be 'the greatest misfortune that could occur ... what a falling off it would be if the consequence of the peace should be a renewal of the war under circumstances of greater difficulty that have hitherto occurred.' Arthur Wellesley accepted that he had been insufficiently informed about the territorial ambitions of the Company in Hindustan during the December negotiations, and that there were arguments for the retention of Gwalior. But he urged conciliation and concession because 'the whole question of the peace of India turns on this point.' If further war with Daulat Rao Sindia was inevitable, it would be successful 'although possibly we might not enjoy all the advantages in carrying it on that we had even in the last war.' But 'I should greatly prefer the continuance of the peace, for the public and for you.'[36]

So far, loyal. Arthur Wellesley had placed, cautiously and in the setting of the career ambitions of Richard Wellesley, the issue of conciliation with Daulat Rao Sindia before his brother. He was writing as one to whom extensive political authority had been delegated, and giving his assessment of the mood of the *darbar* of Daulat Rao Sindia. He was also content to leave the final decision to Richard Wellesley. Publicly to Malcolm he urged an attempt to avoid discussion of the matter at the *darbar* until Richard Wellesley had been given an opportunity to consider the approach that had been made, and also suggested a possible concession on the return of captured forts. But with the freedom with which the two corresponded in private, he set out to Malcolm his total reservation from the position into which he felt that the Governor-General was moving his Maratha policy.

'The Governor General will I know bring forward an ingenious argument in which he will claim the fort but I am afraid that it will be too ingenious.... The fair way of considering this question is that a treaty broken is in the same state as one never made ... when that principle is applied to this case it will be found that Daulat Rao Sindia, to whom the possessions belonged before the treaty was made and by whom they have not been ceded by the treaty of peace, or by any other instrument, ought to have them.'

Malcolm did not succeed in limiting the continued statements of concern at the court of Daulat Rao Sindia on the interpretation of the peace settlement. As he soon realised, ministers had assured Daulat Rao Sindia that Gwalior would be retained, while conducting negotiations in which ambiguous wording had left the issue unresolved. On 4 March Malcolm was taken over the ground again; Gwalior had been captured by the Company after news of the conclusion of peace would have reached the Commander-in-Chief; Sindia was alarmed by the contrast between this conduct and the professions of conciliation which Arthur Wellesley had made during the discussions in December, when he had implied that the operation of the treaty article in question would be as restricted as possible.

Malcolm countered strongly; this position had arisen because of the conduct of Ambaji Inglia; it was he who had separated his interests from those of Sindia and negotiated separately with the Company. He had then broken this agreement with the Company when he heard that a rapid peace settlement had been concluded with Daulat Rao Sindia and had 'used his endeavours to prevent the English Government taking possession of forts and districts which he had ceded as the price of his protection.' The Company would not be restrained by the peace treaty with Sindia from proceeding against Ambaji Inglia, who had so acted as to show that he no longer regarded himself as a servant.

Kavalnyn powerfully stated the case for the *darbar*: Ambaji Inglia was a mere renter of land and the commander of the forces of Daulat Rao Sindia; if he had proved a traitor, the troops in Gwalior had been right to resist the forces of the Company. Daulat Rao Sindia rested his case on the spirit and not the letter of the Treaty of Sarji Arjangoan. What was at issue was income of Rs. 30 lakhs and the future of one of the strongest forts in India, and on the decision 'depended whether the Maharajah was to retain his rank among the powers of India, or be reduced to a *jagirdar*.'[37]

By mid-March, at the point at which Arthur Wellesley was urging Richard Wellesley to reconsider the question, Malcolm noted that he did not propose to raise the matter again, although he would respond if the court did so, until he received a full list of the treaties and agreements which had been reached in Hindustan by Mercer and Lake. He warned of the potential for disharmony in the topic, and was obviously unable to prevent discussion, 'worse and worse about Gwalior' he noted to Arthur Wellesley on 15 March. He added that 'Ambaji Inglia I have reason to believe is moving heaven and earth to irritate this government against the English, but he will not succeed to the extent of persuading it to replunge itself into a war.' Writing to Mercer at the camp of the Commander-in-Chief about the extensive territories in Hindustan involved in the issue, Malcolm commented that

> 'Daulat Rao Sindia cannot be allowed to keep up any troops in these provinces, which he has perhaps gained by deceit, but such is natural to a Maratha and were we to declare all engagements in which they use it null and void we might at once abandon all connection with them.'

In a phrase which directly echoed the view of Arthur Wellesley Malcolm suggested that forthright and honourable methods of dealing with the Marathas would 'make ample amends for any temporary loss we may sustain.'[38]

Malcolm continued to write freely on the importance of conciliation of Daulat Rao Sindia, knowing that the contentious issue was not only the Gwalior fortress itself, but also the extensive lands regarded by the Company as the hereditary lands of the Rana of Gohad. When he read both the public and the private letters which Arthur Wellesley had written, especially those to Richard Wellesley, he was for a time reassured 'should your most able letter to the Lord dispose him to be generous' by establishing the right of the Company to acquire Gwalior 'we shall make our generosity more apparent.' To Mercer, who had been directly responsible for the treaty concluded with Ambaji Inglia, Malcolm pointed out that

> 'this court certainly expects that their losses from the ninth article will be confined to such as are rendered indispensable to enable the Company to keep its faith to those with whom it is pledged ... our retaining Gwalior in our own hands will of course be a cause of great discontent and jealousy and may in some degree interrupt the happy operation of the late alliance which was established with Daulat Rao Sindia... I should give my voice for the cession of Gwalior to this state, and I should do that in

a conviction that it would add little or nothing to its strength in a war against us.'

Matters looked very different viewed from the headquarters of the Commander-in-Chief, who commented on

'these extraordinary demands of Daulat Rao Sindia, he might in my opinion just as well have asked for Agra and Delhi... I fear he will not be content until he tries for Hindustan again... Daulat Rao Sindia tells of the treachery of Perron and Hessing. I know of none in either case. Certain I am that this army bought everything they got, dearly as the Gazettes will show.'[39]

In the first days of April, in a long private discussion with Kavalnyn, Malcolm commented that his optimism on future relations had been much 'clouded' by the recent attitude of Bapu Vithal the Chief Minister

'he had not only persisted in opposition to the most clear evidence in asserting the right of this state to the fortress of Gwalior and the country of Gohad, but to my knowledge continued to assure the Maharajah that these places could never be alienated but by a departure from the treaty of peace on the part of the English Government.'

Malcolm reported that he would soon be required to present a list of the feudatories with whom agreements had been reached, and he was anxious that this should be promptly accepted. Kavalnyn said that neither he nor Bapu Vithal had ever expected the loss of Gwalior and Gohad. They had given the Maharajah the fullest assurances both during the peace discussions and subsequently that this would not happen. Kavalnyn pressed the claim of Sindia for generosity. To this Malcolm asserted that he could not admit this claim upon the justice of the Company; the decision was not one that could be reversed and it was therefore necessary to prepare the mind of Daulat Rao Sindia on this subject.

In comment to Richard Wellesley, Malcolm stressed that 'Gwalior is the chief cause of the discontent of this government'. He believed that the personal pride of Daulat Rao Sindia was implicated, and was certain that Bapu Vithal was 'pledged' on this issue. While the minister was favourably disposed to the connection

with the Company, he would not be able to sustain his position if
the points at contest were not resolved in Sindia's favour.[40]

Malcolm continued to accompany his official reports with extensive personal correspondence. On this he had expected his friends
to exercise a measure of discretion, while believing that the free
expression of his views would be helpful in Calcutta. He wrote to
Shawe that the question was whether there was a desire

> 'for the alliance with this chief to be cordial sincere and useful,
> or is that a consideration of which you are independent. If the
> former you must make an arrangement which will satisfy this
> government on the points at issue.... If every man had my
> sentiments on a hill fort that should be no obstacle. If you do
> not want this man's aid and mean to have no hold upon him but
> that on his apprehension why the point is clear. Keep what you
> have got and make haste to get more.'

When this letter reached Calcutta it was seen by Richard
Wellesley, who wrote vigorous comments in the margin ('scandal-
ous ignorance ... false insinuation') adding for good measure at the
end of the letter 'the sooner he quits Daulat Rao Sindia and Bapu
Vithal the better for his country.' It was ironic that it was Malcolm
who had noted to Arthur Wellesley some three months earlier of
Richard Wellesley that he was 'too much inclined to listen to reports
which make him uneasy and operate strongly on his temper.'[41]

Despite his illness and his vexation both with the court of Daulat
Rao Sindia and with the Calcutta Secretariat, Malcolm prepared in
early April 1804 a detailed analysis of the position of the Company
as against the 'country powers' in central India. He saw it as a
statement that would aid Josiah Webbe, soon to be his successor
at the *darbar*. He set out the political case for conciliation of Daulat
Rao Sindia to which both he and Arthur Wellesley attached such
importance. He noted that the only danger to the authority of the
Company was that of the exposure of its own lands and those of
its allies to 'bodies of irregular horse'. Malcolm stated that it was
the allies of the Company, rather than the Company itself, which
could take some of these horsemen into employ, although at the
same time he was reporting that Daulat Rao Sindia seemed to be
disbanding his army. Daulat Rao Sindia had lost nearly two-thirds
of his territory by the peace settlement. By the subsidiary treaty that
had been concluded, the *darbar* of Sindia was committed 'to

abandon its Maratha habits'. If Sindia could be firmly attached to the Company's interest, this would 'secure the tranquillity of India from being disturbed by plunderers and freebooters, and we should also be certain that no circumstance could ever again revive the idea of a Maratha confederacy against our power, an idea which however impracticable will not for a long time be abandoned.' Such stabilisation of central India would be delayed if Daulat Rao Sindia was not reconciled to the alliance; his army if unpaid 'will clamour loudly to be led to plunder'. It was in line with this advice that Malcolm should comment a few days later to Shawe that restraint alone could produce a peaceful settlement.[42]

Observing from Bombay, Arthur Wellesley was not optimistic of the prospects of a change of Maratha policy; 'I have but faint hopes that I shall succeed in inducing the Governor-General to alter his intentions.' Richard Wellesley had just determined a rather similar issue on the peace settlement with Berar in a markedly arbitrary manner. 'My dear Malcolm, we shall have another war, and the worst of it will be that all these questions will not bear enquiry.' In discussion in Bombay with Goorparah, who had been the first *vakil* of Daulat Rao Sindia to reach his camp in November 1803, and whom the Company was to pension, Arthur Wellesley roundly commented that Ambaji Inglia had 'destroyed Daulat Rao Sindia and deceived General Lake.' He gave it as his view of Ambaji Inglia that Lake would have 'entertained doubts of his sincerity in every communication.' A little later he noted to Webbe that he believed that the Calcutta Secretariat were asking for recognition of the list of treaties and engagements 'to afford a ground for the claim of Daulat Rao Sindia's country' and added sourly that 'a man who negotiates a treaty in this country ought to have the power to carry it into execution, or he does more injury than benefit, and loses his character as well as his time.'[43]

Arthur Wellesley was right; the policy instructions from Calcutta were not to be varied. Malcolm was told, in a letter of which he was not to inform Arthur Wellesley, that the Governor General was 'by no means satisfied with your arguments in favour of the restoration of Gwalior and Gohad to the authority of Daulat Rao Sindia... these possessions ought to have been specifically secured by the Treaty.' If the Company did not secure its rights, Bapu Vithal would be seen to 'triumph' over Arthur Wellesley. Any 'liberality' of the British government could only follow the full acceptance by the court of

Daulat Rao Sindia of the legal position as Richard Wellesley saw it. In an extended formal despatch, John Malcolm was given a detailed rebuttal of the 'pretences' of the court of Daulat Rao Sindia, instructed to report in full to Calcutta the replies that he had given in *darbar* discussion, told that the record of the conferences in December, at which he had been present, gave no support to the contention of Sindia's ministers, and required to state the British case 'directly to Daulat Rao Sindia himself in the most explicit terms.'[44]

Malcolm had contended in his official despatches and his extensive private correspondence that Daulat Rao Sindia had been gravely weakened as a result of the war of 1803, but also that his government retained the capacity to be an effective ally of the Company. On these grounds he had argued for conciliation, both generally and specifically in relation to the whole issue of ownership of Gwalior and Gohad. This approach had been categorically turned down at Fort William. Perhaps there had never been either the potential for a close working alliance, or indeed the prospect of it. Quite certainly, however the courtesies or evasions of a Maratha court might hide the point, it had now been destroyed. In the setting of the hostilities with Jaswant Rao Holkar which now loomed, the consequences were soon all too clear.

NOTES

1. Malcolm-AW 12 Jan 04 WP 3/3/70: Malcolm-GG 12 Jan 04 PRC x 196.

2. Malcolm-AW 19 04 WP 3/3/70.

3. Malcolm-GG 30 Jan 04 PRC x 196: Malcolm-Shawe 6 Feb 04 Add Mss 13747 f.41.

4. AW mem 7 Jan 04.

5. Malcolm-Shawe 15 Feb 04 Add Mss 13747 f.58.

6. Edmonstone-Mercer 22 Jul 03 Martin iii 224: RW-Lake 28 Jun 03 Martin. iii 164, 167: the correspondence to Lake was copied to AW WP 3/3/11.

7. Collins-GG 23 Oct 01 PRC ix 64: Edmonstone-Collins 15 Jan 02 PRC ix. 73: Collins-GG 24 Jun 02 PRC ix 116.

8. Notes behind Lake-RW 9 Jul 03 Add Mss 13742 f.46: RW comment 18 Jul 03: RW-Lake 18 Jul 03 and attached notes by Lake: Martin iii 188.

9. Collins-GG 31 Aug 03 PRC x 132.

10. Lewis Ferdinand Smith 'A Sketch of the Rise, Progress and Termina-
    tion of the Regular Corps ...' (Calcutta 1805) p.31. Smith had been a
    major in the service of Daulat Rao Sindia.

11. RW-Lake 19 Oct 03 Martin iii 409.

12. Undated set of terms A Mss 13775 f.27, WP 3/3/10.

13. Mercer-Edmonstone 6 Nov 03: draft articles 4 Nov 03 Add Mss 13775
    f.25 WP 3/3/10.

14. C.U. Aitchison 'A Collection of Treaties Engagements and Sanads ...'
    (Calcutta 1932) iii 418: AW was sent a copy of this treaty, now in WP
    behind Edmonstone-AW 7 Jan 04 which he received on 30 Jan 04.

15. RW-Lake 28 Jun 03 Martin iii 167 PRC ix 298: copied to AW behind
    Shawe-AW 2 Aug 03 WP 3/3/11.

16. Aitchison op.cit.iii 422.

17. The Treaty of Sarji Anjangaon 30 Dec 03 Aitchison iii 384 PRC x 268
    Martin iii 634.

18. Shawe-AW 8 Dec 03 WP 3/3/5: RW-AW 11 Dec 03 Martin iii 497.

19. AW-Shawe 14 Jan 04.

20. AW-Shawe 13 Jan 04 (two letters): AW-Shawe 14 Jan 04.

21. Malcolm-AW 16,18 Jan 04 WP 3/3/70: Malcolm-Shawe 22 Jan 04 A Mss
    13747 f.26.

22. Malcolm-AW Jan 04 WP 3/3/70: AW-Malcolm 20 Jan 04.

23. Edmonstone-AW 7 Jan 04 Ben Sec Cons 2 Mar 04 (393): AW-Malcolm
    30 Jan 04 (second letter of this day's date).

24. RW-AW 17 Jan 04 Ben Sec Cons 2 Mar 04 (397) WP 3/3/1: AW-Malcolm
    10 Feb 04.

25. Malcolm-AW 5 Feb 04 WP 3/3/70: AW-Malcolm 16 Feb 04.

26. AW-Malcolm 16, 18, 21 Feb 04: the reference is clearly to a copy of
    RW-Lake 24 Jan 04 Martin iv 16.

27. Shawe-AW 7 Feb 04 A Mss 13778 f.67 WP 3/3/5: Edmonstone-J A
    Kirkpatrick 12,13 Feb 04 Mss Eur F.228/71.

28. Malcolm-AW 18 Jan 04 WP 3/3/70 sent AW a draft treaty, a text not yet
    found: AW-Malcolm 26 Jan 04 'I return the treaty which I think will
    answer well': Shawe-Malcolm 27 Feb 04 A Mss 13602 f.72 reports the
    general approval of Richard Wellesley of the draft alliance treaty sent
    to Calcutta. Malcolm's discussion with Kavalnyn is in Malcolm-AW 27
    Jan 04 WP 3/3/70: Malcolm-GG 30 Jan 04 PRC x 196.

29. Malcolm-GG 6 Feb 04 PRC x 199.

30. Malcolm-GG, Shawe 17 Feb 04 SNRR i 381 A Mss 13747 f.64: list of
    pensioners SNRR i 385: AW-Malcolm 21 Feb 04 'your sanad will
    answer well'.

31. The treaty 27 Feb 04 PRC x 278: Malcolm-Dowdeswell 27 Feb 04 Bentinck Mss Pw Jb 13: Malcolm-Shawe 27,28 Feb 04 A Mss 13747 f.98, 108: Malcolm-GG 28 Feb 04 PRC x 219:Malcolm-AW A Mss 13747 f.104.

32. Malcolm-Shawe 17,18 Feb 04 A Mss 13747 f.64, 68: Malcolm-Edmonstone 17 Feb 04 Parl Pps (19 Jun 06) p.169: Malcolm-AW 17,18 Feb 04 WP 1/148 WP 3/3/70: Malcolm-Lake 18 Feb 04 A Mss 13744 f.195.

33. Malcolm-GG 24 Feb 04 Parl Pps (19 Jun 06) p.172: Malcolm-Shawe 22 Feb 04 A Mss 13747 f.82.

34. RW-Lake 13, 20 Feb 04 Martin iv 21,25: Edmonstone-Malcolm 15 Feb 04 acknowledged in Malcolm-Edmonstone 16 Mar 04 Parl Pps (19 Jun 06) p.178.

35. Malcolm-AW 5,6 Mar 04 WP 3/3/70: AW-Malcolm 2,3 Mar 04: Address and reply 10 Mar 04: Malcolm-AW 18 Jan 04 WP 3/3/70.

36. AW-RW 15 Mar 04.

37. Malcolm-GG 4 Mar 04 Parl Pps (19 Jun 06) p.175.

38. Malcolm-AW 15 Mar 04 A Mss 13747 f.147: Malcolm-Edmonstone 16 Mar 04 Parl Pps (19 Jun 06) p.178: Malcolm-Mercer 20 Mar 04 A Mss 13747 f.170: Malcolm-Shawe 20 Mar 04 A Mss 13747 f.164.

39. Malcolm-Mercer 20 Mar 04 A Mss 13747 f.20: Malcolm-AW 24 Mar 04 WP 3/3/70: Lake-Malcolm 29 Mar 04 WP 3/3/72.

40. Malcolm-GG 3 Apr 04 Ben Sec Cons 7 Jun 04 (58) PRC x 230.

41. Malcolm-Shawe 4 Apr 04 A Mss 13747 f.182: Malcolm-AW 16 Jan 04 WP 3/3/70: RW would have seen Malcolm's letter of 4 Apr 04 on 22 Apr 04.

42. Malcolm 'Hints for a memorandum on the present state of India' 6 Apr 04 A Mss 13747 f.121 Bentinck Mss Pw Jb 32 f.11. The memorandum was copied both to Calcutta and to Madras: Malcolm-Shawe 10 Apr 04 A Mss 13747 f.210.

43. AW-Malcolm 30 Mar 04, 1 Apr 04; AW-Webbe 12 Apr 04.

44. Shawe-Malcolm 30 Mar, 4 Apr 04 A Mss 13602 f.82, 88: Edmonstone-Malcolm 8 Apr 04 PRC x 236.

8

'Alliances pushed too far'
(April–August 1804)

Jaswant Rao Holkar had stood aside from the war of 1803. Despite the attempted alliance against the Company of the three Maratha rulers, which Raghuji Bhonsle had been at such pains to create in May and June 1803, Jaswant Rao Holkar had been unwilling to join the two Maratha rulers in an attack, fearing that their objective might rather be to prepare later to turn on him. Much later Malcolm recounted a version of these events which he doubtless learned in informal *darbar* discussions, that Jaswant Rao Holkar had at some point in August 1803 set out to join Daulat Rao Sindia and Raghuji Bhonsle, but that one of his key advisors had reminded him of their record of broken faith and that he had then turned back. There was certainly in August 1803 a recorded exchange of recrimination and accusation of lack of candour in the carrying through of promises made in earlier negotiation. In this setting Arthur Wellesley had attempted to open a relationship with Jaswant Rao Holkar, but this venture had come to nothing, and the authorised agent had been forced to withdraw, after he had failed to secure any undertaking of a safe journey to the camp of Jaswant Rao Holkar.

Holkar had meanwhile begun to plunder lands to the south of the Jumna previously tributary to Daulat Rao Sindia and in December 1803, Lake sought guidance from Richard Wellesley as to his response. He forwarded a friendly letter from Jaswant Rao Holkar but noted that the actions of Jaswant Rao Holkar did not 'appear to accord with his words'. Lake reported that the new frontier of the Company was too well protected for Holkar to do harm, and that he was determined to watch him 'at every turn' as he was 'so little to be depended upon'.[1]

At about the same time Arthur Wellesley was prepared to write afresh to Jaswant Rao Holkar, informing him of the peace settlements with Daulat Rao Sindia and with Raghuji Bhonsle, congratulating him on having remained at peace with the Company, and inviting him to receive an agent. The letter was prepared as if that agent would be John Malcolm, but such an embassy did not occur. Later, at Burhanpur on 24 February, John Malcolm received a boastful reply from Holkar addressed to Arthur Wellesley, apparently dated about 1 February. This warned that 'countries of many hundred *kos* would be overrun and plundered and burnt' and that 'calamity would fall on lakhs of human beings.'[2]

Richard Wellesley set out directions for the handling of relations with Jaswant Rao Holkar, making the assumption that peace settlements with both Daulat Rao Sindia and with Raghuji Bhonsle were near. He started from the premise that the rule of Jaswant Rao Holkar was an usurpation of the hereditary rights of Kashi Rao Holkar, but argued that the Company was not bound to attempt to restore him. To attempt to do so would involve 'difficulties and embarrassments which would not be compensated by the probable benefits.' Alternatively it would be possible to limit matters to the protection of the lands of the Company and its allies against the 'encroachments and exactions' of Jaswant Rao Holkar. 'With a circumscribed territory and a confined field of action, Jaswant Rao Holkar's military power would probably decay': this was a parallel forecast to that being made at about the same time by Arthur Wellesley. General Lake was instructed by Richard Wellesley to open a negotiation with Jaswant Rao Holkar, the aim being to avoid the 'extremity' of a move of force against him. Richard Wellesley expected that after the conclusion of peace with Daulat Rao Sindia, Holkar would 'anxiously solicit the countenance and favour of our government ... the fame of the British power will deter Jaswant Rao Holkar and every adventurer in Asia.'

These instructions Gerald Lake followed in opening a negotiation with Jaswant Rao Holkar at the end of January 1804. Lake required proof of the sincerity of the protestations of peaceful intention. He asked for the withdrawal of forces and abstention from the exaction of tribute from the allies of the Company. Agents were to be sent by Jaswant Rao Holkar to the camp of the Commander-in-chief. Lake hoped to move to Hindoun, from which he could both cover the passes into Company territory and give support to the Raja of Jaipur; the news of the conclusion of peace with Daulat Rao Sindia seemed to make it likely that these negotiations would have a peaceful outcome.[4]

The response of Jaswant Rao Holkar to Lake was to announce that he proposed to send agents to the camp of the Commander-in-Chief: there was no advance indication of the message which they would be authorised to transmit. Lake wrote afresh, disingenuously saying that he did not retain any suspicion of hostile intent by Holkar, but adding that should Holkar 'injure or attack any of the allies of the British government' the steps that the Company would be forced to take would be imposed by necessity. He added that he was aware of letters from Holkar to 'certain short sighted persons in the Doab and in this quarter': these were attempts to stir the new found allies of the Company to revolt. Lake assured Richard Wellesley that he would 'keep a vigilant eye on those persons until I am enabled to punish them effectively for their misconduct.'[5]

The propositions from Jaswant Rao Holkar when they came were hubristic. Lake was invited to accept them, 'if not, my country and my property are upon the saddle of my horse, and please God, to whatever side the reins of the horses of my brave warriors shall be turned, the whole of the country shall come into my possession.' When the *vakils* arrived on 18 March, Lake asked whether they had powers to negotiate and gathered that they had not. The role of the *vakils* was limited to stating the demands of Jaswant Rao Holkar. 'As the government had granted favours to the Jats and other chiefs, Holkar expected from the difference of his power and rank that his demands would be readily granted.' They were that he should continue to be allowed to collect *chauth*, that some former lands of his family in Haryana the Doab, and Bundelkhand should be granted to him, that his tenure should be guaranteed by the Company, and that he should be granted a treaty on the same terms as that recently concluded with Daulat Rao Sindia.

Beyond this, the *vakils* limited themselves to recommending that the Company accept these demands because of the size of the force of Jaswant Rao Holkar, 40,000 Rohillas and 150,000 horsemen, the Rohillas having 'offered to serve three years without pay for the sake of plundering the country.' They added that Jaswant

Rao Holkar had heard from Daulat Rao Sindia that the French had landed in India with a powerful force. Lake and Mercer replied that the conduct of Jaswant Rao Holkar did not justify the terms he had sought, that he would find that he had overestimated his own power, and that the demands of the *vakils* were out of line with the content of Holkar's letter. After the *vakils* had left, they sent back a message implying that they were authorised, despite their tone in discussion, to vary the proposed terms. To this opening, if it were one, Lake and Mercer responded by suggesting that further embassies should be granted full powers. There was one further discussion on the following day. In this the *vakil*, in a markedly more moderate tone, sought 'the grant of some country' and if this could not be conceded, at the least that Jaswant Rao Holkar should be allowed an annual sum in lieu of an increase of territory. To this the response of Lake and Mercer was that such a request could be taken further, but only after Jaswant Rao Holkar had returned to his own country.[6]

At the same time as these exchanges, Jaswant Rao Holkar had sent an agent to the court of Daulat Rao Sindia. His activities were reported to Malcolm, not necessarily fully or truthfully. The Resident was informed that the objective had been 'to engage Daulat Rao Sindia to accommodate his differences with Jaswant Rao Holkar and unite in an attack on the British possessions.' Sindia was reported as having rejected this, adding that 'the character of Jaswant Rao Holkar and the experience which Daulat Rao Sindia had acquired of his utter disregard of the most solemn engagements would effectually prevent him forming any connection.'

Late in February, as he was concluding the subsidiary alliance, Malcolm was hopeful that there would be 'hearty cooperation against Holkar... if that chief should be mad enough to provoke hostilities.' He sent copies of letters from Holkar 'in a very exceptionable style. I should have supposed that the events of the late war would have put such Maratha boasts out of fashion.'[7]

A few days later Malcolm understood that the *vakil* of Holkar had left the camp of Daulat Rao Sindia, although such messages were often false. He learnt later from the court of Daulat Rao Sindia that they had in turn sent an agent to Jaswant Rao Holkar. The *darbar* explained the objective of this embassy (about which at this stage, following the requirements of the subsidiary treaty, probably half-truthful information was being given) as being

> 'to apprise Jaswant Rao Holkar that Daulat Rao Sindia was disposed to overlook his past conduct and to maintain with him the relations of amity and peace, provided that Jaswant Rao Holkar would in future refrain from plundering the territories of Daulat Rao Sindia and those of his tributaries, but that Holkar's disregard of that amicable proposition ... would compel Daulat Rao Sindia to resort to arms.'

The *vakil* was reportedly admitted to a private conference with Jaswant Rao Holkar, at which the latter 'declared his intention to direct his predatory force against the British possessions.' The steps he had taken so far, which included an attack on Adjmir, a fortress of Daulat Rao Sindia, were adopted solely to 'enable him to prosecute a war ... against the Company which involved the independence of the Maratha empire.'[8]

By mid-March at Bombay, Arthur Wellesley had realised, both from letters from Malcolm and from other sources, that hostilities with Jaswant Rao Holkar were probable.

> 'The war against him must be carried on to the northward, and from Gujarat. It will not answer to allow the subsidiary forces (with Peshwa Baji Rao and the Nizam of Hyderabad) to quit the Deccan. We must take Chandor and his possessions in Khandesh, and open a communication through the hills between the Tapti and the Narbada with the corps which will advance towards Indore from Gujarat. This will keep him to the northward, where General Lake must beat him.'

To Richard Wellesley he explained the arrangements he had in hand to reinforce Gujarat. In deciding not to move forward Company troops from the Deccan, he was almost certainly concerned principally about incipient lawlessness in the southern lands of Peshwa Baji Rao.[9]

In the first days of April, Lake reported to Fort William that he saw little prospect of peace with Holkar. Forbearance had been remarkably ineffective, and the continued uncertainty had forced an advanced deployment at high cost. Were the Company's army to advance and force Holkar from his position at Adjmir on the borders of Jaipur, his forces would withdraw into Malwa, and reform after the British withdrawal. 'The cooperation of a British force from the southward, when joined with the forces of Daulat Rao Sindia, would not only effectually prevent his protracting the war by his evading any decisive engagement with this army, but would be the immediate means of withdrawing from him the troops and countenance of the Rajas in that quarter.'[10]

It was on receipt of this letter that Richard Wellesley determined to initiate hostilities against Jaswant Rao Holkar. He sent orders to both Lake and to Arthur Wellesley, leaving them almost complete discretion. Detailed instructions, it was stated, were to follow, although this did not happen in the event. The action taken by Arthur Wellesley to reinforce Gujarat was specifically approved, as was also the scheme of military action in the northern Deccan which he had outlined. Instructions were sent also to the Resident with Daulat Rao Sindia 'directing him to prepare Daulat Rao Sindia to act in concert with the British forces in Hindustan and the Deccan.'[11]

Had a genuine opportunity to negotiate with Jaswant Rao Holkar been lost? A different negotiating team on the Company side might have established a measure of rapport with the *vakils* of Jaswant Rao Holkar and perhaps, after a prolonged period of attitude-taking, have been able to secure an agreed measure of pacification, even taking into account the relatively inflexible instructions of Richard Wellesley. The two days of discussion in the tent of Gerald Lake at Hindoun on 18 and 19 March were to have fateful consequences, not least for the Governor-Generalship of Richard Wellesley.

It was one thing to determine that peace with Jaswant Rao Holkar could not be maintained, but what were the intentions of this campaign? In 1803, as is clear from his instructions of June and July, Richard Wellesley had been prepared to fight Holkar if that had been necessary, although he had been equally content with his eventual neutrality. Perhaps the hidden agenda of the 1804 campaign can best be found in the instructions sent at this stage to Malcolm as Resident with Daulat Rao Sindia. These explained that if the power of Jaswant Rao Holkar was reduced as a result of the war just initiated, there was no intention to acquire any part of his territory for the Company.

'Chandor and its dependencies will probably be given to Peshwa Baji Rao, and the other possessions of Jaswant Rao Holkar situated to the south of the Godavari to the Subadar of the Deccan (the Nizam). All the remainder of the possessions of Jaswant Rao Holkar will accrue to Daulat Rao Sindia provided he shall exert himself in the reduction of Jaswant Rao Holkar.'

The instructions listed some territorial demands in the area near the Ganges-Jumna Doab, but the central approach was that of transfer to Daulat Rao Sindia of the lands captured from Jaswant Rao Holkar. Clearly the war was seen as a joint venture of the Company and Daulat Rao Sindia. Further, the form of the conciliation of Daulat Rao Sindia proposed by Richard Wellesley was not that which both Arthur Wellesley and John Malcolm had sought, but the bribery of Sindia with the lands of Holkar, before they had been captured.[12]

Still in Bombay, Arthur Wellesley commented on the necessary strategy of a war with Jaswant Rao Holkar, before he knew of its outbreak. Presuming, correctly, that it was the intention of Lake 'not to quit Hindustan and not to follow Holkar' he roundly described this strategy as 'fatal'. To Malcolm he commented that Lake had forgotten 'the nature of our tenure, and our present state in the Deccan, the distance we are from Holkar, and the difficulty amounting almost to an impossibility of subsisting an army to the north of Pune owing to famine.' To Lake, Arthur Wellesley pointed out that the country between Pune and Indore 'either from extraordinary circumstances or from nature cannot afford subsistence to an army for a day.' Even if it were possible to move Company force out of the Deccan, there would be a risk of irregular force forming to the south of it on the frontier of Hyderabad. If at all possible, hostilities should be postponed 'if the operations are not to be active until I can arrive in Hindustan (north of the Narbada) to take part in them' until August, when the monsoon rains would have renewed the forage. The alternative was to rely on the force under Murray advancing from Gujarat, and that provided by Daulat Rao Sindia. Holkar could be destroyed by these forces to his rear, provided that Lake attacked him vigorously from the north.[13]

Malcolm reported the movement north from Ujjain of an army owing allegiance to Daulat Rao Sindia, commanded by Bapoji Sindia. It consisted of '20,000 horse, eleven weak battalions of infantry and a few guns.' Its commander was instructed to 'attend to the instructions of General Lake and to cooperate with his army in the event of a rupture with Jaswant Rao Holkar.' It had marched from Rajgarh in the direction of Jaipur. Malcolm warned Lake that the forces of Daulat Rao Sindia were not 'in their present weak and dispirited state a match for Jaswant Rao Holkar.'[14]

The orders from Fort William initiating hostilities with Jaswant Rao Holkar reached Lake at Tonga before Jaipur on 28 April, Arthur Wellesley at Bombay on 7 May, and John Malcolm near Burhanpur on 9 May. Lake was already advanced into Hindustan and was uncertain of how far active hostilities could be pursued. He did not yet appreciate the extent of the famine in central India and was therefore still hopeful that Arthur Wellesley would 'soon have all his forts and country', although he added that he was 'not without hopes that we may be able to disperse or destroy the army of Holkar on this side: his brigades and artillery are in Malwa, and ought to be kept there if not taken by the army of Sindia.'[15]

Uncertainty about the intentions of Jaswant Rao Holkar, which had been aroused in November, had led to the armies in Hindustan being deployed in the field at heavy expense. While the negotiation with Jaswant Rao Holkar took the unpromising cast just narrated, Lake and Mercer having enlarged the alliance system of the Company during the previous year, now set themselves to give it substance and perhaps even further to extend it. An agent was sent forward from the army to the Raja of Jaipur, whose lands were threatened by Jaswant Rao Holkar, with instructions to 'urge personally to the Raja the necessity of the vigorous cooperation of his troops in an object of which the safety and welfare of his own dominions forms the principal feature.' A detachment under Colonel Monson moved forward to Jaipur, 'to encourage that part of the *darbar* friendly to the alliance and to advise and promote the necessary preparations for hostilities with Jaswant Rao Holkar.'[16]

Mercer also set himself to attempt alliances with Kota and Udaipur, far to the south and west of the recently acquired military and political frontier of the Company. An attempt had already been made to negotiate with Udaipur but this had been frustrated by the presence nearby of the forces of Jaswant Rao Holkar. When these proposed subsidiary alliances were known to Malcolm, he protested at their incompatibility with the scheme of partition of the

territory of Jaswant Rao Holkar with Daulat Rao Sindia, and therefore of a degree of conciliation of Sindia, which had been ordered
from Fort William. Richard Wellesley needed, John Malcolm added,
to determine 'the precise system on which this alliance is to be
pursued'. The Company must either deal with Kota and Udaipur
only through Daulat Rao Sindia, or 'we must roundly assert our
right to interference and maintain it at the hazard of losing this
alliance.' Otherwise, the *darbar* of Daulat Rao Sindia would pre-
sume 'that you are very deliberately laying a plan for their execution
after the gentleman you have now in hand is finished.' In any event,
alliances with insignificant rulers were of uncertain value. 'They are
weak and alarmed and intrigue with all parties ... a reverse or even
the absence of our troops would probably make them revert to
their former condition of dependence without a struggle.'[17]

When Arthur Wellesley learnt of the decision to declare war on
Jaswant Rao Holkar, he wrote from Bombay to Murray in Gujarat,
giving instructions on the scale of operations which Murray was to
attempt by moving northeastwards. These orders were necessarily
tentative, because Arthur Wellesley did not know the intentions of
Gerald Lake. Assuming that Lake would seek to defeat Holkar, or
that if Jaswant Rao Holkar was seeking to avoid an attack he would
be pressed by Lake in a way which would lead to a dispersion of
his forces, Murray should so post himself as to stop Holkar, embarrass and impede his flight, and if possible engage him. Murray
should aim to join the army of Daulat Rao Sindia, and take with
him such forces of the Gaekwar of Baroda as were available. Arthur
Wellesley explained that he was suggesting to the Resident at the
court of Daulat Rao Sindia that any siege artillery available at Ujjain
should be moved towards Gujarat, although Murray should not
plan siege operations until Jaswant Rao Holkar was defeated.
Arthur Wellesley discussed alternative routes which Murray could
follow. Political commitments to tributary rulers were to be avoided
because 'it is probable that the greatest part of the territories of
Jaswant Rao Holkar will be given over to Daulat Rao Sindia.' Arthur
Wellesley was himself moving back to the army north of Pune,
hoping to secure the lands and forts of Jaswant Rao Holkar in the
Deccan, but he doubted whether he would be able to operate north
of the Tapti.[18]

The guidance to the Residence with Daulat Rao Sindia, where
the relief of John Malcolm by Josiah Webbe was about to take place,

was in line with these instructions. Arthur Wellesley had little knowledge of the extent of preparedness of the army of Daulat Rao Sindia, or of its location, but assumed that it would be more effective if linked with British troops, although whether this should be the detachment commanded by Murray or one moved south by Lake he did not propose. He believed that the ministers of Daulat Rao Sindia, once they were aware of the intention to transfer to Sindia the lands of Jaswant Rao Holkar would 'exert themselves to bring the war to a speedy and honourable conclusion.'[19]

In writing to Merrick Shawe in Calcutta, Arthur Wellesley stressed 'the state in which we are in the Deccan. The accounts which I receive are every day worse ... I do not usually make complaints. I struggled through difficulties in the last year ... but in this year I really fear that I shall not be able to keep the army together.' Writing with greater freedom to his brother Henry in England, Arthur Wellesley commented

> 'The government of Daulat Rao Sindia, although it has con-
> cluded the defensive alliance, is not satisfied with us, and the
> misfortune is that between ourselves I think we are in the wrong
> ... I am convinced and so is Malcolm that we should have
> renewed the war ... (with Sindia) if the Governor-General had
> not determined to give Daulat Rao Sindia the whole of the Holkar
> possessions, and this concession will probably reconcile Sindia's
> mind to the disappointment respecting Gwalior .... The system
> of moderation and conciliation by which whether it be right or
> wrong I made the treaties of peace and which has been so highly
> approved of and extolled is now given up. Our (former) enemies
> are much disgusted and complain loudly of our conduct and
> want of faith, and in truth I consider the peace (with Daulat Rao
> Sindia and Raghuji Bhonsle) to be by no means secure.'

It was in this frame of mind that Arthur Wellesley set out to rejoin the army of the Deccan.[20]

As Arthur Wellesley moved from Bombay to the north of Pune to rejoin the army of the Deccan, in Hindustan Jaswant Rao Holkar was retreating before Lake. At first everything seemed to confirm the analysis of the position of Jaswant Rao Holkar that Arthur Wellesley had given earlier to Murray that 'his power and even his existence appear to depend ... on his avoiding a contest with the

British armies, and his conduct shows ... plainly that he is fully sensible of the state of his affairs.'

In northern India, Lake and Mercer were understandably greatly encouraged.

'All accounts I receive of the army of this chief agree in representing its strength as very contemptible,' Lake wrote to John Malcolm on 9th May. 'The approach of my army has thrown it into the utmost consternation, and extreme distress and dissatisfaction prevail from the scarcity of provisions and want of pay. The desertion is in consequence so great that every day produces a considerable diminution of his numbers.'

Lake reported that a detachment sent forward from his main army had captured Tonk, and that he planned to place a protective force in the Bundi pass to safeguard the route northwards. At the same time Lake gave Malcolm the first warning of a forthcoming withdrawal. 'The period of the season and the unprotected state in which my advance would leave the country in my rear will prevent the possibility of my prosecuting offensive operations much further.' Mercer wrote in similar terms, not understanding the reference made by Malcolm to the difficulties of operations in the Deccan.

'You seem however to have formed a very different opinion of Holkar's force and its efficiency than we have here. His present force is absolutely nothing, in a state of the greatest distress disorder and mutiny. What his brigades are I know not, but by all accounts they are not nearly so disciplined as were those of Daulat Rao Sindia ... Monson's brigade with some Hindustani cavalry is ordered on towards Bundi and if Bapoji Sindia will cooperate spiritedly, much might be done... If Daulat Rao Sindia should not be contented with the new plan of vesting him with large lots of his old enemy's country I see no chance of pleasing him. A couple of months in the cold weather would settle him in his ancient *jagir* of Ujjain and Holkar in his grave, and settle all Rajputana to a quiet equilibrium under the protection of our government.'

An attempt at this time by Jaswant Rao Holkar to open negotiations with Lake was rejected, the obstensible reason given by Lake being that the Company would need first to consult its allies. This again was a moment at which a negotiated settlement with Jaswant Rao Holkar could have been attempted, a door presumably closed by the forthright nature of the instructions of Richard Wellesley in mid-April.[21]

A detachment under Lt. Col. Don sent forward from the main army captured Rampura, a fortified town belonging to Jaswant Rao Holkar, who had thus lost his one foothold north and west of the Chambal river. Lake was now at his most forward position in this campaigning season, at Nawai, south by east from Jaipur. He sent forward a detachment of native cavalry intended to cooperate with Bapoji Sindia, but Lake and Mercer were at the point of losing faith in any independent action of the forces of Daulat Rao Sindia. A permanent detachment under Colonel Monson was also to be located near Rampura to prevent any northward return of Jaswant Rao Holkar.[22]

Lake was anxious to withdraw the bulk of his force into cantonments before the onset of the monsoon, and for this there was not much time.

> 'If the rains set in, I fear my army will find it difficult to get supplies, which must come from our own provinces... I think this robber is quite off from this quarter, and do not now apprehend he can do much mischief anywhere. If Bapoji Sindia chooses to act properly, he has a force with him perfectly sufficient to destroy his army, but these people are so dilatory, and so little to be depended upon, that it is difficult to guess what they will do.'

Lake reminded Richard Wellesley that the 1803 season had been unusually dry, and that 'an army in this country cannot act in the rainy season.' He sent to the Governor-General the letter in which Arthur Wellesley had stated the difficulties of operating northwards from the Deccan until after the rains, and noted that it would be difficult 'for the Gujarat army to do anything before the rains set in.'[23]

Richard Wellesley had relied on the advice of Lake in reaching the decision to initiate hostilities against Jaswant Rao Holkar. In late May 1804 he again relied on the judgement of the Commander-in-Chief. Following from the deployment which had been initiated,

Richard Wellesley determined that it was wise to phase down the Company military effort, at least until after the monsoon. Reports reaching Fort William at the end of April had encouraged the view that Lake was 'expected to be able to break up his army very soon, leaving Colonel Monson's detachment at Jaipur.' Richard Wellesley assured Bentinck, the Governor of Madras, that either 'Jaswant Rao Holkar will speedily be compelled to retire within the limits of the possessions which he has usurped from Kashi Rao and to disband his predatory army, or ... his power will be destroyed.' The decision now taken in Calcutta was that it was no longer necessary for the Company forces in Hindustan to attempt to operate against Jaswant Rao Holkar. It would be the force under Bapoji Sindia that could be relied upon 'to accelerate Holkar's ruin.'[24]

Letters from the forward field position of Lake as Commander-in-Chief would have taken about twelve days to reach Fort William. Towards the end of May, Richard Wellesley was aware that Holkar had withdrawn. This had removed the outstanding anxiety, that of the safety of the frontier of the Company, at the time at which there could be no prospect of the furtherance of hostile operations against the power of Holkar. The Governor-General now determined on an extensive scheme of withdrawal, which Arthur Wellesley was told had been in preparation before his own full statement of the difficulties in the Deccan had reached his brother. The Madras troops were to be withdrawn from the area of Pune and Ahmednagar, the subsidiary force at Pune was to be provided from Bombay, and the force in Cuttack from Bengal. Bengal was to provide a subsidiary force for the Rana of Gohad, and probably that for Daulat Rao Sindia also, which Richard Wellesley saw as ultimately best placed in Gujarat. Lake was to be ordered to withdraw his army and place it in cantonments along the Jumna, perhaps with Monson's detachment as an advanced force near Jaipur. The suggestions that Arthur Wellesley had made in late April of the form that operations in Hindustan should take were specifically approved. The motivation of this deployment was economic. Richard Wellesley hoped in two months to reduce very markedly the strain on the finances of government from large military establishments, and in this way to allay the concern of Ministers in London, and to a lesser extent that of the Court of Directors.[25]

The premise of these orders was that it was 'unnecessary and unadvisable that any part of the British army should attempt in the present season to advance further towards the central or southern parts of Hindustan.' Effort should rather be devoted to 'effecting such arrangements as may enable us to oppose the most powerful permanent restraint to any possible designs of Jaswant Rao Holkar, of Daulat Rao Sindia or of Raghuji Bhonsle, at the least possible expense.' Immediate deployment was required 'of such a force in a position in Hindustan as shall, under the denomination of the subsidiary force for Daulat Rao Sindia, serve either to protect Sindia's dominions against Holkar, or to frustrate Sindia's treachery, if Sindia should pursue measures equally repugnant to his interests and public faith.'[26]

Just at the time that Richard Wellesley in Calcutta had determined that hostilities with Jaswant Rao Holkar could be wound down, the Resident at the court of Daulat Rao Sindia was attempting to give reality to the supposed military alliance between Sindia and the Company. To this his attention had been directed by Arthur Wellesley, who in writing from Bombay on 7 May had urged that a mandated delegate from the *darbar* should be sent to cooperate with Murray as he advanced from Gujarat, that Sindia's army should, if possible, be reinforced by a body of British troops, and that these forces should be urged to attack Indore.[27]

At the *darbar* of Daulat Rao Sindia, Josiah Webbe replaced John Malcolm as Resident on 12 May, and was formally received by Sindia on the following day. He took up the three current issues of the embassy, the dispute over Gwalior and Gohad—which Richard Wellesley regarded as closed but the court did not—the issue of the enlargement of the group of subsidiary alliances including territories regarded by Sindia as subordinate to him, on which Malcolm had already disagreed with Mercer, and that of the degree of support which Daulat Rao Sindia was to give to the Company in its war with Jaswant Rao Holkar.

Directly after taking over as Resident, Webbe had been concerned to open his embassy by replies to both the Commander-in-Chief and to Calcutta on the proposal that the Company should attempt to secure subsidiary alliances with Udaipur and Kota. As Webbe explained to Arthur Wellesley, 'any proposition at present for withdrawing the feudatories of Daulat Rao Sindia from his authority must necessarily indispose him to the impending war.' He had followed the line taken by Malcolm earlier; lands subordinate to Daulat Rao Sindia could not be transferred to independence by the action of granting to their rulers a subordinate treaty with the Company. To do so was to erode the state of Sindia to quite as marked an extent as had dispute over the content of the peace settlement. The matter, Webbe pointed out to Lake, could not be considered in isolation from the recent altercations about Gwalior. There was also 'the strong degree of jealousy hitherto manifested by Daulat Rao Sindia regarding the independence of any feudatory not actually provided for in the late treaty of peace.' Webbe had felt bound to recommend postponement of the issue.[28]

Webbe soon realised that the *darbar* of Daulat Rao Sindia was most disinterested in active measures against Jaswant Rao Holkar, whose agent was still in camp. 'They seem very loth (sic) to attack the lands of Jaswant Rao Holkar in the present state of their armies compared to his, because it will bring on the certain plunder of their own lands, before Colonel Murray can arrive for their protection.'

The court also expressed concern that Bapoji Sindia was in danger, placed as he was between the armies of Mir Khan and Jaswant Rao Holkar. An attempt was also made to revive the issue of the cessions of territory following the peace settlement. Webbe and Malcolm together sent a written request to the *darbar* for cooperation with the detachment commanded by Murray.[29]

Protest was followed by promises that the steps urged would be taken, ministers giving 'the strongest assurances of their disposition to cultivate the alliance and prosecute the war with sincerity and vigour' but at the same time seeking both military assistance to assert the authority of Daulat Rao Sindia over Ambaji Inglia, and financial aid in the form of advances of the pensions granted in the peace settlement, both of which Webbe had to refuse. In almost daily reports to Arthur Wellesley, Webbe stated his uncertainty.

> 'If Lake returns to Agra and Holkar remains to the southward, there is no hope that Bapoji Sindia will act offensively against him, until Colonel Murray arrives to protect him. It might indeed be better that he should not, for if he attacks Holkar's lands he will probably plunder them of the resources which would otherwise support our army.'

By the end of May, the *darbar* of Daulat Rao Sindia was expressing to the Resident doubts about the ability of the detachment under Colonel Monson to be able to withstand Jaswant Rao Holkar. It felt that Daulat Rao Sindia had been placed in an exposed position because of its alliance with the Company. Webbe remained optimistic; 'everything was well-humoured ... I understand privately that the Maharajah was pleased at the desire I had expressed to give satisfaction to his mind. I talked directly to him in his own language.' But to a fellow political he spoke of 'the great difficulty which I foresee of satisfying Lord Wellesley and at the same time conducting matters in such a manner as a gentleman I think ought to conduct them, for I have an abhorrence of the thought of being in a constant state of altercation with these people.' He had 'no intention of qualifying ... for what Mr Woodfall calls the Bear Garden in Leadenhall Street,' a reference to the Court of Proprietors of the East India Company.[30]

Arthur Wellesley travelled from Bombay to the Deccan army, encamped north of Pune, joining it on 22 May. He doubted whether forward operations against the limited possessions of Jaswant Rao Holkar in the Deccan would be possible.

'In the present exhausted state of the Deccan, I very much doubt whether I shall be able to move from the neighbourhood of Pune till the new grass shall have appeared above ground... If the result of certain enquiries which I have set on foot throughout the country towards Chandor should be that I can march the army there, I shall set out from Pune... in about ten days.'

On the campaign in the north, he continued to recommend moves to Webbe which were designed to keep up the pressure on Jaswant Rao Holkar, but which were soon to be impracticable. 'I have no doubt that Holkar intends to attack Bapoji Sindia, particularly if General Lake should omit to press him with activity, Bapoji must move towards Colonel Murray, unless he should see a fair opening to join General Lake.'

Daulat Rao Sindia had appealed afresh to Arthur Wellesley on the issue of Gwalior, and received a reply which perforce was in line with the decision that the Governor-General had taken. In discussion with agents of Sindia who were with the army, Arthur Wellesley 'pressed them to discontinue their angry discussions, (and) to advise Daulat Rao Sindia from me to bring this question to a close by confirming the treaties.' But he added to Webbe

> 'I am afraid that I have been the means of placing you in a situation in which you will pass but an unpleasant time... The Governor General may write what he pleases in Calcutta. We must conciliate the natives or we shall not be able to do his business, and all his treaties, without conciliation and an endeavor to convince the native powers that we have views besides our own interests, are so much waste paper.'[31]

For a few days Arthur Wellesley was in hopes of being able to march northwards almost at once. He believed that 'everything promises fairly excepting the famine in the Deccan.' Rather presuming on his own experience, both in the pursuit of a *pindari* force in Hyderabad in February 1804, and more generally, he explained to Lake his view of the way that Jaswant Rao Holkar should be handled.

> 'I have served a good deal in this part of India against this description of freebooter, and I think that the best mode of operating is to press him with one or two corps capable of moving with tolerable celerity, and of such strength as to render the result of an action by no means doubtful if he should venture to risk one.'

Jaswant Rao Holkar was more than a 'freebooter.' He was rather a guerilla leader of genius and of total ruthlessness. The importance of this letter is not in its recommendations on operations against Jaswant Rao Holkar, for they were soon irrelevant. It is rather that this analysis in its tone and content made it certain that Arthur Wellesley would never be invited to serve under Lake. Arthur Wellesley had set out his judgement of military objectives for the Hindustan army. He had done this without detailed knowledge of the ground, or even instinctive understanding of the climatic conditions of the area, which he had never experienced. Within two months the style of this correspondence was to be of significance. What Arthur Wellesley thought privately at this time of Lake was clear from a letter to Webbe, in which he asked 'what can have induced the General to press for the commencement of the war with Holkar, being entirely unprepared to follow him, or to carry the war beyond the Company's frontier?'[32]

In camp at Pune, awaiting a feast to be given by Barry Close to Peshwa Baji Rao, Arthur Wellesley set out for his brother the position to the northwards as he knew it at that time, and the deployment he had instituted following the first set of instructions. 'The delay occasioned by the famine in the Deccan will not I hope be of any material consequence in the end. It does not appear to be possible for Jaswant Rao Holkar to bring his army into the Deccan and his possessions in this quarter must be in the power of the British government.'

But within a few days it was clear that the word from the northern Deccan was indeed of conditions in which no army could move. The subsidiary force from Hyderabad, stationed in the lands which the Nizam had acquired from Raghuji Bhonsle of Berar, was forced to move eastwards to safeguard its forage. Just before the monsoon broke, in the detachment that Arthur Wellesley would have commanded, there was a heavy loss of cattle, markedly reminiscent of the difficulties on the Goor river almost exactly one year before. A new scheme of deployment was devised; the siege train and provisions were to be moved forward to Ahmednagar, and if possible to Aurangabad, and the subsidiary force from Hyderabad was to move towards Chandor when conditions made this possible.[33]

Arthur Wellesley was without military employment. He had made some provision against this contingency, but his arrangements were about to be overruled by Richard Wellesley. The time at Bombay and the delay in the initiation of operations against Holkar, in which he was so placed that he could achieve little, led him to reflect on his own future. He had now been a Major General for almost two years, and had been placed on the staff of the Presidency army in Madras by its Commander-in-Chief, a necessary preliminary to the command of a significant detachment, for almost the same length of time. It was at this point that he received word that the staff appointments in India had been under consideration in London and another officer had been selected. Late in April while still at Bombay, Arthur Wellesley had written to Lake setting out these points, and stating that he was 'upon the whole very anxious to return to Europe' and seeking the authority of the Commander-in-Chief to do this. If this permission was obtained, he intended at the appropriate time to resign the appointments which he held from the Madras government. To this Lake responded. While reluctant to lose his services, he would not withhold the permission sought. Lake made contingent arrangements for the replacement of Arthur Wellesley.[34]

This letter reached Arthur Wellesley near Pune at the end of May, and was described by him as being 'in remarkable civil terms'. He now informed Richard Wellesley of his 'very strong desire to return to Europe ... I have served as long in India as any man ought, who can serve anywhere else, and I think there is a prospect of service in Europe, in which I should be more likely to get forward.' He added that he could 'do but little in the Deccan, and that little may as well be done by anybody else.' He wished to leave for England in October and to settle various money matters in both Mysore and Madras before then. There was an important qualification, that if Richard Wellesley 'should have any desire that I should remain in this country, or should think I can be of the smallest use to his plans' he was prepared to remain.

The tentative offer of Arthur Wellesley was to be dramatically answered within a few days, by a letter already on its way from Calcutta. Richard Wellesley now invited Arthur Wellesley to come to Calcutta. Arthur Wellesley decided to undertake this journey via Seringapatam and Madras, since he wished to consult both Stuart, his Commander-in-Chief at Madras, who had stood down in his favour at the time of the advance to Pune the year before, and also Bentinck, the Governor of Madras who had taken up his appointment in September 1803. Arthur Wellesley was also still the officer commanding all forces in Mysore. During his movements south, he planned to undertake discussions with some of the southern jagirdars of the lands of Peshwa Baji Rao, and to set in train what he hoped would be the final settlement of that area.[35]

Although Richard Wellesley regarded the Company as still at war with Jaswant Rao Holkar, in his orders of 25 May, he had determined upon a limited holding operation at least for the monsoon period. He wished to improve his standing with Ministers in London by effecting the economy that would follow from a recall of armies to cantonments. Both Royal and Company units received heavy field allowances, and an army in cantonments was markedly less costly than one in the field. Richard Wellesley may also have hoped that the extensive incorporation of irregular forces, to which

Lake had necessarily committed the Company during the later months of 1803, could be cut back now that it appeared that Jaswant Rao Holkar was prepared to accept the position of Company predominance in Hindustan. The military justification for this withdrawal into cantonments was the assumption at the end of May 1804 of markedly reduced danger of aggressive action by Jaswant Rao Holkar.

The position of the detachment commanded by Monson in advance of the main army of Lake was intended to be the placing of a forward detached corps, not the uncertain probing thrust that it subsequently became. The journey of Arthur Wellesley to Calcutta as an adviser was seen by Richard Wellesley as designed to give assistance in the working out of political rather than military planning. It was associated with a plan for Richard Wellesley to visit the upper provinces, certainly going to Agra and apparently also to Delhi. In March Richard Wellesley had written to Addington in London, assuming that he would still be Prime Minister when this letter arrived, confirming the hope of leaving for England in December 1804.

> 'In the present moment it is impossible for me to quit India, or to fix the precise period of my departure, but I shall hope that I may be able to complete all the arrangements associated with the general pacification of India by the month of December. In June I propose to proceed by water to Agra and to arrange all affairs in that part of Hindustan visiting Delhi and the venerable Shah Alam. I hope to be able to return to Calcutta in December and probably to embark in January 1805.'

In Calcutta the staff of the Governor-General attempted to work out the timings of the extended river journey. In the event, by the time that Arthur Wellesley had reached Fort William in mid-August 1804, the decision was about to be taken that Richard Wellesley was not to visit the Upper Provinces. It had by then become very clear that a severe reverse had occurred to the detachment commanded by Monson. The circumstances had changed so dramatically that Arthur Wellesley found himself involved at Calcutta essentially in the tendering of military advice to his brother, whatever may have been the earlier intention.[36]

In late June, Arthur Wellesley was in camp near Pune. It was here that he received the detailed instructions issued from Fort William on 25 May, which ordered the armies of the Company into cantonments, and were designed to suspend Company operations against Jaswant Rao Holkar. Arthur Wellesley was able to confer with John Malcolm, returned from his unhappy stay near Burhanpur as Resident with Daulat Rao Sindia and with Barry Close. The orders of 25 May from Fort William were based on the presumption that the resources of Jaswant Rao Holkar were diminishing and war with him need not be pursued by any part of the ring of Company forces in three locations that had been formed. It was the force commanded by Bapoji Sindia which was to 'accelerate the ruin' of Jaswant Rao Holkar.[37]

Further pursuit of the armies of Jaswant Rao Holkar was now seen in Calcutta as impracticable at least during the monsoon, and the Company frontier in Hindustan as in no danger. Richard Wellesley had accordingly resolved to rely later on the military and political effect of the subsidiary force with Daulat Rao Sindia, which had not at that stage either been created or located, to provide a barrier against aggression from either Jaswant Rao Holkar or Daulat Rao Sindia. He planned to withdraw the troops from the Madras establishment from the area of Pune and Ahmednagar, and to create a subsidiary force from the Bombay establishment to serve with Peshwa Baji Rao at Pune. Richard Wellesley intended that the subsidiary force to be provided for Daulat Rao Sindia should be stationed in Gujarat, but should be drawn in the first instance from the Bengal establishment and reach their position by a movement across central India. Lake was directed to withdraw his army and canton it along the Jumna, leaving the detachment commanded by Monson near Jaipur.

At the same time, Richard Wellesley wished Arthur Wellesley to travel to Calcutta to discuss with him 'a variety of important questions connected with this plan and the political state of India.' Arthur Wellesley was specifically assured that his earlier suggestions to Lake, on the method by which the campaign against Jaswant Rao Holkar should be conducted, were approved. It was in this letter of 23 April that Arthur Wellesley had recommended that 'if the operations are not to be active in Hindustan' until forces from the Deccan had moved north 'it would be best to delay the commencement of the war ... at least to the month of August.' The scheme of withdrawal into cantonments, already in draft before this letter arrived at Fort William, was decided upon and sent out, once this analysis by Arthur Wellesley had arrived. Letters from Lake to Richard Wellesley had shown him a prospect of a period at the least of suspension of hostilities. The Governor-General hoped in two months to relieve the strain on the finances of the Company caused by large military establishments in the field.[38]

To Malcolm, Shawe wrote at the same time pointing out that the contention in his recent letters to Mercer, that it was not appropriate to conclude subsidiary agreements with lesser rulers in Rajputana, was not approved. These letters had shown that Malcolm was still seeking to maintain the argument in favour of the policy of strengthening and consolidating the position of Daulat Rao Sindia. On this the opinion of the Governor-General was diametrically opposite to that of Malcolm, and Shawe stated this.

The instructions of 25 May from Calcutta, which stood down the ring of Company forces that had been created against Jaswant Rao Holkar, had reached Webbe in camp with Daulat Rao Sindia a week before they reached Arthur Wellesley. Webbe forecast correctly that the resulting deployment 'will probably leave Jaswant Rao Holkar at liberty to do what he pleases and we shall have to assemble the troops again to suppress insurrections.' Of the *darbar* of Daulat Rao Sindia he wrote that 'this government will be distracted at being left at the mercy of Jaswant Rao Holkar and their ill-humour will be insupportable ... It is at present bad enough.'

Webbe still hoped that it would be possible to urge Vithal Pant, the chief minister of Daulat Rao Sindia, that the court needed to call forward the subsidiary force into the territory of Daulat Rao Sindia.

'This is the only mode of preventing Daulat Rao Sindia from being entirely overrun by Jaswant Rao Holkar, for the army of Sindia is under no command and they have not a farthing of money to pay it. Bapoji Sindia has been recalled, but Colonel Murray says that nothing has been done to assist his entrance into Malwa. Daulat Rao Sindia should ask for the subsidiary force; the troops with Colonel Monson would do admirably, and I shall probably be able to prevent his return to Hindustan.'

Webbe was here making an assumption that he would be able, should the *darbar* accept his recommendation, to persuade Lake that it was appropriate that the detachment commanded by Monson should be regarded as the subsidiary force with Daulat Rao Sindia. He was also assuming that Monson had the ability as a detachment commander to handle forces in the vicinity of Jaswant Rao Holkar. As he wrote, he suspected that an agent of Jaswant Rao Holkar was still in residence in Burhanpur. 'It may really mean nothing, but if I should be obliged to report it to Bengal there would be a thundering dispatch to widen the breach.' On the deployment that would follow from the orders of 25 May now received from Fort William, he commented that these seemed 'more like the distribution of troops after the conclusion of peace than like a disposition during the actual existence of war.' It would 'disappoint all the expectation of advantage from the war' held by the *darbar* of Daulat Rao Sindia and 'induce them to believe, what they have already hinted at, that after compelling them into the war, we have compromised with Jaswant Rao Holkar for our convenience.'

A day later Webbe added that it was

> 'most unfortunate... that the war should have been commenced in Hindustan with so little forethought of the means of prosecuting it, and I think it equally unfortunate that the Governor-General should have adopted Lake's opinion, in respect to the smallness of Holkar's power, as the ground of breaking up the several armies, which were intended to press upon him after the rains... The consequence will be that he (Jaswant Rao Holkar) will acquire an increase of reputation, and all the unprovided soldiers of fortune will flock to his standard, and produce that very description of danger which it was our main policy to avoid.... From the beginning there has been a mistake about making the war defensive.'

To Richard Wellesley Webbe reported that the *darbar* had asked him for written advice on the proposed recall of Bapoji Sindia. This was perhaps designed to safeguard a claim for equal division of territorial gains if the Company subsequently gained ground, in the most literal sense, from Jaswant Rao Holkar. This advice was given, and it led on to a desultory discussion on the case for the stationing of a Company subsidiary force within the territory of Daulat Rao Sindia. A few days later discussion turned on the acute financial difficulties which Sindia faced. The point had been reached, as

Webbe stressed in writing to Calcutta, that it was the presence of Company force alone, if it were to be requested, that could render the state of Sindia effective as an ally.[40]

Lake, the various components of his force now withdrawn into cantonments along the Jumna, with his headquarters at Kanpur was concerned in letters to reassure Webbe that Jaswant Rao Holkar seemed unlikely to return to Hindustan although he accepted that there was still the danger of attempts to plunder the unprotected parts of Malwa, the centre of the territory of Daulat Rao Sindia. As political assistant to the Commander-in-Chief, Graeme Mercer, endorsed this, although hopeful that Holkar's forces might be suffering from acute supply shortages. He saw the complaints of the *darbar* of Daulat Rao Sindia as 'ill-judged'. The assessment of the power and position of Jaswant Rao Holkar and of the potential support from Daulat Rao Sindia made by Lake and Mercer was to have serious consequences for the political prospects of the Maratha policy of Richard Wellesley. The Governor-General trusted Lake, having in mind his notable military achievements of the previous year. But transference to Lake of confidence in his combined political and military judgement of the prospects of the Company against Jaswant Rao Holkar was misplaced.[41]

A few days later Webbe felt bound to protest in writing to the *darbar* of Daulat Rao Sindia, giving the substance of the complaints of non-cooperation made by both the detachment commanders, Murray now in Malwa, and Monson advancing southwards from Kota. He reported that Murray had reason to complain of the lack of support from the officer in temporary charge at Ujjain, who had not responded to a request for information on the degree of possible defence of the town, and had simply urged Murray to hasten his advance. Monson's complaint was against Bapoji Sindia; he had ignored orders either to join Lake, when that had earlier been relevant, or to move southwards to support Monson. Instead, he had crossed the Chambal and plundered territory on which Monson was dependent for supplies. He had also rendered ineffective the arrangements which Monson had attempted for the defence of Mundasore, a major city in the territory of Sindia which Jaswant Rao Holkar plundered at this time. Webbe commented to Arthur Wellesley that the reply he received 'might justify more than a suspicion of the insincerity of this government.' He felt that the response followed from the 'embarrassments of this government and particularly from its pecuniary difficulties.' He added that Bapoji Sindia's movements were dictated more by the prospect of securing revenue from Bundi than any intention of contributing to the defeat of Jaswant Rao Holkar.[42]

It was at this point, on 1 July 1804, that Murray who had been advancing from Gujarat towards Ujjain, the destination to which Arthur Wellesley had directed him, decided that he must withdraw behind the Myhie river some one hundred miles to his rear, rather than advance further. He took this decision in the light of letters which he had received from Monson. Writing from camp at Budnawar, Murray reported that he had now learnt that Lake had placed his army in cantonments and that the report from Ujjain was that there were only 2000 cavalry there; in fact the numbers were far fewer. Murray believed that should he continue to advance, he would risk the safety of his force of 3000 effective men, and could 'foresee nothing but the total loss of this army.' He stated that he intended again to move forward 'when the armies from Bengal shall commence their operations or ... such a division of the army of Jaswant Rao Holkar shall take place as shall enable me to act with the smallest prospect of success.' He appreciated the consequences of his action but believed that these were 'preferable to the destruction of this army, and so laying Gujarat entirely open to invasion, which I think would be the inevitable consequence of occupying Ujjain.' He noted that Arthur Wellesley had warned him to avoid exposing his detachment 'to the sole operation of the army of Jaswant Rao Holkar.' He believed that he was destined for some months, until Lake again moved the army of Hindustan from cantonments, to be 'in the very situation' which Arthur Wellesley had warned him to avoid. 'As I am now, with 3000 infantry only I could never hope to engage his numerous bodies with success.'[43]

Murray was not, in fact at this time, directly threatened by the whole force of Jaswant Rao Holkar, although he could perhaps be pardoned from believing that he was. His withdrawal, which he reversed some eight days later, he considered should be attributed to the composition of his force, infantry without cavalry, and to the absence of support, that is primarily Maratha cavalry, from the subordinate authorities of Daulat Rao Sindia in Ujjain. The measures which he considered at this time, which included the incorporation of Maratha cavalry as irregular forces attached to his own, were measures of desperation. They at the least show that he consistently acted in the belief that it was his deficieney in cavalry that rendered his position acutely dangerous. In a letter designed to justify his conduct to Arthur Wellesley he commented that he foresaw the loss of his detachment if he advanced further.

> 'Jaswant Rao Holkar's position at Mundasore threatens Gujarat no less than Ujjain, and as Jaswant Rao Holkar is at liberty to divide his army as he shall think proper, it appears to me not at all improbable, if he could confine me to Ujjain, that he would detach a division to that country which is now quite unprotected.'

Murray attributed part of the blame for his movement on the inactivity of the forces of the Gaekwar of Baroda. Had they been able to move with him, he thought it might have been possible to defend 'a very considerable and fertile part of Malwa', that east of the river Myhie.[44]

Throughout this time the court of Daulat Rao Sindia remained between Burhanpur and Asirgarh; no move northwards had ever proved possible, because of a total lack of resource. In any event, the monsoon had now broken. Writing to Webbe, Murray set out the total disappointment of his hopes of support at Ujjain, nominally Sindia's capital. Here the agent deputed by the court to assist Murray had refused the help of the small body of Maratha cavalry that were available, and seemed to prefer that Murray remain at a distance from the town, perhaps considering that this would lessen the danger from Jaswant Rao Holkar. The subordinate officers of Daulat Rao Sindia were probably by now so acting as to preserve their position if events were soon to move to an alliance by Daulat Rao Sindia with Jaswant Rao Holkar.

At the same time Murray was in negotiation with the Raja of Dhar, seeking to secure, on the advance of a loan of two lakhs of rupees, the addition of 350 cavalry and 500 infantry. Murray had not quite two months expenditure for his existing detachment in his camp, and he sought from Webbe bills of exchange for a substantial sum. Murray wrote to Monson, who he had already urged to advance towards Hislanghar; he reported that he himself still planned to move to Ujjain, but only after he had received news of the advance of Monson, or if he were joined by the forces of either the Raja of

Dhar or those of the Gaekwad of Baroda. He needed an early indication of Monson's intentions.[45]

By 5 July Murray had resolved to resume his advance. He contended that his position had been so altered by the prospect that Bapoji Sindia would now be joining his detachment rather than that of Monson, and by the instructions to Monson, of which he was now aware, to cooperate with him. If Bapoji Sindia now joined his own detachment, he professed himself hopeful that 'with our united forces we may make a serious impression on the force of Jaswant Rao Holkar during the monsoon.' He remained anxious to secure his communication with Gujarat, because of his need for continued provision of supplies and treasure.[46]

Monson meanwhile had probably endangered his detachment more by his own incautious advance, both beyond Bundi and later southwards from the Mukhundra pass, than by any reaction to the news that Murray had temporarily withdrawn. At the point at which Murray was hesitating to continue his advance to Ujjain, Monson had advanced southwards far beyond the line of hills which he had been recommended to guard. He approached and assaulted the fortress of Hislanghar. Jaswant Rao Holkar was believed to be within forty miles, and the onset of the monsoon seemed to call for urgent action. A heavy cannonade greeted the assault on the fort, but this 'from the great expertness of our artillery was in the course of an hour completely silenced.' The fort was seized on 2 July with slight loss of life, after the walls had been scaled. It had been in the possession of the Holkar family for fifty years, and Monson reported that it stood 'on the summit of a hill surrounded by a deep ravine 250 feet in breadth and 200 in depth and a mile and a half in circumference. The garrison consisted of 300 cavalry 800 infantry 28 heavy guns and about 300 gingal pieces.'[47]

Although Monson had already advanced dangerously far, had he acted with vigour here he might have preserved his position; he soon found himself facing an attack which proved to be that of almost the whole force of Jaswant Rao Holkar. Holkar had withdrawn rapidly from Jaipur to a position where his infantry and artillery were deployed, and he had gained irregular cavalry adherents. He now crossed the Chambal towards Monson, who failed to take advantage of this opportunity to attack him. Monson now determined upon retreat, at least as far as the Mukhundra pass. He moved his infantry first, leaving the irregular cavalry, supported by some 1500 of the cavalry of Bapoji Sindia, to face Holkar. In a desperate engagement on 9 July, an estimated 40,000 of the cavalry of Jaswant Rao Holkar fell on both Lucan, commanding the irregular horse recruited by the Company, and on Bapoji Sindia. At least 2000 horsemen were killed or missing in this encounter. The whole of the force of Jaswant Rao Holkar, rumoured to be in total strength 19 battalions of infantry and 174 guns, were reported to be in the field within ten miles of Monson. Monson had only two days of provisions in his camp, and a supply of treasure amounting to Rs 3 lakhs was only a few marches away. He determined on a further withdrawal and sent off the infantry. He then turned to rejoin the cavalry. As he did this 'Bapoji Sindia came riding into camp and told me all was over.' Eventually, after a march of 47 miles in 26 hours, his infantry were again located at the Mukhundra pass.[48]

It was now the turn of Jaswant Rao Holkar to challenge Monson with the suggestion of peace terms. Monson was invited to surrender all his guns and his small arms and retire to his 'former country' and so save himself. To this Monson sent a spirited reply, which challenged Jaswant Rao Holkar to seize the guns, and on 12 July Monson successfully repulsed an attack on his camp. But he again felt impelled to withdraw further, since he feared that Holkar would be able to interrupt his supply line from Kota. Retreating in heavy rain, which filled a *nullah* between the two armies, the detachment reached Kota in two marches, the first of 22 hours without a halt.[49]

At Kota Monson had the humiliation of being refused supplies by the Raja, on whose earlier recommendation (when taken together with his own assessment of the resources of Jaswant Rao Holkar) he had undertaken his ill-judged advance. The Raja had now evidently determined that the Company was the prospective loser in a contest to be fought in part over his territory, precisely as John Malcolm had predicted. As the withdrawal proceeded north of Kota, Monson was forced to abandon his artillery. By 17 July the detachment had reached a tributary of the Chambal, enlarged in the monsoon rains, and had great difficulty in effecting a crossing. It was not until the last days of July that the detachment reached Rampura, which Lake had reinforced and to which he had sent forward supplies on first hearing of the reverse. Monson lamented to Lake the treachery of the Raja of Kota, and added that he 'could not bear the idea of attempting to fall back all the way to Agra... Alas my sun is set forever ... while writing to you I give way to the fullest and bitterest pangs of my heart... but rely on it, it is not apparent to a soul besides and in no instance can my appearance give cause for either fear or despondency.'

Maybe not, but the desperate state of the detachment must soon have been very evident to its members.[50]

But the withdrawal to Rampura was not to be the end of the disaster. Monson knew as he arrived there that the fortress did not contain sufficient supplies for the whole detachment. By mid-August Jaswant Rao Holkar had, despite the monsoon conditions, almost come up with Monson, and after three weeks a further retreat was determined upon. At the Banas river Holkar using all three arms, infantry cavalry and artillery, all but destroyed the detachment, part only surviving a contested crossing, and that portion forced to abandon almost all its baggage. Monson withdrew onto a fort where he hoped to find forces of the Raja of Jaipur, but word of the reverse had travelled ahead of him, and these forces had been withdrawn. At this point there was desertion both of sepoy companies and of irregular horse from the detachment. Constantly pressed by Maratha cavalry and harassed by effective artillery fire, the survivors made their way through the Biana pass and straggled into Agra on 31 August. Those sepoys who were lost from the detachment and did not turn their coats were not treated gently.[51]

The planned campaign against Jaswant Rao Holkar had failed. Murray, without supplies or support and unable to advance further during the monsoon, was at Ujjain. Daulat Rao Sindia had never moved from his camp near Burhanpur; he had contributed almost nothing to the campaign against Holkar, and would certainly be able to deny to Holkar the little help he had given. The alliances with lesser Rajput rulers, on which Mercer and Lake had earlier set store, had indeed proved to be worthless. The comment of Josiah Webbe to Arthur Wellesley two months before was apposite now: 'I am afraid that these alliances have been pushed too far and that instead of being useful to the tranquillity of India we shall be involved by them in constant military operations.'[52]

The outcome was therefore that Jaswant Rao Holkar had regained the initiative for the members of the Maratha confederacy, and had placed the Company in a critical position. What could have been a small-scale withdrawal had become a rout, which would lose nothing in the telling in its transmission to one *darbar* after another, with political consequences which would linger for months. For Richard Wellesley this setback had come at the time of a critical breakdown of his support in London. News of the outbreak of war with Jaswant Rao Holkar would almost certainly have been ill-received in England, but this could perhaps have been weathered if the declaration of hostilities had been rapidly followed by a successful settlement, as had indeed seemed possible in early May.

Arthur Wellesley was about to join the Fort William Secretariat in Calcutta when the Maratha policy of his brother was in crisis.

NOTES

1. Lake-RW 28 Dec 03 Martin iii 556.
2. AW-Holkar 5 Jan 04: Holkar-AW undated ? 1 Feb 04 Parl Pps (19 Jun 06) 292 also quoted in RW-Sec Ctee 15 Jun 04 Martin iv 99 at p.107: WP 3/3/70 fldr 7.
3. RW-Lake 17 Jan 04 Martin iv 3.
4. Lake-RW 30 Jan 04 WP 3/3/70 fldr 6: Lake-RW 11 Feb 04: Martin iv 20.
5. Holkar-Lake 19 Feb 04: Lake-Holkar 28 Feb 04: Lake-RW 28 Feb 04: WP 3/3/70 fldr 6.
6. Holkar-Lake 4 Mar 04: Conf 18, 19 Mar 04: Lake-RW 19 Mar 04 Parl Pps (19 Jun 06) p. 287: Lake-Holkar 19 Mar 04: Lake-Malcolm 18, 19, 20 Mar 04 WP 3/3/70 fldr 9.
7. RW-Sec Ctee 15 Jun 04 Martin iv 99 at p.113: Malcolm-Lake 24 Feb 04 A Mss 13744 f. 277.
8. Malcolm-RW 19 Mar 04 Parl Pps (19 Jan 06) p. 300: RW-Sec Ctee 15 Jun 04 Martin iv 99 at p. 114-15.
9. AW-Malcolm 17 Mar 04: AW-RW 18 Mar 04.
10. Lake-RW 4 Apr 04 Parl Pps (19 Jun 06) 293 Martin iv 48.
11. GG-Lake, AW 16 Apr 04 Parl Pps (19 Jun 06) 302: Martin iv 57.
12. Shawe-Malcolm 16 Apr 04 Parl Pps (19 Jun 06) 303.
13. AW-Webbe 20 Apr 04: AW-Malcolm Apr 04: AW-Lake 23 Apr 04.
14. Malcolm-Bentinck 24 Apr 04: Bentinck Mss Pw Jb 32 p.98: Malcolm-Lake 28 Apr 04 A Mss 13747 f. 237: Malcolm-GG 2 May 04 PRC xi 4.

15. Lake-RW 29 Apr 04 Martin iv 58.

16. Lake-GG 22 Apr 04 A Mss 13742 f. 173.

17. Mercer-Malcolm 30 Apr 04 WP 3/3/93: Malcolm-Mercer 2,9 May 04 A Mss 13747 f. 253,250.

18. AW-Murray 7 May 04 Parl Pps (19 Jun 06) 306.

19. AW-Resident with Daulat Rao Sindia 7 May 04.

20. AW-Shawe 7 May 04: AW-HW 13 May 04.

21. AW-Murray 30 Apr 04: Lake-Malcolm 9 May 04: Mercer-Malcolm 9 May 04 WP 3/3/93: Holkar-Lake 8 May 04: Lake-Holkar 9 May 04 Parl Pps (19 June 06) 308.

22. Mercer-Malcolm 13,16 May 04 WP 3/3/93: these letters were received by Webbe and copied to AW.

23. Lake-RW 12 May 04 Martin iv 63: AW-Lake 23 Apr 04.

24. Shawe-AW 7 May 04 A Mss 13778 f. 85: RW-Bentinck 10 May 04 A Mss 13633 f. 75.

25. Shawe-AW 23,25 May 04 A Mss 13778 f. 90, 98 WP 3/3/5.

26. RW-Lake, AW 25 May 04 Ben Sec Cons 19 Jul 04 (37) Parl Pps (19 Jun 06) 362 PRC xi 15 Martin iv 67.

27. AW-Webbe 7 May 04.

28. Webbe-Lake 13 May 04 PRC xi 9: Webbe-AW 15 May 04 WP 3/3/93.

29. Mem by court of Sindia 16 May 04 PRC xi 11: Webbe-AW 16, 17 May 04: Mem by Webbe to Sindia's court 17 May 04 WP 3/3/93.

30. Webbe-AW 22, 23, 31 May 04 WP 3/3/93: Webbe-GG 31 May 04 PRC xi 21: Webbe-Sydenham 1 Jun 04 A Mss 13770 f. 88.

31. AW-J A Kirkpatrick 21 May 04: AW-Webbe 23 May 04.

32. AW-Lake 27 May 04: AW-Wilks 30 May 04: AW-Webbe 26 May 04.

33. AW-Shawe 1,4 Jun 04: AW-RW 2 Jun 04: AW-J A Kirkpatrick 5 Jun 04 AW-Haliburton 5 Jun 04.

34. AW-Lake 23 Apr 04: Lake-AW 12 May 04 Grwd (1844) ii 1153.

35. AW-Webbe 6 Jun 04: AW-Shawe 8 Jun 04.

36. RW-Addington 1 Mar 04 Sidmouth Mss Devon RO 152M/C1804/OC3: staff advice on the river journey is at A Mss 13533.

37. Shawe-AW 23,25 May 04 A Mss 13,778 f. 90,98 WP 3/3/5.

38. Shawe-AW 23,25 May 04 A Mss 13,778 f. 90, 98 WP 3/3/5 : RW-Lake, AW 25 May 04 Ben Sec Con 19 Jul 04 (37) Parl Pps (19 Jun 06) 312 PRC ix 15 Martin iv 67: AW-Lake 23 Apr 04.

39. Shawe-Malcolm 25 May 04 A Mss 13,602 f. 135.

40. Webbe-AW 16, 18, 19 Jun 04 WP 3/3/93: Webbe-GG 18,22 Jun 04 PRC xi 30,35.

41. Lake-Webbe 20 Jun 04 04 WP 3/3/93: Mercer-Webbe 25 Jun 04 WP 3/3/48

42. Webbe-AW 30 Jun 04 WP 3/3/93 note to *darbar* 30 Jun 04 PRC xi 42.

43. Murray-Webbe, Lake 30 Jun 04 PRC xi 45 A Mss 13740 f.6 WP 3/3/93.

44. Murray-AW 1 Jul 04 Beng Sec Cons 23 Aug 04 (62).

45. Murray-Webbe, Monson 2 Jul 04 WP 3/3/93.

46. Murray-Webbe 3,5 Jul 04 WP 3/3/93.

47. Monson-Lake 3 Jul 04 Beng Sec Cons 9 Aug 04 (212) A Mss 13,277 f. 340: Monson-Webbe 3 Jul 04 04 WP 3/3/93.

48. Monson-Lake 10 Jul 04 Beng Sec Cons 23 Aug 04 (59) A Mss 13,230 f. 38 13,740 f.3.

49. Monson-Lake 12 Jul 04 Beng Sec Cons 9 Aug 04 (218) A Mss 13,227 f.343 13,740 f.10.

50. Monson-Lake 20 Jul 04 A Mss 13,740 f.19.

51. Lake-RW 2, 8 Sep 04: Monson-Lake 2 Sep 04: Nicoll-Monson 31 Aug 04 Martin iv 197, 198, 199, 202.

52. Webbe-AW 31 May 04 WP 3/3/93.

9

Fort William Interlude
(August - November 1804)

When Richard Wellesley had left England for India in 1797, the long
ascendancy in British political life of the younger Pitt had seemed
perennial. The interrelation of the scheme of union with Ireland
and the hesitation of George III over the significance in that context
of his coronation oath had brought his Premiership to an end, and
Richard Wellesley in India had to come to terms with the government of Addington. Given the nature of his appointment, and his
own political ambitions, it was to the Ministers of the Crown rather
than to the Court of Directors of the East India Company that he
looked. As has been seen, the response to his preferred resignation
of March 1802 had been a somewhat conditional request to stay in
India for a further year, 1803, although this extension had been
accompanied by warnings about the need to achieve economy in
the administration of the affairs of the Company. The response of
Richard Wellesley to these approaches had been to accept the
mandate and reject the warning.

Before the conflict with the Marathas had opened, Henry
Wellesley had left India for England. In London he had at once
made it his business to seek out Addington and Castlereagh,
President of the Board of Control. It was essential to assess ministerial support for Richard Wellesley; the attitude of the East India
Company in Leadenhall Street could be assumed to be hostile. But
this latter point was all; Addington needed support, and the Company interest in the House of Commons was worth many votes. In
consequence the message that Henry Wellesley had to send to Fort
William was not one that Richard Wellesley wished to hear. In a

letter of 31 August 1803, read in Fort William on 4 January 1804, Henry Wellesley reported on a discussion with Addington of 30 August. He noted that while ministers appreciated the value of the services of Richard Wellesley 'they are not strong enough to support you, or not disposed to risk anything in your support.' He reminded his brother than 'Indian influence in Parliament is now greater than ever, and there is nothing Addington would not do to save a vote.' Henry Wellesley in London drew from this the conclusion that he could not advise Richard Wellesley to stay 'beyond the present year.' He was clearly advising the Governor-General to leave India almost as soon as the letter he was writing would arrive.

Henry Wellesley reported that he had stressed to Addington in conversation the importance of the appointment as Governor-General of 'a man of rank and influence in his own country and [one] connected with Ministers.' This related to the contingent appointment of Barlow, a Company servant, as the successor to Richard Wellesley, and the known preference of Richard Wellesley for an eventual appointment other than that of a Company servant. Giving his own projection of political events at home, Henry Wellesley forecast that Pitt 'must I think come in again in the course of a year, and there can be little doubt that you may have any situation in his administration which you chose to accept.' He noted that there had been no contact with the Chairman of the Court of Directors, and that Addington had stated his intention to secure for Richard Wellesley an English Marquisate.[1]

A week later Henry Wellesley saw Castlereagh again, and was informed that Addington and Castlereagh could not have brought the question of a continuance of the Governor-Generalship of Richard Wellesley before the Court of Directors 'without risking a very unpleasant discussion.' All this now led Henry Wellesley directly to advise his elder brother that he hoped that he would return to England in January 1804, 'as I think that if you remain the Directors will torment you as much if not more than ever.' He made this recommendation despite reporting the stated preference of Addington and Castlereagh that Richard Wellesley should remain in India. Henry Wellesley reported on a further meeting, noting that there had been an attempt made by Bosanquet, the Chairman of the Company, to limit the stay of Richard Wellesley by official instruction, but that the Deputy Chairman had been supportive of

Richard Wellesley and wished him to have the opportunity to determine the timing of his departure.[2]

But Richard Wellesley had already made his decision. In December 1803, he sent to England many copies of the extensive *Notes on Maratha affairs* which had been prepared as a statement of the military events of the year. He informed the Court of Directors that he saw it as his public duty 'to relinquish my intention of embarking for Europe in the month of January 1804.' At the same time, as President of the Board of Control, Castlereagh was informed that Richard Wellesley had determined to remain in India.

'My departure would occasion the utmost embarrassment to General Lake, to General Wellesley and to every person concerned in the conduct of the war, or the negotiation of peace. My own wishes would lead me to return to Europe... but I should sacrifice my own character as well as the public service, if I abdicated the duty of completing my own plans.'

Two earlier letters had reviewed policy other than that concerned with the Marathas, attempted to give a reassurance on financial prospects, and expressed confidence that Castlereagh would

'approve the measure which became absolutely necessary for the maintenance of our alliance with the Peshwa against the aggression violence and encroaching spirit of two of the Maratha chieftains. Although these measures have occasioned the most extensive military operations... I trust that the great work of pacifying India, and establishing the British dominion on solid foundations is now accomplished.'[3]

It was on 30 January 1804 in camp that Arthur Wellesley read the first instalment of the correspondence from his brother Henry, copies of which the Governor-General had forwarded to him. His comment was vigorous, describing the Ministry as not sufficiently strong to support Richard Wellesley or as not choosing to incur the risk of supporting him against the attacks of the Court of Directors. Ministers, he contended, were guilty of a breach of faith, as they had promised support and then refused to give it, and were in fact indifferent whether Richard Wellesley continued in office in India or not. He recommended that Richard should 'fix a time' and decide to leave, and inform London of this. The time of departure should be October 1804; to delay and fail to declare this date would be to risk the dismissal of the Governor-General 'and I need not point out the bad efffects which that will have in this country.' When he restated his view, on the assumption that his first advice had miscarried, it was put still more strongly:

> 'you ought to determine to go in October [1804] as being the first opportunity and to announce that determination to the Court of Directors and the King's Ministers at an early period, grounding it in your communication to the latter on the knowledge that you were not to have the benefit of their support.'

Richard Wellesley could have ended his Governor-Generalship in a markedly more upbeat fashion if he had weighed and accepted this advice. To do so would have required acceptance that the restructuring of the political map of India which had been attempted had probably been taken as far as was possible in one period of office, certainly if Richard Wellesley sought to transfer to the centre of English political life while the prestige of victory in India was his. The decision which Arthur Wellesley recommended, if taken, would also probably have required a compromise on the total scheme of subordinate alliances on which the Governor-General had set his sights. Perhaps to his personal disadvantage, this was not a step that Richard Wellesley was willing to take.[4]

In a later letter, written on 8 January 1804, and which could have reached Calcutta before May 1804, Henry Wellesley reported his doubts as to whether Addington had ever sought an English Marquisate for Richard Wellesley from the King, noting that 'in the meantime two Garters have been disposed of.' The Wellesleys lived in a world where the 'loaves and fishes' were important; Addington was made of different metal, and had just refused the Garter when it was pressed upon him personally by George III. Henry Wellesley now commented that he had totally altered his view of Addington, who he saw as 'a compound of absurdity vanity and weakness' and reported that he believed that 'a coalition of Pitt Fox Grenville and Windham must very soon hurl Addington from his throne.' On the basis of a letter from Shawe of 28 June 1803, which he had just received in London, Henry Wellesley had reflected the confidence of the Governor-General by forecasting to Castlereagh that if 'Sindia and Bhonsle commenced hostilities the war would be over in three months.' Castlereagh had commented that he had encountered a degree of grumbling from the Court of Directors at the high cost of the deployments of 1803. This would have been seen at Fort William as scarcely supportive comment, since the whole Maratha policy, although initially costly, was seen as ultimately a measure of economy.[5]

Once Arthur Wellesley had travelled to Calcutta, where he arrived in mid-August 1804, he was at once caught up in discussion on military and political matters. We are not so well-informed by these unrecorded exchanges as we are by terse letters written during the 1803 campaign and on his journeys in early 1804. It becomes more difficult to reconstruct his own contribution to policy. There remain some hints in letters written while at Fort William, and a formidable body of 'staff writing' on a range of topics, which were clearly of some effect at the time, and some of which have entered into the historiography of the period.

In mid-August, the latest information from Hindustan at Calcutta was that Monson had 'made his retreat to Rampura'. The Governor-General had instructed Lake in one of his most forceful communications, that nothing would end the warfare initiated by Jaswant Rao Holkar 'excepting active offensive operations carried forward to the heart of the province of Malwa if it should be necessary.' The scheme for Richard Wellesley to visit the upper provinces was about to be abandoned. Arthur Wellesley found himself reassuring the hesitant Duncan, Governor of Bombay, that despite the forward position of Murray in the territory of Daulat Rao Sindia in Malwa, Gujarat was not in danger, and that before Jaswant Rao Holkar could reach Surat 'he must beat Colonel Murray, pass through the Gujarat... and cross the rivers Mahie, Narbada, and Tapti.'[6]

Arthur Wellesley's letters to Malcolm tell us more, but contain an uncertainty.

'I arrived here on the 12th (August) and was received in great style by the Governor General... (he) does not go up the country and orders have been sent to (for?) me to go to Lake and carry on the war in reality and with activity... (the GG) has been ill since I arrived and I have not been able to do more than go into the question of the war with Holkar (and) the mode of carrying it on.'

About ten days later the message has altered, still to Malcolm. 'You may depend upon it that the Commander-in-Chief will not allow me to undertake the settlement of affairs in Malwa. Indeed it would be improper to propose such an arrangement to him and unreasonable to expect that he would propose it himself.' In an aside, evidently deeply felt, he added 'Would to God that I had come round here in March, and Holkar would now be in the tomb of all the Capulets!'

Does this mean that Arthur Wellesley believed that had he journeyed to Fort William early in 1804, as both Malcolm and Webbe had urged, he would have been appointed to the position in the army of Hindustan to which Lake appointed Monson, and that he would therefore have been in command of the detachment sent forward in early May? Or it is rather than Arthur Wellesley believed that better preparation by Richard Wellesley for war with Jaswant Rao Holkar, aided by his personal briefing, could have so changed its course that it would by August have achieved defeat?

In a further letter to Malcolm Arthur Wellesley noted that 'the Governor-General gave him (Lake) an opportunity of desiring that I should join it (the army) of which he did not avail himself. On the contrary he desired that I might return to the Deccan.'

Of the reality of the crisis there was no doubt; if matters were not brought quickly to a solution 'it will be the most serious affair... and one which will require the exertions of all of us. In such a case, I have no objection to go back to the Deccan... The countries to the northward (the Ganges-Jumna Doab) are in great alarm, but it is to be hoped that the Governor-General's luck will not leave him in this crisis.'[7]

At this stage the retreat to Rampura was known, but not that to Agra. 'Affairs in Malwa have gone on very badly indeed, and a great effort is necessary to regain our character,' Arthur Wellesley explained to Barry Close at Pune. He summarised the plan sent to Lake by Richard Wellesley in mid-August, and hoped himself to be permitted to leave Calcutta and join either Wallace, placed in command of the detachment which was to capture Chandor, or Murray in Gujarat. This intention should be announced at the *darbars* of both Peshwa Baji Rao and Daulat Rao Sindia as it might enhance confidence in the continuing military power of the Company. Care should be taken to prepare against the contingent risk that Jaswant Rao Holkar would again move into the Deccan.

During the next few days, as he read the despatches coming in from Hindustan, Arthur Wellesley prepared what has become one of the source documents on the retreat of Monson. In review of the whole episode he established in his own mind, and in this he has been followed by later historians, that the detachment under Monson was not strong enough to be able to engage Holkar, that it was without provisions and was dependent on local rulers for its supplies, had failed to provision a fort to its rear, and lacked its own boats collected at posts upon rivers. Arthur Wellesley believed that the detachment would have been lost even if Holkar had not attacked it with his infantry and artillery. He stated these conclusions to both Wallace and Murray, as deliberate guidance to each of them against the contingent risk that they might face Jaswant Rao Holkar themselves.[8]

In June two sets of instructions had been sent from the Fort William Secretariat to Webbe at the court of Daulat Rao Sindia. In the first, stress had belatedly been laid on the objective of conciliation 'by every concession compatible with the principles on which the late glorious war was undertaken and prosecuted and the peace concluded.' It was further suggested that it would be possible both to secure more Company territory, and assist the financial difficulties of Sindia, if a lease could be secured on the border fortresses and districts of Dholepur Bari and Rajakerrah.

At the end of June, in a clear variation of instructions given at the outbreak of the war two months before, the suggestion was made that the military reverse which it was then assumed that Jaswant Rao Holkar had received near Jaipur in late May would lead to his being prepared to accept a limited territorial settlement. The form of this proposed settlement made little concession to the pride of Holkar, since it was planned for presentation to him at a time of his assumed military defeat. Nor was there to be any change in the attempt earlier initiated to secure the independence from either Daulat Rao Sindia or Jaswant Rao Holkar of various lesser rulers. The terms of settlement for Jaswant Rao Holkar were to be the subject of negotiation with Daulat Rao Sindia.

All this was probably unrealistic, even though it harked back to the suggestions made by the *vakils* of Jaswant Rao Holkar in March.

The suggestion was also made that there should be a settlement in which both Jaswant Rao Holkar and Kashi Rao Holkar, seen by Richard Wellesley as the legitimate claimant but who was mentally retarded, should receive 'suitable provision.' There should also be a settlement between Jaswant Rao Holkar and Daulat Rao Sindia of which the British Company should be the guarantor. Much of this was a reversion, presumably to be attributed to the influence of Barlow and Edmonstone, to the proposals made in early 1803, when the intention had been to offer Jaswant Rao Holkar 'the grant of a fort, with a jagir' to effect his withdrawal from Pune.[9]

The *dak* lines of communication had been much lengthened by the war. When he received these instructions, Webbe could see at once that if they had any validity at the time they were written, they had none now. He prepared a detailed critique, and suspended the operation of his orders. It was doubtful, he reported to Arthur Wellesley, whether Daulat Rao Sindia would be prepared to negotiate with Jaswant Rao Holkar on behalf of the company, or whether Holkar would accept such mediation. While it was true that in theory Sindia could benefit from a negotiated peace by relief from the expenses of war, in reality he had spent nothing, because he had nothing to spend. The troops sent northwards under Bapoji Sindia had not obeyed orders and were 'now actually endeavouring to subsist by indiscriminate plunder.' Those forces still near to the *darbar* were in a near mutinous condition from lack of pay or plunder. Famine in Malwa and the neglect by Sindia of management of his land revenue income during the years of his stay in Pune before 1802 meant that he did not suffer 'the anxiety which every European statesman might consider it to be natural for him to feel for the restoration of order in his affairs.' The natural condition of the relation between Daulat Rao Sindia and Jaswant Rao Holkar was that of rivalry, not cooperation, and this condition had only temporarily and incompletely been reversed by the attempted cooperation against the British Company in June and July 1803.

Webbe surmised that earlier in the year 'if Daulat Rao Sindia could have relieved himself from the fear of the power of Jaswant Rao Holkar by involving us in a war with that chief he would probably have preferred that mode to that of submitting to a state of protection under the operations of the subsidiary alliance.'

Daulat Rao Sindia had certainly been encouraged, once war with Holkar had been declared, to expect territorial gain following a favourable ending to the conflict. To change objectives now to that of a negotiated settlement would disappoint these hopes. It seemed most unlikely that Daulat Rao Sindia would negotiate with Jaswant Rao Holkar 'with sincerity or at least with zeal.' As matters stood in Malwa at mid-August 'no considerable effect' had been made on the power of Jaswant Rao Holkar. He had subsisted his forces in Malwa and levied contributions. He had 'as little reason to distrust his own fortune as at the time of his provoking the war... circumstances as they now stand are of a nature rather to inflame than to abate his madness.' From the standpoint of the *darbar* of Daulat Rao Sindia there had always been the fear of a Company deal with Jaswant Rao Holkar at their expense, and they considered their failure in the war of 1803 as due to the treachery of Holkar and of the European officers in their service rather than to the superiority of British arms.

Taking into account the sum of the 'uneasy reflections' that events would have stimulated in the mind of Daulat Rao Sindia, Webbe felt that 'his chagrin at the loss of Gohad and Gwalior, his disappointment of a compensation from the partition of the territory of Jaswant Rao Holkar, a sense of injury arising from the sacrifices he has already made in the war, a diminution of his respect for our dignity, and a confirmation of his own ideas relative to the possibility of success against our arms... are powerfully calculated to excite and preserve sentiments... which may disturb the plan of settling the peace of India systematically.'

Webbe was concerned to suspend orders received from the Fort William Secretariat, but explained to Arthur Wellesley that he could see no alternative. He had deferred opening the negotiation which he was ordered to attempt because it was not consistent with the policy of Richard Wellesley 'to offer terms under the circumstances which have actually occurred' and because pacification could not be obtained by the mediation of Daulat Rao Sindia 'before the time when the Governor-General will have the power of dictating the plan and conditions of the peace.' Webbe relied on the assistance of Arthur Wellesley in the 'hazardous procedure' of deferring action on instructions; it was his duty to 'depart from a mere ministerial capacity and incur the present responsibility.' When these papers reached Arthur Wellesley at Fort William he was reassuring in reply; the memorandum and letter that Webbe had sent him had enabled

him to explain in Calcutta the realities of the situation in Malwa.
Webbe received a message from the Fort William Secretariat explaining that the reasons why he had suspended action on the
instructions were entirely approved.[10]

In the event the return of Arthur Wellesley to the Deccan, which
he had indicated to Close was imminent, was delayed. Richard
Wellesley was subject to periods of poor health and mental exhaus-
tion and one of these would seem to have been in part the cause
of the delay in permitting Arthur Wellesley to leave for Madras and
contingently for the Deccan. It was also probable that the departure
was delayed from day to day pending news of the operations under
the command of Gerald Lake. The journey to the Deccan did not
begin until early November.

At the end of July 1804, Richard Wellesley had received from
London orders from the Secret Committee of the Court of Directors
on Maratha policy, and also a letter from Castlereagh. As Merrick
Shawe commented to Henry Wellesley in England, the Secret
Committee orders were 'happily impracticable.' They were in total
divergence from an earlier expression of views on the Treaty of
Bassein. They represented 'a gross infraction of the promise of
support' made in September 1802. The despatch was seen as
having 'been calculated for the foundation of a defence in Parliament in the event of any failure in the war and to cover the retreat
of Ministers.'

In optimistic tone, which was to be cruelly invalidated within a
few weeks, Shawe had added

> 'the peace acquires more solidity every day. The utmost
> cordiality subsists between this government and the *darbars* of
> Daulat Rao Sindia Berar and Pune... Sindia appears to lean more
> and more every day upon the British government for support...
> his jealousy wears off in proportion as he perceives our disincli-
> nation to intermeddle in his affairs more than we are bound to
> by treaty. (Daulat Rao Sindia) cannot move a gun or a man
> without our assistance. He has recently shown a great inclination
> to apply to have the subsidiary force stationed at least for a time
> within his territory.'[11]

In London Castlereagh as President of the Board of Control
knew by May 1804 of the outcome of the campaign of 1803.

Overland despatches from Bombay took about four months to reach London. Castlereagh set himself to examine the despatches fully, and prepared for the first time what can be described summarily as the minimalist case against the Maratha policy of Richard Wellesley, that is the prescription of the limited objective of watching the Maratha confederacy rather than selecting allies within it. He went to considerable length to give his own version of events since 1790, and then turned to his own proposed scheme of action. It was all totally irrelevant to the position reached by August 1804, when Richard Wellesley and Arthur Wellesley read it. But viewed in its own terms, and assuming that the clock could have stopped at November 1802 (which Richard Wellesley and Barry Close had taken good care did not happen) it was an analysis worthy of consideration.

Castlereagh gave considerable emphasis to the extent to which Richard Wellesley had weakened the willingness of the Maratha chiefs to accept the concept of the subsidiary alliance by pressure on them to accept it.

'The eagerness with which we appeared to press our connection upon all the leading states in succession might naturally lead them to apprehend that we meant more than we avowed, that our object was ultimately to be masters instead of allies, and that having obtained either possession of or absolute influence over every state except the Marathas with whom we had been in connection, our object was to obtain a similar influence over their councils.'

In comment markedly close to that which Arthur Wellesley had expressed privately the previous year, Castlereagh noted that 'it appears hopeless to attempt to govern the Maratha empire through a feeble and perhaps disaffected Peshwa', asked whether 'the future effect (was) likely to add so much to our prospects in point of security and tranquillity as to counter-balance the immediate inconveniences of war with the several Maratha powers,' and concluded that to talk to the Marathas 'of the advantage of our guarantee for preserving the peace of Hindustan assumes that the genius of their government is industrious and pacific, instead of predatory and warlike.' The letters from the court of Daulat Rao Sindia from Malcolm and Webbe during early 1804, even though they were written in the very different situation created by the campaign of 1803, serve as a striking illustration of the validity of some part of these comments.

The minimalist approach is then outlined. It would have been possible to have left Peshwa Baji Rao without immediate support, and to have offered the contingent availability of British troops normally kept within company frontiers. Alternatively a 'disinterested mediation' of the disputes of the Maratha could have been offered. By placing an army of observation on the frontier, and not becoming involved in what John Malcolm on another occasion had called 'Maratha clan affairs', it would have been possible to have escaped war 'while the Maratha powers wasted their strength.' Castlereagh added that 'events have latterly accelerated our progress so much as in itself... to give an impression with regard to our policy which if heightened may be productive of serious embarrassment... we must now be studious of giving our councils a complexion of moderation and forbearance.' This was to restate the message that Henry Wellesley had sent from London in September 1803, in letters received in January 1804, that the political mandate in London of Richard Wellesley had expired.[11A]

The detailed criticism of the policy culminating in the Treaty of Bassein must have been read in Fort William in August 1804 with scant patience. Had Richard Wellesley wished to do nothing in November 1802 he could have so arranged. Jaswant Rao Holkar and Daulat Rao Sindia could have been left to determine by action or inaction the fate of the Deccan, and indeed of the Maratha confederacy. Peshwa Baji Rao could have spent the balance of his days as a pensioner of the Company, as was to be the fate of Amrit Rao, held by many including Arthur Wellesley, to be a far abler man. The reconstructed system of the country powers which Richard Wellesley had envisaged years before as a junior member of the Board of Control could have been postponed for years. Castlereagh was analysing a fantasy world which could have been created in 1803, but was far removed from the realities of the monsoon season of 1804. Richard Wellesley turned the document over to Arthur Wellesley to prepare a counter-memorandum.

As has been shown earlier, some part of the view of Maratha affairs taken by Castlereagh matched closely that of Arthur Wellesley in 1803. But in mid-1804, as a staff officer for the Governor-General, he now set himself to make the case for the policy which had been selected in November 1802. There is a distinction between the occasional comments in his personal letters, which show his evolving view of Maratha policy from November 1802 to June 1804, and the prepared and coordinated defence brief which Arthur Wellesley wrote at Fort William in September or October 1804. There are contrasts of emphasis, but the purposes of the two sets of documents were different, and it does not follow that either were hypocritical. The terse remarks of private letters have their own validity, as well as their occasional overstatement: the formalised justification included shrewd comment.

Arthur Wellesley began his refutation with a conventional statement of the continuing threat to British India from the French.

> 'the French have never ceased to look to the reestablishment of their power in India, and although they possess no territory themselves on the continent, they have at all times had some influence in the council of the different native powers, and sometimes great power by means of the European adventurers... French influence was powerful... To have omitted to guard against the French would have been ruinous to the Company... the necessity of guarding against French influence was one of the principal causes of the Treaty of Bassein.'

Arthur Wellesley then turned to the more credible contention that once the Company had determined to give to the Nizam of Hyderabad a full defensive guarantee, only a similar arrangement with Peshwa Baji Rao could avert eventual war. 'The policy of a connection with the Marathas ... originated in the necessity of preserving the state of the Nizam in independence, the unjust claims of the Maratha nation on the Nizam, (and) in the certainty that these claims would be asserted in arms.'

Turning to the position in October 1802, Arthur Wellesley then noted the intention of Jaswant Rao Holkar and Amrit Rao to create an alternative Peshwaship, or as he described it, 'the government of the Peshwa administered by the ablest Maratha in the civil affairs of the empire and served by a formidable army commanded by the most enterprising chief.' He argued that the venture failed because Amrit Rao saw that the British government was determined to oppose it and to support Baji Rao, and that for the rightful Peshwa there was a 'large party in the empire attached to his person.' Because of this attachment, the southern *jagirdars* 'were in arms awaiting the arrival of the British troops.' It followed that 'the close of the year 1802 was the most favourable period that had ever occurred, or that would occur, for the admission of Peshwa Baji Rao to the defensive alliance without a war.' Had the opportunity not been taken to replace Peshwa Baji Rao on the throne at Pune 'the most probable result would have been a war with the Pune state under the government of Jaswant Rao Holkar and Amrit Rao, and it is not improbable that this war might have extended to the whole of the Maratha states.' This would have happened, on the scenario that Arthur Wellesley was postulating, because the Maratha armies would have needed to secure sources of plunder, and these could probably have been found only within the existing territory of the Company, or that of the Nizam of Hyderabad.

Arthur Wellesley then reviewed the minimalist policy which Castlereagh had proposed. It would not have been possible 'to frame a concert' with Daulat Rao Sindia and Raghuji Bhonsle against Jaswant Rao Holkar, in part because of the inevitable delays in negotiation, and in part because there would have been 'a counterplot conducted by certainly the ablest Maratha in the empire, I mean Amrit Rao,' with at its centre Raghuji Bhonsle 'the most determined enemy of the British government.'

There were sound points here, stated in a forthright manner. Although the contemporary European evidence for the administrative ability of Amrit Rao appears to be almost entirely the word of Arthur Wellesley, it is certain, as he had said elsewhere, that Baji Rao 'feared and hated his brother.' The combination of Jaswant Rao Holkar and Amrit Rao would indeed have been a potentially formidable one, and the forces from which it would have drawn its military power would assuredly have been tempted to plunder in lands either belonging to the Company or guaranteed by it. The reservation on this whole analysis, certainly when the contrast is drawn with the letters of Arthur Wellesley in 1803, turns on the validity and significance of the support of the southern *jagirdars* and the strength of personal support for Peshwa Baji Rao. On both these points, when set against the evidence of the previous year, Arthur Wellesley was straining to make a case for the Maratha policy of Richard Wellesley.

The paper by Castlereagh was also sent anonymously to John Malcolm. During a time of estrangement from Richard Wellesley after the embassy with Daulat Rao Sindia, following the controversy on Gwalior and Gohad, his comments on Maratha policy remained pertinent. In private he described the document as 'an unprincipled compound of false facts and false reasoning.' In a more formal treatment, he argued that the Treaty of Bassein gave to Peshwa Baji Rao 'a degree of real power and importance as a ruler which he never before possessed' and that it had never been the intention that through it the Company would control the Maratha confederacy; both these points, as had been seen earlier, are directly contradicted in papers created in early 1803. More generally, he accurately noted that the wars which followed from 'the rapacity and violence' of the country powers would lead ultimately to 'the paramount establishment of the influence and power' of the Company throughout the subcontinent.[12]

'I rejoice in the intended movement against Jaswant Rao Holkar' Malcolm had written to Shawe from Visakhapatnam on 30 August, 'that freebooter must fall whenever close pressed. He has no resources and none of his adherents are personally attached to his fortunes, and the moment their plundering is stopped they leave him.' A month later he was markedly more cautious; the reverses of which he was now fully informed were due to an underestimate of the effectiveness of Jaswant Rao Holkar and trust in 'petty Rajput chiefs.' Once Holkar had been defeated, policy should be 'directed to the support of great acknowledged states and to repress instead of reviving obsolete claims of independence and dominion in those who may help to disturb but can never promote the reestablishment of tranquillity in India.' Writing from Ganjam a little later, where he expected to be joined by Arthur Wellesley on a sea journey to Madras, he sent his comments on the anonymous observations, having 'strictly attended to your observations about secrecy. The enclosed is written by a native, an admirable word painter and consequently the safest of all amanuenses.'[13]

Although physically weakened at this time, there was no hesitation in the approach of Richard Wellesley to this crisis in his Maratha policy, as stated to Lake.

'Every hour that shall be left to this plunderer (Jaswant Rao Holkar) will be marked by some calamity. We must expect a general defection of the allies, and even confusion in our own territories, unless we can attack the main force of Jaswant Rao Holkar immediately with decisive effect... In the event of your giving Jaswant Rao Holkar a signal defeat, I leave you at liberty to propose terms of peace to him in the basis of the propositions contained in my instructions to Webbe... but I advise you by no means to treat with him unless he will come into your camp, and disband his forces... We cannot trust him with any power... and if we cannot reduce him, we have lost our ascendancy in India.'

Richard Wellesley authorised Lake to undertake new levies of either regular or irregular infantry and cavalry. Lake determined upon the immediate creation of two further regiments of infantry from existing provincial forces in Oudh.[14]

From the worst of the consequences of the defeat of the detachment commanded by Monson, Gerald Lake in military terms rescued the Maratha policy of Richard Wellesley with energy and tactical flexibility. Marching from Kanpur on 2 September, he was at Agra by the end of the month, and moved forward in pursuit of Jaswant Rao Holkar. Holkar besieged Delhi, and its capture was averted only because of a skilled defence commanded by Ochterlony and Burn. When Jaswant Rao Holkar attempted an irruption into Company territory east of the Jumna, Lake with a cavalry force made some noteworthy forced marches and defeated him at Farrukhabad on 17 November. At the same time Fraser with a predominantly infantry force defeated a major infantry and artillery concentration before the fortress of Deig. In this latter battle, once again, as at Assaye and Laswari, infantry prepared to accept casualties had overcome powerful artillery concentrations.[15]

But in diplomatic terms the achievement of 1803 lay in ruins. The relationship of conciliation with both Daulat Rao Sindia and Raghuji Bhonsle, which Arthur Wellesley and John Malcolm had urged should be created, if ever in prospect, had been lost. Certainly the Maratha rulers were about to act at least for some time on the assumption that the Company had suffered a major defeat. There had been a loss both of prestige and of the aura of victory, what Arthur Wellesley had called 'character.' Over the next six months, the British diplomatic situation was significantly restored, in part as a consequence of the indecision and hesitancy of the Maratha powers. The final journey of Arthur Wellesley in India took place against the background of an aborted attempt to recreate the Maratha confederacy. Once again events can be observed from the standpoint of the Company Resident with Daulat Rao Sindia. Events at the *darbar* of Daulat Rao Sindia had always, as Arthur Wellesley had noted in his initial instructions to John Malcolm in January 1804, been the sport of rival counsellors. Late in August, Sarji Rao Ghatke had returned to the court. He had served as principal minister in 1802, his daughter was one of the wives of Sindia and he could be relied upon to advocate extreme and unscrupulous policies, now aimed by him as vigorously against the Company as they had been directed against Perron in 1802. Earlier in 1804 he had been active in military operations against Arthur Wellesley in the southern Deccan. The politicals needed no warning that the return of Ghatke to the *darbar* was a threat to Company interests, even though in the first instance it was assumed that he had not regained full ministerial authority from the ailing Vithal Pant, with whom Arthur Wellesley and John Malcolm had negotiated in the last stages of the discussions which had led to the Treaty of Sarji Anjangaon.

When Josiah Webbe attempted to protest at the direction in which affairs at the court of Daulat Rao Sindia appeared to be moving, he made little progress. He was assured in early August that Vithal Pant felt 'no jealousy with respect to the stability of his own power and influence.' Later, it seemed that Sarji Rao Ghatke had already been admitted to the councils of Sindia, and was in negotiation with an agent of Jaswant Rao Holkar, who had earlier been reported to have been dismissed. Webbe sought reassurance on the intentions of Daulat Rao Sindia, but this he did not secure. He commented to the *darbar* that the secret dealings of which he had word, when taken together with 'the utter failure of Daulat Rao Sindia to furnish his contingent of troops according to treaty' would seem to justify 'uneasy reflections' on the possible collapse of the alliance. The reply from Vithal Pant, 'delivered under the oppression of much bodily infirmity' attempted to place a favourable construction on each element in the indictment, and countered with a renewed request for Company financial assistance. This alone, it was argued, would make it possible for Daulat Rao Sindia to march to support operations against Jaswant Rao Holkar.[16]

On 8 September Webbe was invited to the *darbar*. In a conference chiefly conducted by Daulat Rao Sindia himself, the Resident received a further request for financial aid; this he countered by asking for his doubts on the stability of the alliance to be set at rest. In particular he sought an explanation for the defection to Jaswant Rao Holkar of the force commanded by Bapoji Sindia which had in early July at first cooperated with the detachment commanded by Monson. Webbe was told that submission to Jaswant Rao Holkar of these forces after the withdrawal of Monson was 'an act of necessity' intended to avert their 'entire destruction.' This version of events Webbe attempted to contest in *darbar* discussion using Monson's own letters, and subsequently set out the British version of the events of the withdrawal, and the complaints of Murray about the lack of support to his detachment. After a prolonged stay in camp near Burhanpur, and without any promise of the financial aid from the Company earlier stated to be needed, Daulat Rao Sindia marched in a direction that suggested a journey to secure plunder rather than cooperation in an attack on Jaswant Rao Holkar.[17]

To Barry Close, Webbe noted that the long illness of the minister had certainly eased the transition to alternative and more extreme counsels. 'We must in the end break. Old Bapu is at the point of death and I hear will certainly go, in which case Ghatke will as certainly step into his place, after having in open contempt of the alliance held avowed intercourse with agents of the enemy.'

Webbe was concerned that he would be seen at Fort William to have been 'precipitate in bringing on a question of the greatest political magnitude' by the protests which he had initiated, at a time when Richard Wellesley had instructed him to attempt negotiation with Jaswant Rao Holkar and Daulat Rao Sindia. Webbe lamented the prospect of his career ending 'just as I supposed, owing to these rascal Marathas, in a way not conformable to my reputation.'[18]

In the first days of October, Webbe reported both the presence in the camp of Daulat Rao Sindia of the agent of Jaswant Rao Holkar, and the advancement to 'supreme direction of the government' of Sarji Rao Ghatke. He felt that there was no intention of giving him satisfaction on the question of the presence of the agent of Jaswant Rao Holkar, and that Daulat Rao Sindia had no serious intention of moving into Malwa. In despair at the direction of policy and his inability to influence it, markedly reminiscent of that of Collins in June and July of the previous year, Webbe doubted whether 'by persisting to agitate these important points I can expect to produce

any change in the plans which Daulat Rao Sindia seems... to have
adopted.' In language close to that of that of Arthur Wellesley he
added that

> 'the Maratha powers seem to have carried on their domestic
> wars less with a view of terminating serious differences between
> independent states than of obtaining trivial advantages over
> their personal rivals. This... may have produced that extreme
> relaxation of the public faith, and that indefinite state of com-
> promise observable in their pacifications, which are unknown
> to the usages of Europe.'

He understood that there were extravagant hopes abroad in the
darbar of 'recovering some of the valuable districts in Hindustan
ceded by the treaty of peace.' There had also been discussion
'calculated to upbraid Daulat Rao Sindia with the diminution of his
power by employing in his councils men of insufficient fortitude.'
Forced contributions had been imposed on some of the officers of
government. Ghatke was not one, Webbe commented, to value the
arts of peace.[19]
It was not only Vithal Pant that was at the point of death; Webbe
was also desperately ill. 'For the last eighteen days I have not been
able to take any sustenance,' he wrote to Shawe on 17 October.

> 'If business of importance had occurred I should not have
> been able to communicate to the Governor-General... If I do not
> find relief from this fever, I must turn my thoughts soon to
> England... Unless General Wellesley returns soon [to the Dec-
> can] we shall be all wrong in this quarter. There is no general
> power, and the communication is too distant for reference.'

Jenkins, the assistant at the Residency, destined soon to be acting
Resident, was sent to the *darbar* to protest that promises about the
direction of march had not been honoured. An elaborate and
evidently contrived response, that the proposed hostilities against
Bhopal were designed to secure revenue that would make hostilities with Jaswant Rao Holkar possible, was given to Jenkins 'in a
spirit of the utmost insincerity and unfriendliness.'[20]
Josiah Webbe died at 4 pm on 9 November 1804. He had in May
assumed responsibility in inauspicious circumstances for one of
the most difficult of the Residences with the country powers, the victim

of the basic miscalculation of Richard Wellesley in 1804, that Daulat Rao Sindia could be, and wished to be, an effective ally of the Company against Jaswant Rao Holkar. He had endured deceit and abuse from the *darbar*, and the discomfort of a moving camp in monsoon conditions. Relations with Daulat Rao Sindia were now in the hands of a young political, appointed to Bombay as a writer in 1798, to whom Richard Wellesley had personally given his degree, at the end of his course at the College of Fort William, in March 1803.

The political setting of the final journey of Arthur Wellesley in India, from Fort William to Seringapatam, was that of a threatened revival of the Maratha confederacy.

NOTES

1. HW-RW 31 Aug 03 A Mss 37415 f. 177 rec 4 Jan 1804.

2. HW-RW 8 Sep 03 rec 29 Feb 04: HW-RW 9 Sep 03 rec 24 Feb 04 A Mss 37415 f. 184.

3. RW-Castlereagh 20, 31 Dec 03 Martin iii 563, 536.

4. AW-RW 31 Jan 04: AW-Malcolm 31 Jan 04: AW-RW 24 Feb 04.

5. HW-RW 8 Jan 04 A Mss 37415 f. 187.

6. RW-Lake 17 Aug 04 RW Notes 17 Aug 04: Martin iv 189: AW-Bentinck, 15 Aug 04: AW-Duncan 20 Aug 04.

7. AW-Malcolm undated, but about 14 Aug 04: 24 Aug 04: 14 Sep 04. The first and third of these letters can be found only in Kaye Malcolm i 288,291. The 'opportunity' of which AW speaks may be the half suggestion of the appointment of a senior officer in RW memorandum 28 Jul 04, sent to Lake, Martin iv 180.

8. AW-Wallace 12 Sep 04: AW-Murray 14 Sep 04.

9. Lumsden-Webbe 11 Jun 04 PRC xi 28: Edmonstone-Webbe 30 June 04 PRC xi 43.

10. Webbe Mem 13 Aug 04: Webbe-AW 13 Aug 04: WP 3/3/93: AW-Webbe 13 Sep 04 Edmonstone-Webbe 19 Sep 04 Add Mss 13603 f.10.

11. Shawe-HW 29 Jul 04 A Mss 13781 f.140.

11A. Castlereagh-RW 4 Mar 04 and attached mem. Martin v (Maratha War Supplement) 302.

12. AW Mem undated: Malcolm Mem 13592 f. 83: Malcolm-AW 27 Sep 04 WP 3/3/72.

13. Malcolm-Shawe 30 Aug, 16,25 Oct 04 A Mss 13747 f. 288, 306, 495: Malcolm-Bentinck 13,20,22 Sep 04 Bentinck Mss Pw Jb 32 p. 104, 106, 110: Malcolm-Sydenham 28 Oct 04 A Mss 13747 f. 308.
14. RW-Lake 11 Sep 04 Martin iv 204: Lake-RW 22 Sep 04 Martin iv 213.
15. Monson-RW 14 Nov 04 Martin iv 233: Lake-RW 17,18 Nov 04 Martin iv 236, 241.
16. Webbe-RW 15,27 Aug 04 PRC xi 69,72.
17. Webbe-RW 9,19 Sep 04 PRC xi 75,80 Webbe-Close 19 Sep 04 PRC xi 83.
18. Webbe-Close 19 Sep 04 PRC xi 83.
19. Webbe-RW 1 Oct 04 PRC xi 84 fuller version A Mss 13740 f. 100.
20. Webbe-Shawe 17 Oct 04 A Mss 13632 f. 269: Webbe-RW 26 Oct 04 PRC xi 98.

10

Justified in not going into the Deccan (November 1804-March 1805)

The last months of the career of Arthur Wellesley in India have been little studied. The Maratha policy of Richard Wellesley was in ruins by mid-August 1804. It was saved by the tactical brilliance of Gerald Lake and the victories of Deig and Farrukhabad. But despite these victories the policy was bankrupt, and Richard Wellesley appreciated this. Although there was continued diplomatic activity, in the sense that the Fort William Secretariat continued to generate directives and plans, these had a decreasing influence on events. The nemesis that Arthur Wellesley had seen in his warning letters to his brother of early 1804 had come. The Marathas had rebelled against the political structure which Richard Wellesley had sought to impose. All three major participants, Jaswant Rao Holkar, Daulat Rao Sindia and Raghuji Bhonsle of Berar, were in different ways seeking to free themselves from the consequences of the year of Company victory in 1803. Further, the Company front of military power, having lost the all-important element in prestige of the appearance of continual victory, was not capable of enforcing a political solution.

In early September 1805, about a year after the events which have just been described, Arthur Wellesley had several meetings with Castlereagh in London. He reported the discussion fully to Richard Wellesley in a letter intended to be read on his arrival in Britain. Castlereagh 'still adhered to the notions which he had formed' when creating his memorandum of April 1804, and wished that there had been 'some middle line between that of leaving the Peshwa entirely at the mercy of the Marathas and taking him out of their hands and into ours.' Arthur Wellesley had responded that 'he was entitled by experience to assert that nothing short of the Treaty of Bassein would have answered at all.' This was the argument he had deployed in his memorandum written as an answer to that of Castlereagh of the year before. In the discussion Castlereagh further insisted, as he had in correspondence of the previous year, that the orders sent to Arthur Wellesley and to Lake in June and July 1803 represented a 'great extension of our political system.' This was the view being pressed upon Castlereagh by the group in the Court of Directors led by Charles Grant, who were to contest the whole policy of Richard Wellesley, including his Maratha policy. In answer, Arthur Wellesley reported to his brother that he had explained 'when you found that your system was not likely to meet with the approbation and support at home which you thought it deserved, and above all when you had experience of the treachery of the Rajputs and others in their conduct towards Monson's detachment... you had determined to narrow the system.'

The possible form of a narrower system can be seen in the letter which Arthur Wellesley had sent to Webbe in September 1804. In this he reported that the Governor-General appeared

'determined to leave the Rajahs of Jodhpur Udaipur Kota and Bundi at the mercy of Daulat Rao Sindia, and to have nothing to say to them. It has been reported that the Jaipur people fired at Monson on his retreat... The Rajahs of Bharatpur and Macheri also are supposed to have corresponded and intrigued with Jaswant Rao Holkar... If any or all of these persons should have broken their treaty with the Company, the Governor General is determined to hand them over to the government of Daulat Rao Sindia in the same situation as they were previous to the late war. He has found out that this barrier is exceedingly dangerous... He appears also to be inclined to give up Gwalior.'[1]

This may well state accurately the longer term intentions of Richard Wellesley towards the Marathas, although in the event they were to be carried through by other hands. Policy in late 1804 was reactive to an inconclusive Maratha attempt to revive the confederacy. This attempted revival was to some degree concerted by the Maratha rulers; the political officers of the Company began to detect it in actions at the *darbars* of Daulat Rao Sindia and Raghuji

Bhonsle, and in the military movements more especially of Mir Khan, still one of the foremost of the guerilla leaders of Jaswant Rao Holkar. The British response could only be restrained, in part because of the scale of Company military effort already deployed against Holkar both in the Deccan and in Hindustan. Arthur Wellesley was to observe and comment on these developments as he returned to Madras and Seringapatam, bringing with him once again the delegated political and military powers which he had exercised in 1803, and which were renewed in November 1804.[2]

After a hesitant acceptance by Raghuji Bhonsle of the view of the contested clause in the peace of Deogaon upon which Fort William had insisted, and against which Arthur Wellesley had argued in vain, the Fort William Secretariat sent markedly firm instructions to the Resident at Nagpur in early September. These noted that Raghuji Bhonsle still appeared to consider as an act of injustice the alienation of the lands of the subsidiary rulers who had completed agreements with the Company. It was impossible, the instructions proceeded, to grant 'that which is offered as a compensation for involuntary injury to the Raja, proceeding from the necessary operation of our public engagements with a third party, to be received as compensation for a deliberate act of injustice on the part of the British government.' There was however a willingness to compensate the Raja for the loss of land revenue he had suffered, once he had acknowledged the Company position on the dispute. These instructions Elphinstone was able to follow in a discussion with the chief minister in early October. The minister gave the fullest assurances that the Raja admitted the justice of the actions of the Company, and stated that the Raja had appeared to act in a different sense solely to please his brother.[3]

Despite this exchange, the Resident had earlier reported to Fort William the interception of correspondence hostile to the Company passing between the Raja of Berar and rulers in his former eastern lands. On this activity Elphinstone was instructed to protest in the strongest terms. Precautions were being taken, the Raja of Berar was to be warned, 'for the eventual purpose of repelling aggression and of punishing treachery'. These measures included the return of Arthur Wellesley to the Deccan 'with orders to march directly to Nagpur in the event of any unquestionable indication which the Raja may manifest of a design to commit acts of hostility against the British government or its allies, or of any proceeding of the Raja in favour of our enemies.' This warning, including the threat that in the event of war the Raja would be 'effectually reduced', was not to be issued until the Resident had heard the results of the first operations of Lake against Jaswant Rao Holkar. Although Elphinstone had begun to be suspicious of the intentions of Raghuji Bhonsle he deferred acting on these instructions, an action for which he was subsequently reproved from Calcutta. Elphinstone was also given contingent instructions on the method of payment of the compensation to Raghuji Bhonsle for his losses in his eastern territories. He was to arrange for the chief minister to receive secretly an allowance from the Company. Elphinstone had discretion to postpone the implementation of these later instructions if appearances at the *darbar* were hostile. This discretion he exercised, when the instructions reached him in mid-November.[4]

Earlier in October 1804, an agent from Mir Khan, at this time operating independently from Jaswant Rao Holkar south of Bundelkhand, arrived at the *darbar* of Raghuji Bhonsle. The British Resident understood from secret sources that he was instructed to seek Raghuji Bhonsle's full cooperation with Jaswant Rao Holkar, or failing that a financial contribution, or at a last resort to request that Raghuji Bhonsle should embarrass the Company by demanding the restoration of the territory ceded to the Nizam of Hyderabad at the peace settlement. Elphinstone warned the Raja against 'the false statements and deceitful acts' of the agents of Jaswant Rao Holkar. An agent from Daulat Rao Sindia also arrived, and shortly afterwards a minister of the Raja moved with a reinforcement to take command of his army some way north of Nagpur.

Elphinstone challenged Raghuji Bhonsle on these military movements and was told that land near Sagaur was threatened by Mir Khan and that the actions taken were defensive. This version of events he doubted. He believed that the supposed threat was a misrepresentation to enable the Raja to assemble his forces near those of Mir Khan and Daulat Rao Sindia. The Raja attempted to support his contention by showing Elphinstone the letters he had received from Mir Khan. These were found 'to contain expressions calculated to excite the Raja's hopes and revive his ambition.' They also contained 'an invitation in plain terms to unite and chastise the enemy.' The view of the correspondence which the Resident had reached was disputed by the *darbar* and Elphinstone felt bound 'again to warn the Raja of the danger of confederating against the British power'. He reported to Barry Close at Pune that he found all the explanations given by Raghuji Bhonsle lacking in credibility, and that he in part believed rumours that a combination of Daulat Rao Sindia, Mir Khan and Raghuji Bhonsle was being created with the intention of an attack on the lands of the Nizam of Hyderabad. He added that 'it is difficult to believe that these chiefs could take a step so full of perfidy and injustice and involving so certain a prospect of the speedy and entire destruction of their states, but I consider my intelligence as sufficiently corroborated by the movements of the Maratha troops.'

He gave this information also to the commander of the Company detachment which had in early October 1804 captured Chandor, the last stronghold of Jaswant Rao Holkar in the Deccan.[5]

Granted on 23 November an audience twenty miles from Nagpur, where the Raja had been assembling his forces, Elphinstone heard again the alleged justification for the assembly of troops. To this he responded both with scepticism since 'military preparation had long preceded any apprehension of Mir Khan's invasion', and with enquiry about the interpretation which the Raja placed on the movements of Daulat Rao Sindia. This latter point Raghuji Bhonsle dealt with by denial of any information. Elphinstone indicated that the conduct of the Raja gave reason 'to doubt the purity of his designs' and that he therefore could not give the detail of the proposition on compensation for the alienated provinces which he had received. The next few days brought news of attacks by the *pindaris* of Mir Khan on the northern territories of Raghuji Bhonsle, and also of the decision of Raghuji Bhonsle to return to Nagpur from the assembly point of his forces.

While Arthur Wellesley was travelling with John Malcolm by sea to Madras, at the court of Daulat Rao Sindia, Richard Jenkins had taken up the task of Josiah Webbe as acting Resident. He had to attempt by argument, with nothing but contingent financial aid as an inducement, to bring the *darbar* back either from covert alliance with Jaswant Rao Holkar, or at the least from total inaction in its supposed alliance with the Company against him. The failure was total. On 10 November Jenkins sent to Fort William secret intelligence of the march of the forces of Daulat Rao Sindia into the territory of the Raja of Berar. From this movement, and other indicators, Jenkins deduced that Ghatke had 'actually invited Mir

Khan to unite with the Maharajah in an invasion of Bundelkhand.'
He also assumed that the objective of the present march of Daulat
Rao Sindia was this union, as were the orders sent to subsidiary
rulers and the leaders of groups of *pindaris* to move to Sagaur, the
proposed point of assembly. Jenkins was in camp some distance
from Daulat Rao Sindia, since it had been impossible to move the
Resident's camp frequently in the last days of the illness of Webbe.
Jenkins would have preferred not to cross the Narbada until it had
been possible to question the *darbar* on the purpose of the
proposed march. The direction of movement appeared to be aimed
at union with Mir Khan, an 'avowed partisan of Jaswant Rao Holkar.'
Jenkins planned to stress in *darbar* discussion the 'absurdity and
danger of the plan' which he believed Daulat Rao Sindia to have in
mind. He proposed also to warn him that the Company 'would not
fail to adopt the most decisive measures to defeat his purposes, if
hostile, and effect the destruction of all our foes.' He intended to
regard the crossing of the Narbada as confirmation of the intention
of Daulat Rao Sindia to join Mir Khan.[6]

Jenkins joined the camp of Daulat Rao Sindia, and received a
visit of condolence on the death of Webbe. In a note to the *darbar*
he expressed surprise that the march had taken Sindia through the
territory of the Raja of Berar, that no discussion had taken place
with him on the content of any negotiations with Raghuji Bhonsle,
a requirement of the subsidiary treaty of February, and added that
the direction of the march 'must appear to all the world to be
unconnected with any object of the war [with Jaswant Rao Holkar]
or of the alliance [against him].' He wished to explain to the *darbar*
what he anticipated would be the reaction of Richard Wellesley
rather than having 'any hope of drawing a satisfactory explanation
of the proceedings.' The *darbar* dealt with the request by evasion.
In a message sent to the Resident late on 19 November, Daulat Rao
Sindia attempted to assure Jenkins of his intention to adhere to the
engagements with the Company. Jenkins hoped soon 'to impress
upon the mind of the Maharajah the extreme absurdity of endeavouring to impose ... trivial excuses.'[7]

A few days later Jenkins reported that the attempt to extort
money from members of the court initiated by Ghatke had failed,
that financial difficulties had made it necessary to reduce the
strength of his infantry battalions, and there was mutiny in the
silledar horse. It seemed probable that much of the army of Daulat

Rao Sindia would desert. At the end of November, in a *darbar* discussion with Daulat Rao Sindia, Jenkins outlined the progress of the Company moves against Jaswant Rao Holkar. In response to enquiry, Sindia 'directly denied' any communication with Raghuji Bhonsle and defended the direction of his march as necessary to secure forage. Jenkins decided not to refer to his suspicions of direct contact between Sindia and Mir Khan, since he still hoped that Sindia would be deterred from effective cooperation with Holkar. He did not respond to requests for financial aid, which took the form of seeking an advance of the pension payments due in January.[8]

Fresh instructions from Fort William, prepared just before Arthur Wellesley had left Calcutta at the beginning of November, now reached Jenkins. These showed it was now appreciated that Daulat Rao Sindia was not able effectively to assist the Company against Jaswant Rao Holkar. Once Sindia had reached Ujjain, the objective to which Webbe had for so long sought to direct him, and once Sarji Rao Ghatke had been dismissed from office, rent for the territories of Dholepur Bari and Rajakerrah, which was due to Sindia, could be paid. A minister of the *darbar* potentially friendly to improved relations with the Company should be made the recipient of this offer. While Daulat Rao Sindia was still encamped on the south bank of the Narbada and still sixty miles from Sagaur, Jenkins set himself to initiate this negotiation. He warned that movement towards an attack on Company territory could lead to the destruction of Daulat Rao Sindia and the ruin of his state. Jenkins himself made the offer of financial aid which had been authorised. The offer was made contingent on the dismissal of Ghatke.[9]

Four or five marches from Sagaur, Daulat Rao Sindia attempted to levy contribution from a small fort, Deoli. He seemed also about to attempt to coerce the Nawab of Bhopal. The Nawab of Bhopal sent an agent to Jenkins to seek Company support, and Sindia protested at this on the grounds that Bhopal was a subordinate ruler. The charges and counter-charges were repeated at a full *darbar* on 14 December, Jenkins commenting that the recent moves 'to this quarter were become most notorious, and that it was by the clemency only of the British government that the destruction of this state did not follow the meditated treachery which it had presumed to entertain.' To a request for financial aid he replied that this could only follow the removal of Ghatke, and the dismissal of the agent of Jaswant Rao Holkar. Jenkins noted that much of the discussion was conducted by Daulat Rao Sindia 'from whose serious attention to every subject which came under discussion, and from the general tenor of the conference, I am led to indulge very favourable expectations of the result.[10]

These expectations were not to be realised. When Jenkins renewed his requests for information on the proposed direction of march of Daulat Rao Sindia and on the continued service of Ghatke as a minister, he received in reply an 'absurd digression' on Company policy earlier in the year, an improbable assurance that the earlier intention to march to Sagaur had been abandoned, and the contention that the revenues of Dholepur Bari and Rajakerrah belonged to Daulat Rao Sindia as of right. Jenkins gave a time limit to his request that Ghatke should be dismissed; if after two days this matter had not been resolved, he would not act on the instructions from Fort William on financial aid. This approach he considered was necessary because of 'the temporising system of Maratha policy, and to confound the presumptuous idea which Ghatke would insinuate into the Maharajah's mind, of our dependence upon their exertions to terminate the war.' The army of Daulat Rao Sindia was now joined by 15,000 *pindaris*, who were plundering lands of Peshwa Baji Rao in the area; these were very probably the *pindaris* who had been driven from the camp of Daulat Rao Sindia in January 1804. Jenkins received renewed promises of the imminent dismissal of Ghatke, and again refused to make 'the smallest advance of money to this state.' In the last days of 1804, he determined that 'an unequivocal spirit of hostility' seemed to indicate 'a decided intention on the part of Daulat Rao Sindia to commence hostilities.' He resolved that he would shortly leave the camp of Daulat Rao Sindia, and so informed Arthur Wellesley.[11]

Arthur Wellesley and John Malcolm had reached Seringapatam from Fort St. George, Madras at the end of November. On 5 December they received the news that they had been fearing and half expecting, that of the death of Josiah Webbe on 9 November. Arthur Wellesley at once urged the need for arrangements to be made that would lead to a speedy replacement at the court of Daulat Rao Sindia. The reality of the crisis of representation was accepted at Fort William, although handled in a different way from that which Arthur Wellesley had recommended. Contingent military and political powers were given to Barry Close, who was instructed to move from Pune to the *darbar* of Daulat Rao Sindia. Captain Thomas Sydenham was appointed as acting Resident at Pune.

Arthur Wellesley was weakened by an attack of fever or ague. As he received in Seringapatam the first of the letters from Jenkins written after the death of Webbe, he remained convinced that Daulat Rao Sindia still detested Jaswant Rao Holkar, and that there was, therefore little danger of the creation of a renewed Maratha confederacy. As Arthur Wellesley saw it, at a time of great distress Ghatke had proposed to Sindia 'the old Maratha game, as a method of relief'. But news of the victories in Hindustan would 'bring all right again in that quarter, and possibly Sarji Rao Ghatke will be blown from a gun'. But, as he commented to Shawe at Fort William, even if temporarily, policy at the *darbar* of Daulat Rao Sindia had undergone a reversal, which seemed inexplicable on the analysis of the Company observers of the best interests of Sindia.

> 'Daulat Rao Sindia, whose enmity to Holkar was become proverbial, who allied himself with the Company for the express purpose of defending himself against, and eventually destroying Holkar, who rejoiced when he found that the war was determined on and [was] inevitable ... and who has everything to hope for from its successful conclusion which the smallest exertion on his part would ensure ... joins his enemy for the purpose of destroying his friend and ally.'

In these changed circumstances, and starting from the premise that 'there can be no doubt that Daulat Rao Sindia has already broken the treaty of defensive alliance,' Arthur Wellesley commented that if Jenkins was correct in assuming that Daulat Rao Sindia had allied with Mir Khan, there was no option open to the Company but to destroy Sindia by capturing Malwa. But, wrongly, Arthur Wellesley doubted whether Sindia would act as if the Maratha confederacy could be formed afresh. If he did not do so, the Company had freedom to plan its future actions and 'the present is of all others the worst to attempt the conquest of Malwa... We have neither troops, money, civil servants, magazines nor any one object which would be necessary... There are other reasons also for delaying to attempt it, referable to the state of affairs in England.' He proposed that Richard Wellesley should call upon Daulat Rao Sindia to seize Jaswant Rao Holkar. Should Sindia refuse to do this, he should be left to himself. There was a reasonable prospect that 'the English party' at the *darbar* of Daulat Rao Sindia would, at a later time, revive.[12]

In early December a fresh flurry of concern about the activities of Raghuji Bhonsle at Nagpur followed from the report of an attack at the frontier with the lands of the Nizam of Hyderabad near Manickdurg. At first it seemed that the forces of the Raja had been clearly implicated, and Elphinstone visited the *darbar* to discuss both 'former suspicious movements' and also this fresh 'open act of perfidy'. The Resident had first been told of this attack by the chief minister of the Raja, who had been at pains to clear the Raja from any suspicion of involvement by the argument that the attack had been the work of Vincaji Bhonsle, the brother of the Raja, the device of supposed surrogate aggression which had been used before. An attempt to argue that the attack had been the work not of troops answerable to the brother of the Raja but of 'some horse out of employ' was brushed aside by Elphinstone. The forces of the Company would continue to move towards Nagpur, and the Raja should accept responsibility for the actions of his brother; 'if he could not control him he should call in the English army for that purpose'. Elphinstone agreed to await both a promised report on the reported plundering of the territory of the Nizam, and also the reaction of Richard Wellesley, but warned that he could not undertake that the Governor-General would 'overlook any insult or injury which should prove to have originated with the Raja.'[13]

In a meeting with the Raja on 6 December, Elphinstone repeated his argument that the Raja could not evade responsibility, the incursion into Hyderabad territory seemed to have been organised by him. 'The English army must advance to punish this gross violation of faith' and the Resident must ask for his passports. The only alternative was a public indication of displeasure at the actions of Vincaji Bhonsle and the seizure of his *jagir*. These harsh terms Raghuji Bhonsle eventually accepted, and Elphinstone dictated the detailed deployment of the forces of the Raja. When the orders were shown to the Resident in an unclear form, he protested afresh.

'If no satisfactory answer to my note arrives', Elphinstone wrote to Richard Wellesley on 7 December,

> 'the party (on the Hyderabad border) will continue its devastation, and the main army will probably follow as soon as

possible. If the Raja attempts to deceive me by further promises, he will not be able to detain me longer than tomorrow without making some show of executing the conditions. If he actually discharges some of his troops and gives out that he intends to disband his new levies, such conduct cannot but have the effect of shaking the confidence of Daulat Rao Sindia and of Mir Khan in him. As Daulat Rao Sindia appears... to be inclined to return to his duty, this step of the Bhonsle's... cannot fail to determine him. Even if the Raja should at present be sincere, the approach of the army of the Deccan before he has thrown off the mask will probably decide him to submit. At least it will prevent his plundering.'

Elphinstone had taken his authority as Resident to the limit, and in the event the gamble paid, but matters stayed in the balance for several days. The deployment on which he had insisted was set in hand, and the *jagir* of the brother of the Raja confiscated. The minister even raised the issue of the provision of a Company subsidiary force, although he had initiated this matter only on his own authority. Elphinstone agreed to put to Richard Wellesley the proposition of the entry of Nagpur into the subsidiary alliance system once the army of the Raja was dispersed into small units. Although it was clear that the Raja was greatly alarmed at the prospect of war with the Company, it seemed possible that 'his brother and some others of his family are still for war.' The Resident wrote setting out the route by which he would attempt to join the Company army if hostilities broke out.

At this point Amrit Rao, who after a stay at Surat had elected to move to Benares and enjoy the very adequate pension of Rs. 7 lakhs which Arthur Wellesley had arranged for him in 1803, and which followed from the partial settlement of the lands of Peshwa Baji Rao earlier in 1804, arrived at Amrauti, and so was approaching Nagpur and the area of the possible junction of the Maratha armies. Amrit Rao wrote to Elphinstone to say that he was withdrawing to Elichpur and planned to send an agent. Elphinstone begged Amrit Rao to withdraw, even as far as Ahmednagar; this Amrit Rao refused to consider, although he was prepared to retreat towards the Company army. Elphinstone at first feared that the reported demobilisation of the forces of Raghuji Bhonsle was no more than a cover to gain time until Amrit Rao could arrive. As Resident he had retained his threat to leave from day to day, but on 12 December agreed to postpone a possible departure for four days. As that time limit expired he began 'to be confident that the Raja will disarm and submit to such conditions as may be thought necessary for punishing his treachery and limiting his future powers of mischief.'[15]

Arthur Wellesley, as the correspondence reporting these matters reached him at Seringapatam, took a markedly less alarmist view of the meaning of the actions of Raghuji Bhonsle at Nagpur than Elphinstone had done. He felt confident that the Raja had been threatened by Mir Khan with devastation of his territories if he was unwilling to attack the Company. He also believed that Amrit Rao had resolved never again to take an active part in Maratha politics. Arthur Wellesley now heard of the interview in which the Resident had reminded Raghuji Bhonsle that he was 'certain of immediate destruction' if he joined any confederacy. At this *darbar* discussion, Elphinstone had attempted to reassure Raghuji Bhonsle that his state was in no danger; a large Company force was 'within a fortnight's march of Elichpur.' The Raja should not despair of the support of the Company, provided his conduct continued to be such as would satisfy the Governor-General. Elphinstone had stressed the danger to which Raghuji Bhonsle would expose himself if he joined Jaswant Rao Holkar.

'Jaswant Rao Holkar had originally been a common horseman and was accustomed from the first to lead a life of danger and fatigue, and it was a great situation for him to be at the head of a band of plunderers, but the Raja had from his youth been a prince, and could not now begin to live like a robber.'

Having read these reports, Arthur Wellesley stated that he felt 'perfectly satisfied that the intentions of the Raja of Berar are pacific... It is very possible that he may have opened a negotiation with Jaswant Rao Holkar or with Mir Khan, the object of which may have been hostility towards the British government, but the design to attack us, if it ever existed, has certainly been relinquished.' Arthur Wellesley directed that authority should be given to the commander of the British detachment in Berar to move to the assistance of the Raja of Berar. This force should only be called forward by the Resident of Nagpur if the danger was 'great and immediate'. It could not be moved very far north of Nagpur without endangering the security of the lands of the Nizam of Hyderabad.[16]

The anxiety of Elphinstone as Resident at Nagpur in early December, and the report of the attack of forces of Raghuji Bhonsle on the lands of the Nizam of Hyderabad, had led the Resident at Hyderabad to seek authority to increase the size of the Company force there. To this appeal the Calcutta Secretariat had responded with orders that would have moved two units, one from the ceded districts north of Mysore, to Hyderabad. Arthur Wellesley could see that a mistake in the deployment of the limited forces available in the peninsula had been made, and set himself to correct this. In doing so he was anticipating accurately revised instructions from Calcutta which were received later. He gave a full explanation to Bentinck, the Governor at Madras, and also to James Kirkpatrick, the Resident at Hyderabad.[17]

There had been evident if understandable over-reaction, Arthur Wellesley explained. The supposed attack on the territory of the Nizam of Hyderabad had never taken place, although the brother of the Raja of Nagpur had assembled troops when not authorised to do so, and Arthur Wellesley continued to assume that the intentions of Daulat Rao Sindia were not hostile. It was not appropriate to send forward to Hyderabad cavalry from the ceded districts. These should be retained as a reserve force on the borders of Company territory.

Within a few days Arthur Wellesley knew of the terms in which the Resident at Hyderabad had sought reinforcement, and stated fully to him the reasons why in his view it was not required. The circumstances at the two Maratha courts were such that in his judgement Hyderabad was in no danger, and the difficulties of the Nizam flowed from his lack of forces of his own; 'this evil is permanent, and requires something more than a temporary remedy, such as the measure of increasing the British corps stationed at Hyderabad.' It had earlier been assumed that British interests at the court of Hyderabad required the presence of Company force, but two crises in that relationship, that culminating in the peaceful accession of the 'young Nizam' in August 1803, and that of the acceptance by the Nizam of Mir Alam as chief minister, had both taken place 'at times when the British detachment has been weakest.' Reinforcement of Hyderabad by British troops could not be borne either by the military establishment of the Company or the finances of the Nizam. The appropriate 'amendment of the system' which Arthur Wellesley had pressed on the Resident at Hyderabad before, would be for the Nizam 'to support a portion at least of those troops which have always served his father's government.' It seemed likely that the use of pressure from the Resident to secure the appointment of Mir Alam as chief minister had weakened the position of the minister and the influence of the Company.

Over the previous fifteen months, James Kirkpatrick as Resident had attempted to interest the *darbar* of the Nizam on the need, frequently the subject of suggestions made by Arthur Wellesley, to recreate the forces of the Nizam. Kirkpatrick remained concerned at the declining influence of the Company at the *darbar* of the Nizam; he had found that his representations had recently been received with 'apparently studied inattention', and that this could be corrected only 'by the proposed measure of reinforcement'. While he would have preferred to operate a 'mild and just system' he doubted whether 'any essential object of reform involving expense or material sacrifices will be effected in the lifetime of the present ruler save from fear and apprehension.' The Nizam had agreed to the elevation of Mir Alam while the Company influence was strong and 'supported by the splendour of our recent martial achievements and by the solid benefits accruing from the advantageous pacifications ... with the subdued Maratha chieftains.' Kirkpatrick continued to feel the need for the 'immediate presence of the grand type of power' when dealing with 'statesmen of so gross a texture as most Asiatic politicians'. It would be possible to raise an adequate force of *silledar* horse on the Berar revenue alone, and any further addition of Company force at the capital could be compensated by additional cession of territory by the Nizam. Kirkpatrick believed that the views of the *darbar* had recently changed and conciliation was now being attempted.[18]

It was time for Arthur Wellesley again to consider his own future. When he had sought in April 1804 from Lake as Commander-in-Chief authority to return to England, he had explained his concern at his career, and noted that there seemed little to do of military note in the Deccan. After the journey to Fort William, from which he had moved back to Mysore with full political and military authority, the degree of defeat inflicted on Jaswant Rao Holkar in Hindustan, and an assessment of the extent to which Raghuji Bhonsle and Daulat Rao Sindia were in earnest in their attempt to

revive the confederacy, brought Arthur Wellesley again to the view
that he could perhaps best serve both his own requirements, and
those of Richard Wellesley, by leaving India. He commented to
Shawe on 19 December, 'I rather think the state of affairs at present
to be such that the Governor-General would prefer that I should
return to England to my going into the Deccan. However, I have
not decided yet.'

But a fortnight later the grounds for taking the decision to leave
for England seemed clearer. Arthur Wellesley had raised with
Richard Wellesley before leaving Calcutta the possibility that the
defeat of Jaswant Rao Holkar might make it unnecessary for him to
travel to the Deccan; and this the Governor-General had accepted.
With this in mind Arthur Wellesley had delayed his departure for
the Deccan from Mysore after recovery from the attack of fever. In
the first days of January 1805 he concluded that 'the object in view
in sending me into the Deccan' had now been secured by other
means, that is the victories achieved by Fraser and Lake. The need
for a cavalry concentration in Malwa, which would have required
a major military movement northwards, crossing both the Tapti
and Narbada, which Arthur Wellesley would have been prepared
to command himself, had gone. The decision not to move northwards into the Deccan, as the start of a more extended military
operation, was one that he had nonetheless taken with 'a considerable degree of doubt and hesitation'.

'I know that all classes of the people look up to me and it will
be difficult for another officer to take my place. I also know that
my presence... would be useful in the settlement of many
points... But these circumstances are not momentary ... very
possibly the same state of affairs which now renders my presence
in the Deccan desirable will exist for the next seven years... I
conceive that I am justified in not going into the Deccan.'

There remained the wider question of the journey to England.
'The Kings's Ministers have as little claim on me as the Court of
Directors.' He therefore would feel justified in giving up his command as a King's officer in India. Perhaps there were real advantages to the collective Wellesley concerns that would flow from his
own prompt return to England, it being now clear that the delayed
total defeat of Jaswant Rao Holkar meant that there could be no

question of Richard Wellesley returning in February 1805, as had at one time been planned and had earlier seemed possible.

'I have considered whether in the situation of affairs in India at present, my arrival in England is not a desirable object. Is it not necessary to take some steps to explain the causes of the late increase of the military establishments, and to endeavour to explode some erroneous notions which have been entertained and circulated on this subject. Are there not a variety of subjects in discussion relating to this country, upon which some verbal explanation is absolutely necessary. I conceive therefore that in determining not to go into the Deccan, and to sail by the first opportunity for England, I consult the public interest not less than I do my own private convenience and wishes.'

Arthur Wellesley was still not taking the decision, and was leaving the issue in the hands of his brother, significantly adding to Shawe that while he was prepared either to sail for England or move northwards, he would not be drawn into the Deccan by 'mere suspicions and unfounded surmises.'[19]

At the end of January 1805, Richard Wellesley and the Fort William Secretariat reached the same view as had Arthur Wellesley on the ending of the requirement for an advanced deployment on the Deccan plateau. It was possible markedly to relax the defensive stance which had been adopted on the presumption of hostile intent by both Daulat Rao Sindia and Raghuji Bhonsle. A statement of general policy prepared at this time, intended for the Resident at Delhi but circulated to all Residents, had within it elements that were strangely moderated or even hypocritical. It was certainly markedly different from the actions of early 1804, and can perhaps best be seen as the rationalisation of the 'narrower system' which Arthur Wellesley had seen as following the defeats of August 1804. The statement set against 'the justice and equity of our principles of action' the contrast with 'the vague and desultory policy of the native powers' in which 'a confidence of their own security in the steady observance of justice and good faith' by the Company could be expected to be but 'slowly inculcated in barbarous and lawless minds'. The principal native states were seen as having understood the validity of the system, although this understanding was not necessarily shared by 'the rude and predatory tribes situated within the vicinity of our new frontier.'[20]

Richard Wellesley was now willing to be convinced that Daulat Rao Sindia and Raghuji Bhonsle, although earlier misled by exaggerated reports of the progress of Jaswant Rao Holkar, had been compelled by events 'to return to a proper sense of their obligations towards the British government.' It remained important to persuade Daulat Rao Sindia to return to Ujjain, and establish his government in Malwa, but he need not be compelled to adopt these arrangements. It was therefore possible to withdraw the force, currently commanded by Colonel Haliburton, which had been advancing eastwards along the Purna valley with the purpose of strengthening the hand of the Resident at Nagpur and contingently protecting Raghuji Bhonsle from Mir Khan or even from Daulat Rao Sindia. The elements in this force which were to be regarded as the subsidiary forces of the Peshwa and of the Nizam of Hyderabad should be withdrawn and deployed in the Godavari valley. It was now seen, as Arthur Wellesley had anticipated, as no longer necessary for him to move into the Deccan. The timing of the relinquishment of the special political and military powers granted to him in November was left as a decision for Arthur Wellesley.[21]

Shawe suggested to Arthur Wellesley that 'the main object of your intended mission to the Deccan was to prevent the renewal of war with Daulat Rao Sindia and the Raja of Berar, or if that misfortune could not be averted to assume the general conduct of the military operations in the Deccan against those chieftains and against Jaswant Rao Holkar.' The changed attitude of both *darbars,* as it then appeared at Calcutta, had removed the principal object of the proposed services of Arthur Wellesley, and there was no reason why Arthur Wellesley should not leave India. It was accepted that he would be able to give valuable information if he reached England ahead of Richard Wellesley. This seemed increasingly probable, since the Governor-General would not be able to leave Calcutta while the war with Jaswant Rao Holkar was in 'a doubtful or unfinished state.' There seemed to be every prospect of opposition in London to the Maratha policy; word had now arrived that Castlereagh had spoken in the House of Commons in July 1804 in terms which echoed his memorandum of March to which Arthur Wellesley had prepared a reply when in Calcutta.[22]

'I now feel an anxiety only about my departure for England, the extent of which I cannot describe,' Arthur Wellesley wrote to Shawe on 3 February, before this revised deployment was known to him.

'I have no confidence in my own judgement in any case in which my own wishes are involved ... I know that my presence in England would be useful; and I am certainly very anxious to go there... The time presses for a decision. If I do not go in the first fleet that sails from Madras I shall lose the season.' He was about to place a deposit on a passage.[23]

Far away to the north the hesitations of the potential revived Maratha confederacy continued. As the new year opened, Jenkins as acting Resident with Daulat Rao Sindia continued to feel that the actions of the *darbar* under the influence of Sarji Rao Ghatke left no prospect of putting directly to Sindia the contention that there was danger in blatant disregard of the subsidiary treaty with the Company and of the supposed alliance against Jaswant Rao Holkar. The army of Sindia had advanced northeast of Saugar and levied a contribution upon the Raja of Kotahghur on the borders of Bundelkhand. Jenkins was waiting 'for an opportunity to quit the camp with safety to our small party.' Once he had stated this intention to the *darbar*, attempts were made to delay this from day to day by specious promises, mainly on the proposed direction of the march, and on the reasons for this. Jenkins decided not to leave the camp, until instructions arrived from Arthur Wellesley 'unless this government should act in such a manner as to render my departure indispensably necessary.'[24]

Altercation on the intended line of march continued, Jenkins challenging the agent sent to him with the inconsistency of the complaints of lack of financial resources and the assembling of forces. It was reported that the army of Sindia was about to move northwards towards Narwar. Jenkins reported that the intentions of Ghatke seemed 'of the most hostile nature' and as 'destined to be carried into execution'. A union of the forces of Mir Khan and Ambaji Inglia (re-entering the Maratha confederacy after his attempted defection to the position of Company ally in December 1803) seemed to be in prospect. Jenkins remained firm in his intention to make the provision of financial aid to Daulat Rao Sindia, the need for which was as usual stated to be desperate, totally conditional on the dismissal of Sarji Rao Ghatke. He now doubted whether Sindia had any intention either of dismissing Ghatke, or of returning to Ujjain, to which he had repeatedly been urged. New levies were being raised, and it was reported that *pindaris* would be sent south to attack the territory of Raghuji

Bhonsle and the Nizam of Hyderabad. There was a direct attack on the Residency, which the Resident saw as possibly instigated by Ghatke, whose object was 'to involve his master in a war as the only means to preserve his present power.' An attempt to force a reply from Sindia led to a request to wait for eight days until consultations with Ambaji Inglia should prove possible: Jenkins countered this by saying that he could not await the actions of 'a traitor to both governments' and restated his intention to leave. On 10 January Jenkins struck camp and assembled his baggage, and then agreed to stay on a promise from Sindia of a march to Ujjain six days later.[25]

The invitation to Ambaji Inglia was extended, despite the comments of Jenkins, who now expected (correctly in the long term) that his influence would displace that of Sarji Rao Ghatke. The Resident reported his intention to leave the camp of Daulat Rao Sindia, where it was evident that the breakdown of trust was now complete. The court of Daulat Rao Sindia arranged for the total collapse of relations to be symbolised by a direct *pindari* attack on the Residency, which wounded some of its members and deprived all of them of shelter. This attack took place while the Resident was again attempting to negotiate in the *darbar* on the proposed movements of Daulat Rao Sindia.[26]

As Arthur Wellesley withdrew from active participation in the Maratha policy of his brother, the relations of the major Maratha rulers and the Company were in a strange condition of 'neither peace nor war.' In early February, Barry Close held cordial discussions with the Raja of Berar in Nagpur, and Elphinstone was able to arrange the secret pensioning by the Company of his key ministers, noting that word of the attack on the Residency with Daulat Rao Sindia had been without effect. At the same time Arthur Wellesley moved from Seringapatam to Madras, and set himself to carry into effect the deployment requested by the Governor-General in late January. He recommended a position for the subsidiary force with the Peshwa, perhaps as far forward as Toka, where he had crossed the Godavari after the capture of Ahmednagar, and for that with the Nizam a stationing further down the Godavari. He had on the evening of 16 February reached his final decision to leave for England, and had with difficulty reconciled the newly arrived Commander-in-Chief, Madras to his imminent departure. News of his knighthood had arrived. He formally resigned both his military and political appointments, recommending to his brother that if necessary Barry Close should be appointed to the same combined position.[27]

Arthur Wellesley was at the point of leaving Madras when he received the letters from the Residency with Daulat Rao Sindia reporting the attack of 25 January. In a final vigorous statement sent both to Barry Close and to Fort William, he commented on the strange impasse in his brother's policy.

'My private opinion has always been that Mr Jenkins was in too great a hurry with Daulat Rao Sindia. Before he received the accounts of our successes over Holkar, he began by pushing him to an extremity, and he threatened to quit his camp unless a certain line of conduct should be adopted. This line of conduct was not adopted, and yet Mr Jenkins stayed, and the only effect of his threats was to give to Daulat Rao Sindia and to Ghatke an opinion of his weakness and indecision. The truth is that Mr Jenkins had no confidence in the propriety of the measures he was adopting, and the consequence was that he changed his intention daily, and was glad to lay hold of any excuse which the promises of Daulat Rao Sindia afforded him to stay in his camp.'

Daulat Rao Sindia Arthur Wellesley declared to be 'very weak in intellect' but overawed by Sarji Rao Ghatke. Wrongly attributing to the Marathas his own view of the total strategic picture, Arthur Wellesley contended that their best policy would have been a rapid attack on Company territory in Bundelkhand. This they had not attempted, partly because Ghatke's objectives were limited to the command of 'an army of plunderers which will give him the power over Daulat Rao Sindia.' Given the need in the changed conditions 'to intervene with a strong hand to save Mr Jenkins and our honour' he suggested a demand to Sindia for the punishment of Ghatke sent either by Richard Wellesley or by Close, followed by deployment of a Company force from Bundelkhand, with the purpose either of securing the safety of Jenkins or of protecting Sindia from Ghatke. Anticipating the suggestion that he should postpone his own departure to England, he noted that he could not reach the centre of possible operations in the Deccan until after the time for moving troops into cantonments prior to the monsoon. 'I wish that affairs were in a more settled state, but I do not conceive that my presence will make any alteration in them.'[28]

Arthur Wellesley boarded HMS Trident on 9 March. Shortly after the vessel sailed, a letter addressed to him by the Governor-General on 24 February arrived in Madras. It begged Arthur Wellesley to stay in India. Arthur Wellesley was urged again to travel to Fort William, this time in the company of John Malcolm. The letter added that Richard Wellesley had 'not entirely relinquished his own intention of embarking this month for England.' Within a few days, Richard Wellesley had requested John Malcolm to travel to Calcutta, warning him to be prepared to be 'employed in a second mission to the *darbar* of Daulat Rao Sindia.' Malcolm was also told that the Governor-General regretted the departure of his brother. Once again able to comment freely on events in his private letters, John Malcolm noted that had Arthur Wellesley stayed as Commander-in-Chief, Bombay, the post to which by rumour at least he had been contingently appointed, but which he had indicated that he would not accept, Malwa could readily have been seized. There were however, as Malcolm saw it, advantages in the outcome, the early departure of Arthur Wellesley for England. He could 'do more good than all others who have gone home both because he has more information, and because his manners and character will enable him to mix with every class of man that it is necessary to reclaim from error.' [29]

More than manners and character would be required to alter the now accepted view in Whitehall of the Maratha policy of Richard Wellesley.

NOTES

1. AW-RW 21 Dec 05: AW-Webbe 11 Sep 04.

2. RW-AW 9 Nov 04 Grwd (1837) iii 538 (1844) ii 1356.

3. Edmonstone-Elphinstone 5 Sep 04 A Mss 13590 f.18: Elphinstone-RW 2 Oct 04 A Mss 13604 f. 59.

4. Edmonstone-Elphinstone 4 Oct 04 A Mss 13590 f. 27 Edmonstone-Elphinstone 17 Nov 04 PRC v 106 acknowledging Elphinstone-Edmonstone 29 Oct 04: Edmonstone-Elphinstone 3 Nov 04 SNRR i 157 Martin iv 230: Elphinstone - Edmonstone 19 Nove 04 A Mss 13604 f. 64.

5. These events can be reconstructed from Elphinstone-Close 28 Jan 05 SNRR i 166: RW-Sec Ctee 22 Mar 05 Martin iv 318: Elphinstone-Close 20 Nov 04: Elphinstone-Wallace 23 Nov 04 WP 3/3/48.

6. Jenkins-Edmonstone 15 Nov 04 PRC xi 107: Jenkins Mem 15 Nov 04:
   Jenkins-Sydenham 16 Nov 04 A Mss 13876 f.31,33.

7. Jenkins-Edmonstone 17, 19 Nov 04 WP 3/3/48: Jenkins Mem 17 Nov
   04 PRC xi 109.

8. Jenkins-Edmonstone 28 Nov 04 WP 3/3/48.

9. Edmonstone-Webbe 5 Nov 04 PRC xi 101: Jenkins-Edmonstone 13
   Dec 04 PRC xi 113 fuller text in WP 3/3/93.

10. Jenkins-Martindale 16 Dec 04: Jenkins-Edmonstone 17, 20 Dec 04 WP
    3/3/93.

11. Jenkins-Edmonstone 29 Dec 04 PRC xi 121: Jenkins-AW 29 Dec 04 WP
    3/3/93.

12. AW-Close 12 Dec 04: AW-Shawe 14 Dec 04.

13. Elphinstone-Edmonstone 4 Dec 04 WP 3/3/48.

14. Elphinstone-RW 7 Dec 04: Elphinstone-AW 8, 9 Dec 04 WP 3/3/57.

15. Elphinstone-AW 10, 11, 12 Dec 04: Elphinstone-Amrit Rao 11 Dec 04:
    Elphinstone-Edmonstone 16 Dec 04 WP 3/3/57: Elphinstone-Halibur-
    ton 11 Dec 04 PRC v 109.

16. Elphinstone-RW 27, 29 Nov 04 WP 3/3/48: AW-Close, Elphinstone,
    Shawe 19 Dec 04.

17. Bentinck-AW 8, 14 Jan 05 WP 3/3/15: AW-Bentinck 11 Jan 05: AW-Kirk-
    partrick 19 Jan 05: the confirming orders are RW-AW 9 Jan 05 G.rwd
    (1837) iii 60 (1844) ii 1395 and RW-Bentinck A Mss 13,633 f. 188.

18. James Kirkpatrick-AW 30 Jan 05 WP 3/3/63.

19. AW-Shawe 4 Jan 05.

20. Edmonstone-Resident at Delhi 13 Jan 04 PRC xi 122 SNRR i 208.

21. RW-AW 24 Jan 05 Martin iv 267 SNRR i 209 PRC xi 128.

22. Shawe-AW 25 Jan 05 A Mss 13,778 f. 181.

23. AW-Shawe 3 Feb 05.

24. Jenkins-AW 1,3 Jan 05: Jenkins-Edmonstone 2 Jan 05: WP 3/3/93.

25. Jenkins-AW 4,9 Jan 04 WP 3/3/93: Jenkins-Martindale 5 Jan 05 PRC xi
    122: Jenkins-Edmonstone 7 Jan 05 PRC xi 126: Jenkins-Edmonstone
    10 Jan 05 WP 3/3/93.

26. Jenkins-AW 12 Jan 05: Jenkins-Edmonstone 16, 17, 18, 26 Jan 05 PRC
    xi 124, 126, 132 WP 3/3/93.

27. Elphinstone-AW 6 Feb 05: Elphinstone-GG 9 Feb 05 WP 3/3/57:
    AW-Malcolm 17 Feb 04: AW-Craddock 19 Feb 05: AW-Bentinck 19 Feb
    05: AW-RW 27 Feb 05.

28. AW-Close, copied to Shawe 4 Mar 05: the passage quoted in full can
    be found in the MSS version in WP 3/3/50. Jenkins was Chairman of

the East India Company at the time of the publication of the first edition of Gurwood.

29. Malcolm-Shawe 23 Feb, 7 Mar, 25 Mar 05 A Mss 13747 f. 384, 378, 386: Shawe-Malcolm 11 Mar 05 A Mss 13602 f. 140: Shawe-AW 6 Mar, 28 Mar 05 A Mss 13778 f.176, 178: RW-Bentinck 11 Mar 05 Pw Jb 48 p. 139.

11

Conclusion

Arthur Wellesley was never to see India again.

In early 1805, the conflict with the Marathas was of uncertain outcome. Daulat Rao Sindia had moved rapidly northwards, with the intention to join Jaswant Rao Holkar, and perhaps even to intervene in the interest of the Raja of Bharatpur in the continuing siege of his fortress. The Raja of Berar had relapsed into acceptance of his position in the Company scheme of paramountcy, although not to the extent of undertaking the obligations of a treaty of subsidiary alliance. Peshwa Baji Rao remained inert, his control of his territories insecure. John Malcolm was again to be involved in a further period of diplomacy, which led at the end of 1805 to treaty settlements with both Daulat Rao Sindia and Jaswant Rao Holkar. In these the outcome of the 'narrower system' which Arthur Wellesley contended that his brother had accepted in September 1804 could be seen, with reversion of the control of Gwalior to Daulat Rao Sindia and the granting of a territorial provision to Jaswant Rao Holkar. 1805 saw the departure of Richard Wellesley after a Governor-Generalship of seven years, the arrival of Cornwallis in failing health and his northward move towards the scene of diplomatic and military action, and after his death in October, the conclusion of this interim settlement with both Daulat Rao Sindia and subsequently with Jaswant Rao Holkar. This outcome was in effect forced on Fort William by a powerful Court of Directors with whom Ministers were not disposed to quarrel. The great venture of Richard Wellesley, at least viewed against its full objective, could be held to have failed.

Arthur Wellesley was to be closely involved, as a member of the House of Commons, in the prolonged defence of the Governor-Generalship. In papers he wrote in 1806, and in speeches in the Commons, he drew on the analysis that he had developed of the events of 1802-4. This analysis, created with an eye to the solidarity of the Wellesley clan, as has been seen, differed significantly from the view which Arthur Wellesley had formed as events were unfolding, and on which he had commented freely in private letters to those involved with him in the direction of policy. Much has often been made of this distinction, and it is certainly possible to condemn the Maratha policy of Richard Wellesley with the words of the letters of Arthur Wellesley. From his emeritus position of the mid-1830s Arthur Wellesley was content to have this evidence made public, although there was strange reticence, particularly with regard to the position of officer colleagues. The publication of the despatches of Richard Wellesley almost at the same time, made available an extensive documentation of the policy of the period, so nearly complete as to render the additional evidence to be gained from archival research sometimes marginal in the additional light which it throws on events.

But much of the material needed to understand and to criticise the events of 1803-5 had been available much earlier. Richard Wellesley had deliberately created in his elaborate published *Notes* of December 1803 a full record of the year of achievement. To this was added for the interested public the material in his letter to the Secret Committee of the Company of April 1804, a copy of which was captured by a French frigate and published in the *Moniteur* of June 1805. There was a ready market in French newspapers in London during the war (arranged by English and French fishermen meeting in mid-Channel) and Stockdale the London printer, who had already sold a version of the *Notes* on Maratha affairs in London the previous year, made available the full text of the dispatch of April 1804 in a pamphlet in August 1805.

A further consequence of the questioning of the policy of the Governor Generalship almost immediately on its close, stimulated by a powerful group of Directors led by Charles Grant, was that there was made public in the first decade of the century, as a result of the traditional call of the House of Commons for papers, much of the evidence on which the Whig case against Richard Wellesley was built up. Criticism concentrated at first on aspects of the Governor-Generalship other than Maratha policy, for instance the seizure of the Carnatic and the policy followed in securing extensive territorial cession in Oudh. But the fear expressed in 1804, that Parliamentary criticism would bring into the public domain much of the Maratha *darbar* controversy of the time, and thus show weaknesses in the policy, was fully justified. Publication served to make available letters passing between the members of the group of political and military officers.

Once this information was available, the extent to which the Governor General had imposed his own view of events, not simply in terms of decision taking but also in analysis, became very clear. Examples have been given in this study. There is to be detected in July 1804, for instance, an inability by Richard Wellesley and the Calcutta Secretariat to appreciate the extent of the failure of military measures. Further, in September 1804 there is a clear hesitation in the control of policy, apparently coincident with a further collapse in the health of Richard Wellesley. By September 1804 this tense and autocratic man of forty-four was labouring in his seventh monsoon, in a land without hill stations.

During the period March to September 1805, Arthur Wellesley was travelling to Europe. Unfortunately for his future happiness one of his objectives was to marry Kitty Pakenham. More to his central purpose, he hoped to further his military career in Europe. The years in India had given to him a corpus of knowledge, civil and military, on which he would draw many times. He would frequently be consulted about Indian affairs in later years as a Cabinet Minister. But the apprenticeship, to some extent given to him by the chance of the appointment of his brother and seized by him with vigour, was of deeper significance. The endless letter writing, representing on average perhaps two hours writing a day for the two and a half years here surveyed, records his direction of military and political events, and his assessment. It shows also his growing capacity to see the whole picture of policy, and to use this vision both on behalf of the policy of his brother, but also on occasion to criticise it with effect and precision.

Arthur Wellesley was always clear that he had learnt his basic trade, that of warfare, in India. But more than this, because he had carried together political and military authority, he had come to appreciate the contrast between potential political power and the often very different and enfeebled reality. He had analysed events from the letters of Residents at the courts of the country powers and acted on this judgement. He had negotiated with Indian agents while uncertain of the condition and even the location of the territories in dispute. All this the despatches show us, with the immediacy of telephone transcripts. When the letters were printed, Arthur Wellesley was surprised as he read the proofs at the range of topics covered. It is possible to set this extensive correspondence against the documentation generated by the Company 'politicals.' From that scrutiny, the Arthur Wellesley of the Indian years emerges with enhanced stature. Writing of wartime Washington, Felix Frankfurter said of political life that it was 'warfare, permeated by people with a zeal to pervert.' The Premier who in 1828, while engaged in Cabinet making, lamented a morning 'assuaging what gentlemen were pleased to call their feelings' had been trained in a hard school.

India had been the making of Arthur Wellesley.

Glossary

Attavesi	Country between the Tapti and Damungunga rivers
Banjara	Dealers in grain and salt who followed armies with supplies for sale
Bheels, bhils	Inhabitants of the hills of Malwa and the northern Deccan
Chauth, chaute	Tribute or protection money imposed by the Marathas
Darbar	The court of a ruler
Doab	The land between two rivers, especially that between the Ganges and the Jamuna
Ghat	A pass through hills, but also a river crossing point
Hindustan	Territory to the north of the Narbada and south of the Jamuna
Hircarrah	A messenger
Jagir	The territory ruled by a jagirdar
Jats	A Hindu agricultural grouping in Rajasthan and elsewhere
Karkun	An agent or messenger
Khas	Land granted by a ruler from which the revenue is collected directly
Killedar	The commander of a fortress
Kos	A traditional measure of distance, about two miles
Munshi	A representative or agent, especially of an official
Pagah	The personal horsemen of a ruler
Parganah	A district
Pindari	Irregular troops paid only by plunder
Rajput	A Hindu warrior caste of northern India

Sanad	A treaty or agreement
Saramjami	Land temporarily assigned for the support of troops or given to the holder of a civil office
Silledar	State cavalry
Vakil	An agent or messenger

Bibliography

MSS sources used

Two sources have been of note; the papers of Richard Wellesley in the British Library, and those of Arthur Wellesley now in the Wellington Collection at the University of Southampton. I have also consulted the Bentinck Collections at the University of Nottingham, the Sidmouth MSS at the Devon County Record Office, and the Oriental and India Office Collections of the British Library.

Printed editions of the letters of Arthur Wellesley

The Dispatches of..the Duke of Wellington...from 1799 to 1818 compiled ...by Lt Col Gurwood, 13 vol, 1834-39, New edition, 13 vol, 1837-39. The pagination is not standardised betwen these two editions. Second edition, 8 vol, 1844-47.

Supplementary Despatches...of FM Arthur Duke of Wellington, 15 vol, 1858-72.

A Selection from the despatches... relating to India of FM the Duke of Wellington, ed. S J Owen, Oxford, 1880.
Wellington at War 1794-1815, ed Antony Brett-James, 1961.
The convention throughout the notes in the present volume is that for letters from Arthur Wellesley the date alone is given.

Important early source material; references are to the first edition only, the place of publication is London unless stated

Aitchison, C.U.   *A collection of treaties, engagements and sanads...relating to India*, 7 vol, 1862-65.
Auber, P   *Rise and Progress of the British Power in India*, 2 vol, 1837.
Broughton, T D   *Letters written in a Mahratta camp during the year 1809...*, 1813.
Compton, H.E.   *A particular account of the European Military Adventurers of Hindustan from 1784 to 1803*, 1892.

Duff, J.C.G. *A History of the Mahrattas*, 3 vol., 1826.

Forrest, G.W.   *Selections from the Letters and Despatches in the Bombay Secretariat: Mahratta Series*, Bombay, 1885.

Fraser, H.   *Our Faithful Ally, the Nizam*, 1865.

Kaye, J.W.   *Life and Correspondence of Major General Sir John Malcolm*, 2 vol, 1856.

Malcolm, J.   *Sketch of the Political History of India 1784 to the present date*, 1811.

Memoir of Central India 1784-1823, 2 vol, 1826.

Political History of India 1784-1823 2 vol, 1826.

Martin, M. ed   *Despatches, Minutes and Correspondence of the Marquess Wellesley during his administration in India*, 5 vol, 1836-7. (cited as Martin)

Mill, J.   *The History of British India*, 3 vol, 1817.

Parliamentary Papers; these are not numbered for this period; the date of the authority of the House of Commons to print is given in the references.

Thorn, W.   *Memoir of the war in India conducted by...Lord Lake...and Sir Arthur Wellesley...from 1803...to 1806*, 1818.

More recent authorities; again the place of publication is London unless stated.

Bidwell, S.   *Swords for Hire: European Mercenaries in Eighteenth Century India*, 1971.

Butler, Iris   *The Eldest Brother: The Marquess Wellesley*, 1973.

Callahan, R.A.   *The East India Company and Army Reform 1783-1798*, Cambridge Mass, 1972.

Chakravorty, U.N.   *Anglo-Maratha Relations and Malcolm 1798-1830*, New Delhi, 1979.

Choksey, R.D.   *A History of British Diplomacy at the Court of the Peshwas*, Poona, 1951.

Fortesque, J.W.   *History of the British Army*. 13 Vols. 1899-1930.

Furber, H.   *John Company at Work*, Cambridge Mass, 1948.

Gupta, P.C.   *Baji Rao II and the East India Company*, Bombay, 1939.

Kanungo, S.   *Jaswant Rao Holkar, the Golden Rogue*, Lucknow, 1965.

Nightingale, P.   *Trade and Empire in Western India 1784-1806*, 1970.

Philips, C.H.   *The East India Company 1784-1834*, 1940.

Poona Residency Correspondence: English Records of Maratha History (cited as PRC).

- vol 6, *Poona Affairs 1797-1801*, Bombay, 1939.

- vol 7, *Poona Affairs 1801-1810*, Bombay, 1940.

- vol 9, *Daulat Rao Sindia and North Indian Affairs 1800-1803*, Bombay, 1943.

- vol 10, *The Treaty of Bassein and the Anglo-Maratha War in the Deccan 1802-1804*, Bombay, 1951.

- vol 11, *Daulat Rao Sindia's Affairs 1804-1809*, Bombay, 1943.

Roberts, P.E.   *India under Wellesley*, 1929.

Sardesai, G.S.   *A New History of the Marathas*, 3 vol, Bombay, 1948.

Sarkar, J.   *Fall of the Mughal Empire*, 4 vol, Calcutta, 1950.

Sen, Surendranath   *Administrative System of the Marathas*, Calcutta, 1923. *Military System of the Marathas*, Calcutta, 1928.

Sinha, H.N. ed.   *Selections from the Nagpur Residency Records*, 3 vol, Nagpur, 1950-53, (cited as SNNR)

Thompson, E.J.   *The Making of the Indian Princes*, 1943.

Weller, J.   *Wellington in India*, 1972.

Ziegler, P.   *A Life of Henry Addington, 1st Viscount Sidmouth*, 1965.

A.S. Bennell bibliography

Southern India under Wellesley 1798-1805, *B.Litt. Oxon*, 1951.

'Wellesley's Settlement of Mysore', *JRAS* (1952)pp. 124-32.

'Governor General of India 1: Wellesley', *History Today* (Feb 1959), vol 9, no 2, pp. 94-102.

'The Anglo-Maratha Confrontation of June and July 1803', *JRAS* (1962), pp. 107-31.

Factors in the Marquis Wellesley's Failure against Holkar, 1804, *BSOAS* (1965), vol 38, Part 3, pp. 553-81.

'The Anglo-Maratha War of 1803-5', *JSAHR* (1985), vol 65, pp. 144-61.

The Road to Poona in *East India Studies* presented to Sir Cyril Philips ed. K Ballhatchet and J Harrison Asian Research Service (1986), pp. 183-206.

'Arthur Wellesley as Political Agent 1803', *JRAS* (1987), pp. 272-88.

Arthur Wellesley the Sepoy General as politician and diplomat 1797-1805, in *The Road to Waterloo* ed. A J Guy, National Army Museum (1991).

JRAS Journal of the Royal Asiatic Society

BSOAS Bulletin of the School of Oriental and African Studies

JSAHR Journal of the Society of Army Historical Research

INDEX

NOTE: The following abbreviations have been used in the body of the Index
DR = Daulat Rao Sindia; JR = Jaswant Rao Holkar; RB = Raghuji Bhonsle;
AW = Arthur Wellesley and RW = Richard, first Marquis Wellesley.